The
HEBREW PROPHETS
AND THEIR
SOCIAL WORLD

The
HEBREW PROPHETS AND THEIR SOCIAL WORLD

AN INTRODUCTION

Second Edition

VICTOR H. MATTHEWS

B
Baker Academic
a division of Baker Publishing Group
Grand Rapids, Michigan

Published by Baker Academic
a division of Baker Publishing Group
P.O. Box 6287, Grand Rapids, MI 49516-6287
www.bakeracademic.com

Printed in the United States of America

A previous edition of this book was published in 2001 as *Social World of the Hebrew Prophets*.

Library of Congress Cataloging-in-Publication Data is on file at the Library of Congress, Washington, DC.

ISBN 978-0-8010-4861-6

The internet addresses, email addresses, and phone numbers in this book are accurate at the time of publication. They are provided as a resource. Baker Publishing Group does not endorse them or vouch for their content or permanence.

Scripture quotations are from the New Revised Standard Version of the Bible, copyright © 1989, by the Division of Christian Education of the National Council of the Churches of Christ in the United States of America. Used by permission. All rights reserved.

Quotations labeled *OTPar* are from *Old Testament Parallels: Laws and Stories from the Ancient Near East; fully revised and expanded third edition*, by Victor H. Matthews and Don C. Benjamin. Copyright © 2006 by Victor H. Matthews and Don C. Benjamin. Paulist Press, Inc., Mahwah, NJ. Reprinted by permission of Paulist Press, Inc. www.paulistpress.com

12   13   14   15   16   17   18   7   6   5   4   3   2   1

Contents

Abbreviations

Old Testament/Hebrew Bible

Gen.	Genesis
Exod.	Exodus
Lev.	Leviticus
Num.	Numbers
Deut.	Deuteronomy
Josh.	Joshua
Judg.	Judges
Ruth	Ruth
1–2 Sam.	1–2 Samuel
1–2 Kings	1–2 Kings
1–2 Chron.	1–2 Chronicles
Ezra	Ezra
Neh.	Nehemiah
Esther	Esther
Job	Job
Ps(s).	Psalm(s)
Prov.	Proverbs
Eccles.	Ecclesiastes
Song	Song of Songs
Isa.	Isaiah
Jer.	Jeremiah
Lam.	Lamentations
Ezek.	Ezekiel
Dan.	Daniel
Hosea	Hosea
Joel	Joel
Amos	Amos
Obad.	Obadiah
Jonah	Jonah
Mic.	Micah
Nah.	Nahum
Hab.	Habakkuk
Zeph.	Zephaniah
Hag.	Haggai
Zech.	Zechariah
Mal.	Malachi

New Testament

Matt.	Matthew
Mark	Mark
Luke	Luke
John	John
Acts	Acts
Rom.	Romans
1–2 Cor.	1–2 Corinthians
Gal.	Galatians
Eph.	Ephesians
Phil.	Philippians

Col.	Colossians	**Apocrypha**	
1–2 Thess.	1–2 Thessalonians		
1–2 Tim.	1–2 Timothy	Bar.	Baruch
Titus	Titus	2 Esd.	2 Esdras
Philem.	Philemon	Jdt.	Judith
Heb.	Hebrews	1–4 Macc.	1–4 Maccabees
Jas.	James	Sir.	Sirach/Ecclesiasticus
1–2 Pet.	1–2 Peter		
1–3 John	1–3 John		
Jude	Jude		
Rev.	Revelation		

General

ANET	J. B. Pritchard, ed., *Ancient Near Eastern Texts Relating to the Old Testament*, 3rd ed. (Princeton: Princeton University Press, 1969) [cited by page number]
BCE	"Before the Common Era"—used in place of BC, but the dates are the same. *NOTE*: all dates in this book are BCE unless otherwise stated.
CE	"Common Era"—used in place of AD, but the dates are the same
OTPar	V. Matthews and D. Benjamin, *Old Testament Parallels: Laws and Stories from the Ancient Near East*, 3rd ed. (New York: Paulist, 2006) [cited by page number]

Introduction

Examining any text in the Old Testament/Hebrew Bible from a social world perspective requires an understanding that this material has a particular place in history and a social context that may be difficult for modern readers to interpret. The authors and editors of the biblical materials reflect their own time period even when they are editing a story or narrative originating from an earlier era. Similarly, when prophets speak, they do so within the social, economic, and historical context of their own time. They are primarily concerned either with current events or recent happenings, and not the far future. Therefore, as we explore the social world of the Hebrew prophets, we must first recognize that these persons, both male and female, spoke within their own time, to an audience with a frame of reference very different from ours. This is not to say that their message had no influence on prophets and writers centuries after their deaths. The many references to earlier prophetic speech (e.g., Jer. 26:18 quoting Mic. 3:12) or the reuse of their words in both the Hebrew Bible and the New Testament (e.g., Matt. 1:23 quoting Isa. 7:14; and Matt. 2:18 quoting Jer. 31:15) demonstrate both the power of these statements and the way in which they became proof texts for events occurring in later periods.

Although the world and words of the Hebrew prophets and their audiences often revolved around urban centers like Jerusalem, Bethel, and Samaria, the country as a whole was rural and agriculturally based. During the period 1000–587,[1] most of the population still lived in small farming communities of 100–250 people. We get an indication of just how pervasive this cultural setting actually was through the large number of pastoral and agricultural images employed by the prophets (Isa. 5:1–7; Amos 8:1–2). It simply would have been worthless to speak of shepherds and herds, vineyards, and summer

---

1. All dates in this book are **BCE** unless otherwise identified.

Insider/Outsider Perspective

Emic = Insider

Modern readers often have difficulty comprehending the perspective of the biblical writers. We lack the "insider" (*emic*) information that functioned as the basic cultural environment of the ancient audience. *Emic* is a term that anthropologists use to indicate the way that members of a culture understand and explain their own society.

Etic = Outsider

Modern readers have a tendency to impose their own cultural perspectives on what they read in the biblical text. Their "outsider" (*etic*) viewpoint therefore can get in the way of exploring the original cultural context of the narrative. Without a sense of what it meant, for example, to be a member of Tekoa's small community of hill country farmers and herders like Amos or to be an exiled Levite from Anathoth functioning as an unpopular prophet in Jerusalem like Jeremiah, the reader only skims the surface of the text.

fruit to people who had had no experience of them. This insider perspective, however, presents some problems for modern readers and scholars. For readers who did not grow up on farms or live in rural areas, many of the images and metaphors employed by the Hebrew prophets will not have as great an impact as they did on the original audience. One task of this survey of the prophetic materials therefore will be to shed some light on what it might have been like to live in ancient Israel during the time of the Hebrew prophets.

With that said, it must be understood that the life of an average Israelite was not an easy one: the Mediterranean climate with which these people had to contend brought rain only during the winter months (October through March), and the land they occupied was hilly, badly eroded, and rocky. Thus their lives were hard, often quite short, and too often dominated by environmental and political forces beyond their control. Their ability to feed their families and occasionally produce a surplus for trade or as a hedge against future privations was often limited. In addition, political and economic forces from outside their immediate area—along with the demands of temple and palace for sacrifices and taxes—added to the pressures of daily existence.

Because few modern students share these aspects of everyday life in ancient Israel, one of the greatest challenges for modern readers is to become acquainted with the social and historical forces that played such an important role in the lives of the prophets and their audiences. To assist with that process, I designed this survey as an introduction for students of the Hebrew prophets and of the basic elements of their literature and their social world. In order to accomplish these goals, I will

- introduce each prophet as he or she appears chronologically in the biblical narrative,
- sketch out his or her social and historical context,
- explain aspects of historical geography where relevant to their message,
- examine the economic and social forces that dominate that particular moment in time,
- explain the literary images and metaphors used by the prophets, and
- make continual references to intertextual links between the prophets.

1

Historical Geography

A close reading of the biblical materials makes it possible to establish some aspects of the spatial perspective of the Hebrew prophets. However, since very few modern readers of the Bible have an intimate knowledge of the historical geography of the ancient Near East, it is important to begin this survey of the world of the Hebrew prophets with a brief examination of the topography and climate of these lands. Keep in mind that when the prophets mention a geographic site or feature, they are generally describing a place that they and their audience know intimately. They have walked over each field, climbed the nearby hills, seen the foliage, and smelled the various aromas associated with herding sheep or with cultivating an olive orchard or vineyard. Because their frame of reference is that of a geographic insider, they do not have to go into great detail to conjure up a picture in the minds of their listeners. And because ancient Canaan is a relatively small place, certain place-names or landmarks will reappear over and over again in the text. Even at that, modern readers often become lost amid the strange-sounding place-names and descriptions of places that are either unknown or so foreign that they cannot even be imagined. In order to acquaint modern readers with this unfamiliar world, I provide here a basic description of the major geographic regions of the ancient Near East and their significance to the Israelites. Additional comments on geography or climate, when necessary to describe the words of a particular prophet, will be given in each chapter.

The ancient Near East can be divided into three primary areas: Mesopotamia (modern Iraq), Egypt, and Syria-Palestine. Adjacent to these regions are the Anatolian Peninsula (modern Turkey), Persia (modern Iran), and the island of Cyprus. Each of these subsidiary areas will figure into the history and the development of Near Eastern cultures during the biblical period. For instance, the Hittite Empire in Anatolia and portions of Syria and northern Mesopotamia provided a firm cultural link to the Indo-European nations of Europe and also influenced the political development of Syria-Palestine just prior to the emergence of the Israelites in Canaan. Cyprus and the Syrian seaport city of Ugarit functioned as early economic links with the burgeoning Mediterranean civilizations based on Crete and in southern Greece during the second millennium. For example, the epic literature from Ugarit (dating to 1600–1200) provides many linguistic and thematic parallels to the biblical psalms and the prophetic materials. The island of Cyprus, located just off the western coast of northern Syria, was also a prime source of copper, a metal essential to the technology of the Near East for much of its early history. Finally, Persia developed in the sixth century into the greatest of the Near Eastern empires just as the Israelites were emerging from their Mesopotamian exile. Persian religion (**Zoroastrianism**) and administrative innovations, including coined money, would contribute to the development of the postexilic community and Judaism both in the **Diaspora** and in the new Persian province named **Yehud**, centered on Jerusalem.

Travel between and within the various segments of the ancient Near East and the eastern Mediterranean required a willingness to face the dangers of the road, political cooperation among nations, and technological advancements that allowed for heavier loads. Early shipping hugged the coasts, but by 2000 ships were making regular stops at the Mediterranean islands as well as up and down the coasts of the Red Sea, Persian Gulf, and Indian Ocean. Evidence for such far-flung travel can be seen in the list of luxury items and manufactured goods found in Mesopotamian and Egyptian records and in the speeches of the Hebrew prophets (e.g., the depiction of the Phoenician port city of Tyre in Ezek. 28:11–19).

Overland trade routes generally gravitated toward the coasts, where seaports (Tyre, Sidon, Aqaba) could take raw materials and grain to far-flung markets. In Syria-Palestine, two highways linked Mesopotamia and Syria to the Palestinian coast and on to Egypt: the **Via Maris** and its extension, the Way of the Philistines, which provided a coastal route; and the **King's Highway**, which extended from Palmyra to Damascus and south through Transjordan to the Gulf of Aqaba. Caravan routes also followed the Arabian coastline and made it possible for traders to carry frankincense, myrrh, and other exotic goods (ivory, gold, animal skins) from Africa and India up the Red Sea and into the heart of the Near Eastern civilizations.

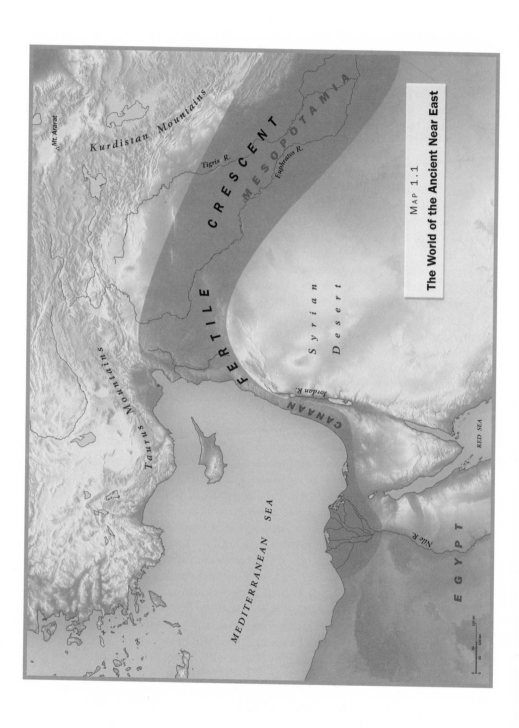

MAP 1.1

The World of the Ancient Near East

Mesopotamia

The Tigris-Euphrates River valley is the dominant feature in the area known as Mesopotamia. Today this region contains the nation of Iraq and parts of Iran and Syria. The dual river system flows over an increasingly flat expanse of land as it travels from north to south. There is little rainfall in much of this land, but the melting snows in the mountains of eastern Turkey feed the rivers. Life therefore was often precarious, dependent on the little rain that fell and the volume of water available from rivers and wells. In fact, the river system comprises a vast floodplain that could be inundated when water over-flowed the riverbanks. Disaster also could strike very quickly in such a fragile environment, where life-giving winds and rain could be replaced by the drying effects of the desert wind, the sirocco. The epic literature of this land attests to the inhabitant's dependence on water sources and the capricious character of their gods: "Enlil prepares the dust storm, and the people of Ur mourn. He withholds the rain from the land, and the people of Ur mourn. He delays the winds that water the crops of Sumer, and the people of Ur mourn. He gives the winds that dry the land their orders, and the people of Ur mourn" ("Laments for Ur," *OTPar* 252).

Given these environmental conditions, cities and towns could be established only close to the rivers, and only the introduction of massive irrigation proj-ects made possible population growth and an increase in arable land. The cooperative efforts necessary to construct and maintain irrigation systems eventually served as a major factor in the political development of the region. **City-states** and monarchies appeared very early in Mesopotamian history, while the formation of empires encompassing all or most of Mesopotamia did not occur until the eighteenth century.

No major geographic features provide natural barriers or defenses for Meso-potamia. As a result, waves of invasions by new peoples and the rise and fall of civilizations mark the history of the entire area from as early as 4000. The land also lacked an abundance of natural resources. What forests may have existed in antiquity did not survive into historical times. Mineral resources were found to the north and east of the Tigris-Euphrates valley, but less so within it. To make up for their lack of natural resources, the city-states of Mesopo-tamia established a brisk river trade to transport goods and large quantities of grain downriver very early in their history. The Mesopotamians also sent caravans into the Arabian Peninsula and east into Persia and the Indus valley of northwestern India. Such widespread trade links brought a further degree of cultural mixing and created a more **cosmopolitan** culture.

The first civilizations to appear in Mesopotamia were in the extreme south-ern area and became known as Sumer (ca. 4000). These people took advantage of the wetlands and trade links associated with the Tigris and Euphrates Riv-ers as they flowed into the Persian Gulf. The city-states of Ur, Kish, Lagash,

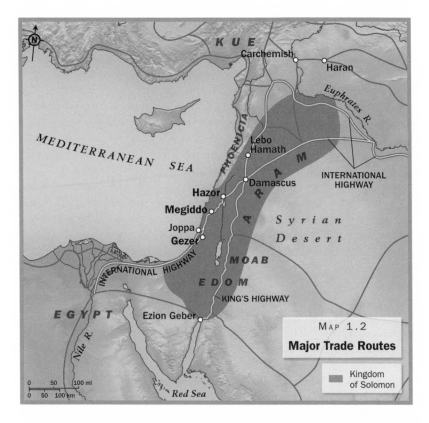

MAP 1.2
Major Trade Routes

Kingdom of Solomon

Nippur, and Uruk dominated this region and were responsible for the invention of the cuneiform writing system, the development of complex irrigation systems, the use of ziggurat towers as part of their temple complexes for their many gods, and the development of strong monarchies, although not empires.

Invaders from the steppes of Central Asia brought the first Semitic culture into the area around 2500. This also led to a spread of the population north into the region known as Babylonia. Babylon, located at the point where the Tigris and Euphrates almost meet as they travel south from the Caucasus Mountains, became the center of this new culture and eventually formed the seat of one of the first Mesopotamian empires, led by Hammurabi (1796–1750).

The Old Babylonian Empire did not survive for long, however. Hammurabi's successors were weak: they were plagued by a corrupt or complacent military, or the ever-present danger of natural disaster could damage an administration and leave it open to the next wave of invaders. Thus, from 1500 to 1000, no nation or city-state was able to dominate the whole area. Instead smaller kingdoms such as the Mitanni in northern Mesopotamia and the Hittite Empire in Anatolia controlled portions of the area. This fragmentation ended with the rise of the Neo-Assyrians about 1000, who occupied the northern reaches of the Tigris River. They took advantage of the petty kingdoms too busy fighting among themselves to resist an organized and ruthless opponent. Gradually, by 800, Assyrian **hegemony** came to dominate all of Mesopotamia and then expanded west to the Mediterranean Sea. At its height in 663 the Neo-Assyrian kings were even able to briefly conquer Egypt. In this case, an empire of this size, stretching across more than 1,000 miles and many different geographic regions, was held together by a policy of systematic terror and immediate retaliation for acts of rebellion: "The hunter cut open the wombs of the pregnant. He blinded infants. He slit the throats of warriors. . . . Whoever offended Ashur was executed. Sing of the power of Assyria, Ashur the strong, who goes forth to battle" ("Annals of Tiglath-pileser I," *OTPar* 166; compare 2 Kings 8:12; Hosea 13:16). When the Assyrian leadership began to fight among themselves and failed to maintain this strict policy throughout the far-flung districts, their empire was doomed, and they were supplanted after 605 by the Neo-Babylonians (also called the Chaldeans) under the leadership of Nebuchadnezzar.

It is possible, however, that the model of empire established and maintained for two hundred years by the Assyrians served as the impetus for another imperial power: the Persians from east of the Tigris. After pushing aside Nebuchadnezzar's weak successors, King Cyrus captured Babylon in 539. The Persians addressed the problems created by Assyrian and Babylonian administrative policies and chose to accommodate their style of empire to the realities of distance and time. They invented a "pony express" system that allowed communication to flow over an area of two thousand miles in five days. The Persians also recognized that terror is effective only when constantly in use. As a result, they chose a more benevolent and bureaucratically based form of administration, allowing freedom of religion and appointing local leaders as Persian representatives whenever possible (Neh. 2:1–8). Only the rapacious ambitions of Alexander of Macedon and the decadence of its rulers could end the Persian Empire (ca. 325).

Egypt

While the Egyptians were able to create an advanced civilization at least as early as that in ancient Sumer (ca. 3500), it was very different in character. The differences arise from the more isolated nature of Egypt in relation to the rest of the Near East. To the east, the Red Sea and the wastelands of the Sinai Peninsula provide an effective barrier to invaders. Once the pharaohs established a line of fortresses to bar the narrow strip of land that connects Egypt and the Sinai, they were able to almost completely control the entrance of armies, migrant peoples, and caravanners. Only the Hyksos invaders (1750–1550) were able to establish themselves as foreign rulers over Egypt, and they too were eventually supplanted by a native Egyptian dynasty. The Libyan and Saharan deserts protected the western border. Although more open to invasion from Nubia in the south (especially after 900), Egypt, for much of its history, was protected by the cataracts, which limited navigation of the southern reaches of the Nile River.

Nearly all of Egypt's culture and history has developed in and been sustained by the predictable inundations of the Nile River valley. The Nile flows north amid arid wastes and rocky desert outcrops, where farmers had to rely entirely on the river for irrigating their fields. As it enters the Mediterranean, the Nile spreads over the land into a fan-shaped delta and is dominated by papyrus marshes. It is customary to refer to the two regions of Egypt as Upper and Lower Egypt. But because the Nile flows from south to north, Upper Egypt is the southern area, from Thebes to Memphis, and Lower Egypt comprises the northern region, including the delta and eastern desert along the Mediterranean coast.

The natural flow of the Nile is interrupted south of Thebes by a series of rocky cataracts that makes river traffic nearly impossible. As a result, caravans bringing goods from Arabia, Nubia, and other African kingdoms were forced to disembark and march alongside the Nile rather than travel upon the river. This gave the Egyptians the opportunity to control the influx of people and products and, of course, to tax them. Although smuggling almost certainly occurred, it would have been much more difficult than along the more open borders of Mesopotamia.

Unlike the Tigris-Euphrates system, which could flood without warning or shift its channel, the Nile was a fairly consistent waterway. Its annual flood cycle was measured early in Egyptian history, and as a result the people and their rulers were able to plan their agricultural and economic activities with greater certainty than was possible in Mesopotamia. The constancy of life from year to year contributed to a culture that built for the ages and assumed a continuity of existence beyond this life into the next. Just as the Nilotic floods brought new layers of rich topsoil to fertilize and reinvigorate the fields each year, the *ma'at* ("peace") of Egypt was believed to come from the goodwill of the gods and their god-king, the pharaoh.

The Egyptian climate is hot and arid. Daytime temperatures range into the upper 90s F nearly year-round, and this is magnified by the cloudless, sunny skies. It is no wonder, therefore, that the sun god Amon is one of the most powerful of the Egyptian deities. The extreme temperatures moderate somewhat in the evenings, with cooling breezes coming off the Nile and from the desert. In fact, in the desert it can be quite cold at night. Throughout the region, architectural and clothing styles are based on accommodation to the extreme ranges in temperature.

The small annual rainfall meant that the people were forced to rely on the Nile and on wells for their water. As a result, waterwheels and other forms of irrigation technology were developed to move the water into channels that could flood the field. The river also served as a travel link facilitating the transport of goods, building materials, and armies. Familiarity with travel on the Nile and its various characteristics also became a common feature in their literature:

> My lover is a marsh. My lover is lush with growth. . . . Her mouth is a lotus bud. Her breasts are mandrake blossoms. . . . Her head is a trap built from branches . . . and I am the goose. ("Egyptian Love Songs," *OTPar* 323)

> Once, a man plowed his field, loaded the harvest on a barge, and towed it to market. At sunset, a terrible storm came up. The man, safe in town, survived, but his wife and children at home perished, lost when their houseboat capsized in the Lake of the Crocodiles. ("A Sufferer and a Soul," *OTPar* 226)

Metaphors involving the marshes, where birds roost and crocodiles and hippopotami are hunted, appear in **genres** as diverse as love poetry and the teachings of sages.

Syria-Palestine

Even though Syria-Palestine is the smallest of the Near Eastern regions, it is characterized by a much wider variety of topographic features, climatic zones, and population centers than either Egypt or Mesopotamia.

Syria

The northern range of this area includes Syria, the other Aramean states, and Phoenicia (modern Lebanon). From 1500 to 1200, the Hittite Empire dominated much of this northern area, stretching its hegemony beyond the boundaries of Anatolia (modern Turkey) and even challenging the Egyptians for control over Canaan. A significant economic power during this period was the port city of Ugarit, which controlled the carrying trade in the eastern Mediterranean. Ugarit is also responsible for the development of an alphabetic cuneiform writing system that would dramatically increase literacy and promote cultural identity within the smaller nations throughout the Near East. Its epic literature has many parallels in the Psalms and prophetic books:

> Ba'al proclaimed, "I alone rule the **divine assembly**. Who but I can feed the Holy Ones? Who but I can feed the peoples of the earth?" ("Ba'al and Anat," *OTPar* 271)

> May Ba'al the Cloud Rider, and El, the creator of the heavens and the earth, and every member of the divine assembly erase the name of that state, and its ruler. ("Karatepe Annals of Azitiwada," *OTPar* 175)

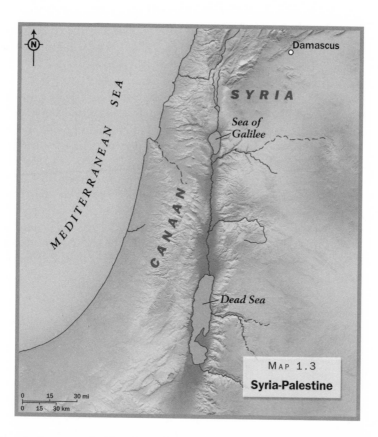

MAP 1.3

Syria-Palestine

In fact, the images of **Yahweh** as the master of the storm, the "Cloud Rider" (Ps. 68:4; Isa. 19:1), and the **transcendent** creator God (Isa. 40:28) were probably borrowed from or influenced by Ugaritic or Canaanite literature and their depictions of the gods El and Baal.

After 1200 a major political and cultural break occurred in the Near East when a mixed invasion force collectively known as the Sea Peoples challenged the power of the major cultures along the Mediterranean coastline. When the dust settled, the seaport city of Ugarit, which had dominated the Mediterranean carrying trade, had been destroyed and was never rebuilt. In subsequent centuries, the Phoenician seaports of Tyre and Sidon followed Ugarit as masters of Mediterranean shipping and planted colonies in North Africa, Sardinia, and Spain. The Hittite Empire in Anatolia was also conquered by the Sea Peoples, leaving that area in a state of political fragmentation that would allow for the Greek colonization of Ionia, the western coast of Anatolia, and the offshore islands, and would also remove one of Egypt's chief political rivals.

Egypt was also severely weakened by the Sea Peoples. The loss of effective control over many of its holdings in Canaan created a political vacuum that would eventually be filled by a variety of peoples, including the Philistines, who settled the southern coastal plain of Canaan. Others may have been new tribal groups, such as Israel, that infiltrated the virtually empty central hill country and established a tenuous village culture there. The royal inscription of Pharaoh Merneptah (1224–1214) provides at least some basis for this claim of Israel's presence in Canaan just prior to 1200: "I have decimated the people of Israel and put their children to death" ("Annals of Merneptah," *OTPar* 98).

Other beneficiaries of the new political situation after 1200 were the Phoenicians and the Syrian kingdom situated around Damascus. These peoples occupied the area immediately north and east of Canaan. Phoenicia was blessed with heavily forested hillsides just inland from a narrow coastal plain that was only eight to ten miles wide. The massive cedars had an almost mystical draw for the nearly treeless countries of Egypt and Mesopotamia and brought great wealth as well as conquering armies to the Phoenicians and their predecessors. In fact, many ancient rulers brag that they had extended their rule to include the cedar forests and Mediterranean coastline:

> The god Nergal did open up the path for the mighty Naram-Sin, and gave him Arman and Ibla, and he presented him (also) with the Amanus, the Cedar Mountain and (with) the Upper Sea. ("Naram-Sin in the Cedar Mountain," *ANET* 268)

> I, Wen-Amon, priest at the gate of the temple of Amun, was dispatched to buy timber for the sacred boat of Amun-Re, ruler of the divine assembly. ("Stories of Wen-Amon," *OTPar* 348)

In addition to its wealth of natural resources, Phoenicia possessed several major deepwater port cities, including Byblos, Tyre, and Sidon. Heavily laden ships were able to lie at anchor close to the wharves of these cities as they off-loaded and took on cargo. The wealth that flowed through these ports made them impressive prizes for the growing superpowers in Egypt and Mesopotamia in the period after 900, but the service they provided to the larger states during these centuries generally left them free to operate and even establish trading links throughout the Mediterranean basin with colonies established in North Africa, Sardinia, and Spain.

Syria (or Aram) was never politically united prior to the Roman period, but the dynasty based at Damascus had influence over much of the region that stretched from the Mediterranean coast on the west to the Taurus Mountains to the north and the Syrian desert on the east. This area encompasses three separate climatic zones: the Mediterranean coastline in the western area, a desert area with less than ten inches of annual rainfall to the south and east, and steppe land between the coast and the desert with sufficient rainfall and other sources of water to support agriculture and small oak forests.

During the eleventh to ninth centuries, Syria was a significant opponent of Israel, as both kingdoms sought to control the lands north and east of the Galilee, which contained the trade routes into and out of Mesopotamia and south through Transjordan. With the advent of camel caravans after 1200 and frequent travel from the Euphrates west to Tadmor/Palmyra (about 145 miles) and then along a depression between low hills to Damascus (another 130 miles), control of these trade routes became even more desirable. Accordingly, Solomon is said to have laid claim to Tadmor and Palmyra (2 Chron. 8:4), while the Syrian kings and their aggressive policies were a major concern of the Israelite kings (1 Kings 11:23–25; 15:16–22) and the prophets Elijah and Elisha. The Israelite kings were not always successful in resisting Syrian aggression; in fact, during the latter part of the ninth century, King Hazael of Syria was able to successfully invade Israel and Philistia and extend his hegemony over both for a time: "With Hadad riding before me, I liberated Israel from two ruthless monarchs by destroying their chariots and cavalry and killing Jehoram, son of Ahab and ruler of Israel, and Ahaziahu, son of Jehoram and ruler of the household of David. I destroyed their cities and left their lands barren" ("Tel Dan Annals of Hazael," *OTPar* 171). During the eighth century, the Syrians also figure quite prominently in the prophetic speech of Isaiah and Amos.

Much of Syria is mountainous. Except in its lower elevations, it is subject to extremes of hot and cold temperatures. Like Israel to the south, it was predominantly a village culture, and agriculture was its prime concern. Not surprisingly, therefore, the storm gods Baal and Hadad were of most importance in their pantheon. The major urban center was Damascus, located on the Barada River, on the southwest corner of Syrian territory and virtually on Israel's doorstep (ca. fifteen miles from the Golan Heights).

Canaan

Strategically located on a land bridge between Egypt and Mesopotamia, Canaan is a cultural crossroads as well as a melting pot for many different peoples. It covers only about 10,000 square miles, approximately the size of Vermont or New Hampshire. From north to south, there are only 145 miles between Dan, just north of the Sea of Galilee at the foot of the Hermon Range, and Beer-sheba, on the desert fringe of the eastern Sinai. Traveling east from the coastal plain to Jerusalem is only about 30 miles, although not by a direct route. From there to the Jordan River is only another 20 miles. Even within this small territory, there are four major geographic zones, each with its own ecological characteristics.

Coastal Plain

The coastal plain consists of a narrow stretch of flat lowlands and sand dune beaches. Because there are no deepwater harbors along this coast, ancient

Canaan's commercial efforts were severely limited except in those periods when rulers were able to establish trade alliances with maritime nations (Solomon in 1 Kings 10:1–22). Just inland are fertile areas that catch much of the rain and sea breeze from the Mediterranean. In ancient times, there were also some meager forestlands and marshy areas in this region.

Just to the east of the coastal plan, the **Shephelah** is a gradually rising plateau that eventually merges with the hill country that bisects the middle of the country. It consists of three fertile plains that provide the bulk of Canaan's arable farmland. The first is the Plain of Acre, which stretches to the north from Mount Carmel about twenty-five miles and extends inland five to eight miles. Since this area was controlled by the Phoenicians during the biblical monarchy, it does not figure prominently in the accounts of the court historians or the prophets.

The second is the Plain of Sharon, which extends to the south of Mount Carmel for nearly fifty miles and about ten miles inland. In antiquity, much of this territory was dominated by marshland, and there were few villages except along the coast. As a result, it likewise does not appear to any great extent in the biblical accounts. Just to the south of the Sharon, however, is Philistia, an area settled after 1200 by the branch of the Sea Peoples known as Philistines. They either conquered or founded many towns and villages and ruled the area from five major city-states. Three of these cities, Ashkelon, Gaza, and Ashdod, were near the coast.

Because much of the coastal plain is quite flat, it naturally became an international trade route used by Egyptians and Mesopotamian merchants and armies. The highway is sometimes referred to as the Via Maris, or "Way of the Sea," but this name probably applies to different links of the road rather than to its entire length. The Via Maris may refer to the portion of the road that extended from the coast east through the valley of Jezreel, south of the Carmel Range, and then on north through Galilee to Damascus. This detour from the northern route was made necessary by the Carmel Range extending to within 150 yards of the Mediterranean. Such a narrow band would have been a perfect place to ambush caravans or military convoys. Consequently, Megiddo, the site where the Jezreel valley opens to the east, became the gatekeeper to this important trade route: "Behold, all foreign countries have been put in this town by the command of Re on this day, inasmuch as every prince of every northern country is shut up within it, for the capturing of Megiddo is the capturing of a thousand towns!" ("The Asiatic Campaigns of Thut-mose III," *ANET* 237).

The summer temperatures along the coastal plain are quite hot, averaging about 100° F during the day. A sea breeze in the evenings makes this more tolerable, but architecture and business practices had to cope with a portion of the day when it was simply too hot to move. During the winter months (the period when most rainfall occurs) the temperatures dip into the 40s and 50s, but there is no danger of frost to harm plants. As a result, two grain harvests can be expected each year, and all types of fruit trees (among them olive, date, fig, and pomegranate) grow well here: "October to sow the barley, December and January to weed. . . . March to harvest the barley, April to harvest wheat and to pay tithes" ("Gezer Almanac," *OTPar* 156).

Central Hill Country

The spine of hills that runs from north to south down the middle of Canaan is called the central hill country. It rises from the rolling hills of the Shephelah Plateau to elevations as much as 3,300 feet above sea level between Hebron and Jerusalem. This narrow region would ultimately form the heart of both Israel and Judah during the monarchy. It began to be settled with any degree of density only starting in the Iron Age (around 1100). The appearance of hundreds of village sites after that point suggests an influx of population, probably related to the settlement of the Philistines along the coast and in the Shephelah. The hills themselves were denuded of trees in antiquity, and many of the hillsides were badly eroded. This may explain why much of the area was not settled by the Canaanites. In any case, it would have provided a safe, if not easy, life for refugees as well as new immigrants.

As is the case with all of Canaan's regions, the central hill country must also be subdivided as one travels from north to south. The climate becomes increasingly hot and dry in the southern reaches. The north, the Galilee region and the valley of Jezreel, has adequate rainfall to support intensive agriculture, and the valleys and basins have sufficient arable land to provide for the needs of both village communities and larger urban centers such as Megiddo and Beth-shean.

The middle portion of the hill country, which stretches from Dothan to Bethel, contains many large cities, including the northern kingdom's capital, Samaria, and the important cultic sites of Shechem and Bethel. Although not as lush as the Galilee, this central area contained a large population during the monarchy and was the location of many important events and battles. Agriculture here had to rely more heavily on the construction of terraced hillsides (Isa. 5:1–7) since there was less flat land. Fig and olive trees were abundant, and there was adequate pasturage for herds of sheep and goats.

The southernmost section of the hill country included the territory of Judah, with Jerusalem, Hebron, Beer-sheba, and the Judean wilderness. Because of the higher elevations, this region experiences greater temperature extremes than the rest of the country. In the hot and dry summers, the temperature is often in the 90s F, while in the wet winter months, the people shiver at night with blustery winds and temperatures in the 30s and 40s. Significant snowfall in Jerusalem is not unusual, and frost is a common morning experience.

Jordan River Valley

The Jordan River valley lies farther to the east. It was created by a gigantic rift or a geological fault that starts in Syria and extends south all the way to the Red Sea and Africa. Much of this huge fold in the earth is below sea level, although there are a few areas, such as the Huleh Basin just ten miles north of the Sea of Galilee, that have a slightly higher elevation (230 feet above sea level). For instance, despite being surrounded by steep hills, the Sea of Galilee is 700 feet below sea level. From that point, elevations continue to decrease along the course of the Jordan River.

The Jordan River originates north of the Sea of Galilee and is fed by springs at several sources, among them Tel Dan and Banias/Caesarea Philippi, and by the melting snows of the Hermon Range. It flows into the Sea of Galilee and then meanders south over a distance of about seventy miles. Its actual course, however, is so circuitous that the banks of the waterway stretch nearly two hundred miles. Several well-known fords along the Jordan are mentioned as strategic sites in the biblical narrative (Judg. 3:28; 12:5–6).

The Dead Sea is the ultimate repository of the Jordan's flow. It is the lowest spot on the face of the earth, about 2,600 feet below sea level at its northernmost end. The mineral-laden water is trapped here without an outlet and quickly evaporates in the extremely high temperatures of the area. The result is an extremely high salt content that transforms the lake into a health spa of great value, but it also deprives the lake of any large life forms. The most important settlement near the northern end of the Dead Sea is the oasis community of Jericho. Since it receives only about two inches of rainfall per year, its existence as a continually occupied site for more than ten thousand years is due to its continuous springs. Other important sites around the Dead Sea that play a role in biblical history—Qumran, the site of the Dead Sea Scrolls, and En-gedi—are also supported by springs.

Unlike the Tigris-Euphrates system and the Nile River, the Jordan River cuts its banks so deeply that it is difficult to create extensive irrigation projects. It is prohibitively expensive in time and funds to raise the water up over the riverbank, and, as a result, there is less irrigation farming and there are fewer settlements along the southern range of the Jordan River. The high temperatures, which average over 100° F for much of the year, and the nearly complete lack of rainfall also cut down on population growth during the biblical period. To be sure, there would be many events in this region, but they tended to center on the idea associated with "wilderness" rather than the normal pursuits of life.

Transjordanian Plateau

The last Syro-Palestinian region to be considered is the Transjordanian Plateau, which runs for about 250 miles from Mount Hermon in the north to the Gulf of Aqaba in the south. The region consists of a narrow plateau and set of hills running east from thirty to eighty miles to the eastern desert.

Transjordan includes two Israelite territories. Farthest north are the Golan Heights, which include the oak forests (Ezek. 27:6) and lush mountain pasturelands of Bashan just to the east of the Galilee region (39:18) and extend south to the Yarmuk River. The other is the region just to the east of the Jordan known as Gilead, where some of the Israelite tribes are said to have settled after the conquest in Joshua's time (Josh. 17:6). It is a mountainous region with many V-shaped valleys lying between the Yarmuk and the northern end of the Dead Sea. It is bisected from east to west by the very steep Jabbok River valley. Like Bashan, the Gilead region has sufficient rainfall to support wheat farming as well as cultivation of olive trees and grape orchards.

Farther south and east, between the Jabbok and the Arnon Rivers, is the kingdom of Ammon. Its capital at Rabbah anchored a state that stretched along a narrow, fertile band of land between Gilead and the eastern desert. While the kingdom was supposed to be bounded by the eastern arm of the Jabbok River, **archaeological** evidence shows Ammonite sites west of this area. Since it lay on the plateau above the hills associated with the Jordan valley, Ammon and especially Rabbah became prosperous as a link on the north-south King's Highway.

The area between the very deep valley of the Arnon River and the Zered River formed the boundaries of Moab. It is mountainous country, with elevations up to 3,600 feet above sea level. Although watered by springs, the average annual rainfall decreases in its southern reaches. As a result, much of this southern region is given over to sheep and goat herding, while agriculture is possible closer to the Arnon. A tableland area, the Mishor, adjoins Moab to the west. It stretches from Heshbon in the north for about twenty-five miles south to Aroer and Dibon, just north of the Arnon valley. Among the important sites located here were Mount Nebo and Shittim. A territory disputed between Moab and Israel, it was controlled by Moab during most of the period of the divided monarchy (Isa. 15:4–9; Jer. 48:2–5; Ezek. 25:8–11): "Chemosh said to me, 'Go! Take Nebo from Israel!' . . . I built Aroer and a highway through the Arnon Valley. I also rebuilt the cities of Beth-bamoth and Bezer for fifty households from Dibon" ("Annals of Mesha," *OTPar* 168–69).

Edom, the southernmost Transjordanian kingdom, was located in a region between the Zered River and the Gulf of Aqaba that provides a sea link to Arabia and Egypt. It is mountainous country, with peaks as high as 5,700 feet above sea level; its cities were built along the narrow ridges of these hills. The living area for Edom was further narrowed by the Arabah, an extension of the Jordan Rift, to the west and by the desert on the east. This left only about twelve or thirteen miles of inhabitable area east to west for the Edomites. The western crest of these mountain ridges receives enough rainfall to support agriculture, but at lower elevations it is quite dry, supporting only scrub forests and marked by the exposure, due to erosion, of limestone cliffs and Nubian sandstone. The red color of this landscape gave Edom its name (the Hebrew name for Edom means "red").

Travel through this rugged land was extremely difficult. Only the pass at Punon (Num. 33:42), twenty-five miles south of the Zered, affords passage from the Arabah east for nine miles. The northern area of Edom, sometimes referred to as Teman, was dominated by fortresses such as Bozrah (Amos 1:12). These sites adjoined and guarded the southern portion of the King's Highway as it extended on to the Gulf of Aqaba.

This overview provides only a cursory description of the major geographical and geopolitical regions of the ancient Near East; nevertheless it should serve as a reminder of the complexity of the world of the Hebrew prophets. The physical world, of which they were a part, is governed like our own, in large part by their interaction with the environment's barriers, potentials, and limitations. Because the prophets constantly refer to geographical regions, cities, and landmarks, a basic knowledge of these features is essential for anyone who studies their words and writings.

2

Defining and Describing the Prophet

How Do We Identify an Ancient Near Eastern Prophet?

There is a long history of prophetic activity in the ancient Near East. Much of this activity is associated with practices of **divination** and the interpretation of omens by professional cultic officials and priests. Because Mesopotamian religion assumes that the gods represent the forces of nature and are therefore both powerful and capricious, the determination of the future through the reading of various omens is critical. No army went to war, no temple or other public building was constructed, and no diplomatic marriage was arranged without first consulting the omens. As a result, a whole industry developed in which persons who could interpret the visible symbols of the gods' intentions obtained high status or were given an audience.

The task of the diviner is to determine the will of a god or gods through various ritualized actions, such as the examination of sheep entrails, consultation with the dead (1 Sam. 28:8), or the study of the astrological configurations. Over the generations, the nature of these omens and their possible interpretations were recorded in what are now called **omen texts**. These texts, along with clay models of sheep livers, were then studied by priests-in-training, who would consult the ancient documents first before making any pronouncement. The standardization of interpretation based on these texts added to the monopoly over divination held by the priestly community.

Ezekiel 21:21 contains a striking example of a Mesopotamian king's use of various forms of divination. Here King Nebuchadnezzar of Babylonia employs three separate techniques: shaking a group of arrows and then choosing one (belomancy), consulting the teraphim or divine images that he has brought with the army, and examining a sheep liver (hepatoscopy).

Israelite law forbade all of these practices because they were associated with false gods and false religions (Deut. 18:10–13). There was also an implicit recognition that the practice of divination could be corrupted by a diviner's desire to please his clients or employer (1 Kings 22:1–8). Thus prophets like Isaiah (8:19–22), Jeremiah (27:9–10), and Malachi (3:5) condemned such practices, declaring the practitioners to be liars and deceivers.

Biblical writers record the activities of some diviners, such as Balaam (Num. 22–24), who were not just religious practitioners following a prescribed set of texts to interpret the will of the gods. At least in Balaam's case, he seems to be deeply moved by dreams and oracles that came to him spontaneously from God. Thus Balaam's reputation for being a "true prophet" serves to bolster the argument for **Yahweh**'s supremacy since the deity is able to manipulate this prophet and elicit from him an oracle condemning Israel's enemies and a disclaimer that he could speak only "the word God puts in my mouth" (22:31–38): "This is the story of Balaam, son of Beor and a seer. At night the divine assembly appeared to Balaam, son of Beor. He dreamed that he heard El pronounce a death sentence on his city. . . . When Balaam got up the next morning, he began to fast and to lament bitterly. The people of the city asked: 'Balaam, son of Beor, why do you fast? Why do you mourn?' So Balaam agreed to tell them about his dream" ("Stories of Balaam," *OTPar* 132–33).

These persons, both male and female, were recognized as prophets or spokespersons for a god or gods and in essence provided an interactive service for those who consulted them. Some prophets are identified as **ecstatic** (having lost conscious control of their bodies or speech), while others present their divine messages in less spectacular or manic ways. But they all deliver messages from one or more gods. Among the ancient texts from Mesopotamia that describe these ancient prophets are the Neo-Assyrian inscriptions (ca. 800–650) and the letters from the eighteenth-century government archive at Mari, a city on the northern Euphrates River where it borders Syria and Iraq today. In these latter texts at least three classes of male and female prophets advised King Zimri-Lim. *Apilum* prophets could move from place to place, spoke for the **divine assembly**, and thus made formal statements and held high status, although these divine messages often came in the form of ecstatic pronouncements. They were not required to serve within a specific temple or cultic community. *Assinu* prophets were temple personnel whose gender became indeterminate during their prophetic performance and whose messages most often dealt with cultic matters, such as the rebuilding of a temple or the making of an annual or memorial sacrifice. *Muhhu* prophets were ecstatics who spoke while in a spontaneous trance. In some cases, the trance may have been brought on by drugs, physical deprivation, or music. It is unclear whether they were always associated with a temple or shrine. In general, the frenzied statements of these prophets were interpreted and then transmitted to the king by priests or government officials.

Since prophetic activity very often included either a trance state or an ecstatic experience, it is not surprising that the Mari word for *muhhu* prophet (*mahu*) means "to become crazy" and the hieroglyphic sign for "prophet" in the Egyptian "Memoirs of Wen-Amon" is a human figure in convulsions. The biblical text also contains examples of prophets transformed into an ecstatic condition by music (2 Kings 3:15), dancing (1 Kings 18:26), or a combination of the two (1 Sam. 10:5, 10). The personal names of the nonbiblical prophets never appear in the Mari letters, which could indicate that they were considered members of a sacred social class whose names could not be spoken.

Who Were the Hebrew Prophets?

Although the Hebrew prophets in some ways resemble the diviners of the ancient Near East, the biblical writers portray them as more than religious practitioners. While some of them were members of the priestly community, the prophets stood outside that institution and came from every class, every profession, and both genders. They occasionally interpreted omens, but they were not strictly diviners, and their message was never totally dependent on the examination of physical clues to God's behavior or intention. Rather, their role was to challenge the establishment and the social order, to remind the leadership and the people of their obligation to the **covenant** with Yahweh, and to warn the people of the punishment that would surely ensue if they violated this covenantal agreement. This is not to say that every prophet simply parroted the words and themes of all previous prophetic figures. Each is unique in his or her own way and each will display a social and theological agenda tied to the concerns of his or her own time. While they do not walk in figurative or theological lockstep, they do share a respect for the covenant and for the task of reminding the people just who really is God.

In the world of ancient Israel, the prophet may *not* be identified as simply a fortune-teller, social activist, doomsayer, messenger, moralist, or even predictor of Jesus. Part of the difficulty stems from the word "prophet" being used in a variety of ways in the Hebrew Bible. Some individuals may not, on first reflection, be considered prophets and yet perform a prophetic role. For example, Abraham (Gen. 20:7), Moses (Deut. 18:18), Aaron (Exod. 4:14–16), and Miriam (Exod. 15:20) are called prophets in the Pentateuch even though they are more properly considered ancestors and **eponymous** heroes. And while Deborah (Judg. 4:4) and Samuel (1 Sam. 3:20) are called prophets, they also function as **wisdom** figures and judges. In the fifth-century compilation of Israel's history found in Chronicles, the Levites, who were primarily temple functionaries, are called prophets (1 Chron. 25). Finally, the **canon** includes the books of Haggai, Zechariah, and Malachi with the prophets even though much of the material in these books suggests that they were visionaries.

Figuring out what a prophet *is*, however, is often more difficult than stating what a prophet is not. The following six propositions will help us define the prophet's role.

First, although some Hebrew prophets experienced ecstasy, it does not appear to have been essential or even common. Ecstasy threw prophets into trance states, seizures, or convulsions and was therefore considered to be a sign in the ancient world of possession by a god. While several biblical prophets experienced such ecstatic states, many others did not.

Second, prophetic speech, in whatever form, was a strategy for crisis management closely associated with the monarchies of Israel and Judah (1000–587). Throughout this period, wars and taxes plunged the two small countries into one crisis after another. Crisis, by definition, often destroys the old rules and throws a culture into chaos. Prophets appeared during these difficult times, and their pronouncements often analyzed and critiqued the nation's prospects for survival.

Third, prophets often challenged the authority of the monarchs of Israel and Judah, even when they were speaking directly to the people. In this respect, their strategy was like that employed by the Assyrian ambassador who challenged King Hezekiah by negotiating directly with the people of Jerusalem during a siege (2 Kings 18:13–37).

Fourth, the confrontations between monarchs and prophets were not simply personality conflicts but were instead part of a sociopolitical process that prevented the monarchs from becoming absolute rulers. It would be wrong to conclude that the prophets spoke for Yahweh and the monarchs did not. In their own way, both were committed to fulfilling Yahweh's covenant with Israel. They would agree that the same God who cared for the ancestors and who fed and protected the Hebrews in the wilderness was responsible for the establishment of the kingdoms of Israel and Judah. They disagreed on which systems best reflected that conviction. These disagreements tended to be played out in the prophet's analysis of economic, judicial, and administrative systems and their call for social justice.

Economic systems. Monarchs wished to portray themselves as Yahweh's stewards, responsible for feeding and protecting their countries; to do this they used the centralized economy common in most Canaanite **city-states**. By contrast, the prophets saw themselves as sentries (Jer. 1:11–13) or heralds proclaiming the ideals of the covenant, and this often ran afoul of the policies and desires of the king and priestly community. The prophets are concerned with issues of social justice and champion the rights of the poor and weak members of society. They will not abide the abuse of power and the use of economic forces to drive small farmers from their land or defraud them in the marketplace (Amos 8:4–6). A similar balance of power between prophet and king existed in Mari, where Nur-Sin, an official of King Zimri-Lim, reported: "An apilum prophet of Addu, God of Halab, said to me: 'Am I not Addu, God of Halab, who has raised you . . . who helped you regain your father's throne? I never ask too much of you. Respond to the appeals of your people when they experience injustice and give them a just verdict'" (translated from G. Dossin, "Sur le prophétisme à Mari," in *La divination en Mésopotamie ancienne et dans les region voisines* [Paris: Presses universitaires de France, 1966], 78).

Royal administration. Monarchs defended the state and advanced their political agendas by collecting taxes, raising armies, and making treaties and alliances with other nations (1 Kings 5:12). In response, prophets asserted that such actions usurped Yahweh's authority and the deity's exclusive right to feed and protect Israel. The confrontation between David and the prophet Gad is typical of these confrontations (2 Sam. 24). David had taken a military census in order to muster an army to protect Israel. But Gad denounced David's action as treason and reminded him that only Yahweh, and not the king, protected Israel. Therefore the king is given a choice of punishments that are peculiarly attuned to a ruler's pride and sense of authority: "Will you flee three months before your foes . . . ? Or shall there be three days' pestilence in your land?" Furthermore, only Yahweh, and not the king, could feed the people: "Shall three years of famine come to you on your land?" (24:13). As if to underscore this point, the climax of the narrative is set at a threshing floor where food is processed and taxes collected. This agricultural installation symbolizes the power of God to feed the nation (24:16–17). Gad's sentence reminds David that without God's help he is powerless to protect and to feed himself and his people.

Judicial systems. There were two judicial systems in ancient Israel. Each was a separate system. Although they functioned side by side, one did not review or appeal to the other. Prophets were associated with both systems, while monarchs figured prominently in just one judicial system.

Monarchs administered courts-martial. In a court-martial, the plaintiff went before the king, who alone heard the petition and rendered a verdict that could be enforced by police power. Courts-martial were concerned primarily with matters of taxation, political crimes, and military service, although they could also touch on social injustices. Verdicts of a court-martial, however, were subject on occasion to review by a prophet. For example, the prophet Nathan (2 Sam. 12:1–25) and the wise woman of Tekoa (2 Sam. 14) were plaintiffs in this type of court, and Elijah appealed the sentence that a court-martial carried out against Naboth (1 Kings 21).

In the other judicial system, prophets occasionally were associated with both the gate court and the court of the divine assembly. The gate court, associated with local justice and the activities of village elders, antedated the monarchy and continued to serve as a rival center of power throughout the monarchy.

When prophets associated themselves with the gate court, they did so to emphasize their function in balancing the power of the monarchs (e.g., Jeremiah's **execration ritual** in Jer. 19). Like any other citizen, prophets could stand at a gate to initiate their course of action (7:1–2). The venue of the trial at a gate court was regularly transferred to the divine assembly (1 Kings 22:1–40; Ps. 82:1), which is analogous to the gate court in several different ways. Powerful landowners made up the body of elders in the gate court, while Yahweh, the heavens, the earth, and the prophets made up the divine assembly. Both courts were convened at crucial boundaries in space: the gate court convened at the boundary between the cosmos within and the chaos outside the city proper, while the divine assembly met at the boundary between the divine and human planes. Both had the task of resolving disputes involving land and children, the primary elements of the covenant between Yahweh and Israel. Residents of a single city appeared before the gate court; nations before the divine assembly.

In addition, the divine assembly convened to renew treaties during elaborate **liturgies** at royal sanctuaries on major feast days. Prophets used a **genre** called "covenant lawsuit" to try monarchs who did not fulfill their treaty obligations or who made treaties without the sanction of the divine assembly (Hosea 12:1). Within this context, the divine assembly served as the jury whose decision the prophets announced to Israel and Judah in the form of an oracle (Mic. 3).

Conduct of warfare. War also brought monarchs and prophets into confrontation. In premonarchic Israel, only Yahweh could declare war. A hero would then be lifted up to help deliver the people with the assistance of the **Divine Warrior** (e.g., David in 1 Sam. 30:1–9). The monarchy replaced these defensive wars with standing professional armies sent into battle as a part of royal strategy and international diplomacy. Prophets remained part of the protocol of war even after the establishment of the monarchy. No king would consider going into battle without making a sacrifice and determining whether Yahweh would assist his army (1 Sam. 13:8–12; 1 Kings 22:1–40). The **oracles against the nations** (Amos 1:3–2:16; Ezek. 25–32), the day of Yahweh traditions (Isa. 13:6; Joel 1:15), and the **motif** of the enemy from the north (Jer. 1:14) all played a part in mustering troops for battle—although not always Israelite troops!

Fifth, messengers were an important part of the biblical world, but the prophet was not just a messenger for the divine assembly. In Mesopotamia, messengers were responsible for communications and negotiations between monarchs. The Mari archives show some messengers carrying letters from one ruler to another, usually announcing the imminent arrival of an important official or a foreign army. Other messengers served as proxies for their monarchs and carried letters of introduction outlining the royal prerogatives that they enjoyed, which could include authorization to draft treaties. Hosts lavished them with food, clothing, and slaves, sensing that to honor a monarch's messenger was to honor that king himself. They also provided bodyguards and escorts to protect them from harm while they were in the country and to prevent them from spying as they traveled through it. Meticulous records from Mari list the names, destinations, and backgrounds of all messengers who came and went throughout the region. For strategic and political reasons, a host could temporarily delay messengers, but not permanently detain them. That was part of the diplomatic game, but it had its rules and limitations.

Royal messengers in the Bible do not always fare as well as those described in Mesopotamian texts. For instance, the messengers that David sends to the court of Hanun the Ammonite are intentionally shamed. The newly enthroned Ammonite king orders that half of their beards be shaved off and their clothing be cut off "in the middle at their hips" (2 Sam. 10:4). Such blatant disrespect for the representatives of a foreign government was an assertion of independence and was designed as a graphic means of dissolving all previous diplomatic ties. To prevent public shame to his administration, David sequesters his messengers at Jericho so their private humiliation would not become public knowledge and the basis for discontent among the Israelite leaders (10:5). The subsequent invasion of Ammon results in a twofold victory, with Ammon and its Aramean allies defeated and new treaties established that enforced Israelite **hegemony** over much of Transjordan (10:15–19).

Only two of the twenty references in the Bible to messengers refer to prophets as messengers (Hag. 1:13; Mal. 3:1). Both messengers and prophets are representatives, but messengers represent monarchs, whereas prophets represent the divine assembly. Both the monarchs and the divine assembly commission representatives with the formula "go to [proper name] and say . . . ," but messengers carry information, whereas prophets are empowered to deliver a legal verdict (Jon. 1:2). Both are treated with the respect or disdain due those they represent, but messengers play no role in the development of or the response to the communications they carry. Prophets take an active part both in the deliberations of the divine assembly and in working out Israel's response (Amos 7:1–9). As such, although they carry a message, they also function as envoys or ambassadors of Yahweh and thus benefit from a form of limited diplomatic immunity (Jer. 26:12–15).

Sixth, prophets generated a wide range of reactions. In some cases, the terms used for the prophetic office are voiced in a derogatory or mocking manner. For example, Amaziah, a priest at Bethel, calls Amos a "seer" (Hebrew *hozeh* in Amos 7:12), and Amos himself refuses to be addressed by the title "prophet" (Hebrew *nabi'* in 7:14). An even more blatant judgment of a prophet's worth is found in the **Septuagint**, the third-century Greek translation of the Old Testament, which refers to Hananiah as a "false prophet" (Greek *pseudoprophētēs* in its translation of Jer. 28:1). In both of these contexts, the term "prophet" is meant to refer to a false prophet, who is not an independent or reliable agent of God. However, what distinguishes true prophets from false prophets is not their means of support, their human employer, or their personal reputation among the people. Rather it is based on recognition that they have the authority to speak in the name of Yahweh and that their message conforms to the terms of Israel's compliance with the covenant (Deut. 18:15–22; Jer. 28:8–9).

Prophets were not eccentrics who plagued the biblical world with their visions or erratic behavior. They were important players in the struggle for survival of the people, their identity, and their relationship with Yahweh. The ecstasy that overpowered the prophets identified them as channels linking the human community with the divine. Their actions and their words offered the human community a fleeting glimpse of the consequences of the actions of their rulers. The Hebrew prophets were powerful because they were sensitive not only to the precarious balance of power between Yahweh and the monarchs but also to the people's obligation to Yahweh under the covenant. They could feel and communicate the repercussions of a single act of royal power on the nations in the days ahead.

Characteristics of Prophecy

The following characteristics are not exhaustive, nor will every prophet exhibit every characteristic. Nevertheless, the reader should become familiar with these factors and be able to recognize them when they appear in the biblical text or in extrabiblical materials.

The Prophet's Call

Not every prophet has a fully detailed **call narrative** in the text. This is not to say that they were not called to become prophets, but for some reason the event is not included in the biblical account. When a call story does appear, it is designed in much the same way as the ceremony in which an ambassador is installed. However, the intention of the stories is to confer authority on the prophet, not to provide biographical information. These narratives authorize the prophets' monitoring of Israel's compliance with its covenant with Yahweh. Thus the call is the distinctive event that marks the occasion when a person makes the transition to become a prophet. Some call stories, such as that of Moses, are quite elaborate, while others, like that of Amos (7:14–15), are very perfunctory and give few details. When the biblical writer includes a detailed description of a call, it is usually intended to enhance the importance of the prophet and the prophet's message.

The stories of the calls of Isaiah, Jeremiah, and Ezekiel were told by Israelites who had witnessed the coronation of monarchs and were influenced by this experience. The literary pattern in these stories includes a recognizable series of steps:

divine encounter or **theophany** (Isa. 6:1–2)

introductory word or greeting (6:3)

objection or demurral (6:4–5)

commissioning statement (6:9–10)

sign or talisman empowering the person who has been chosen (6:11–13)

The call transforms the individual. This person, who may have been engaged in some other pursuit or undistinguished to this point in his or her life, now becomes a dynamic spokesperson for God. The call invests the new prophet with special powers, a message, and a mission.

In addition to describing the prophet's call, the call story also highlights the majesty of God. In the more elaborate call narratives, mountains shake upon their foundations, clouds or fog obscure human vision, earthquakes rumble, and divine beings, including angels, appear in theophanic manifestation. The immediate reaction of the human to all this power is abject fear. For example, Ezekiel falls to the ground, Moses hides his face, and Isaiah stands in amazement that he has survived this encounter.

The introductory word or greeting that follows the theophany discloses God's name and God's reason for appearing at this time and place. The naming is necessary because the Israelites lived their entire existence within a polytheistic milieu. All the other nations had many gods, and it would have been only natural to wonder which god had appeared. Moses, for example, asks God's name because he knows that the Hebrews will want to be able to distinguish this one from the many other deities (Exod. 3:13).

The reason for appearing establishes the basis for the prophet's mission. Yahweh has identified a problem, and since it is always the role of the "chosen people" to deal with their own problems (especially if they are the cause of the problem), one of their own people will be sent to provide a warning. The warning is necessary since Yahweh is a righteous God. Although Yahweh may indeed destroy the wicked, it is necessary that righteous humans be given a warning that will allow them to rectify the problem and thereby save their own lives. A good example of such a warning is God's disclosure to the righteous Noah that a flood is coming in order to cleanse the earth of wickedness (Gen. 6:9–18). The deliverance of the righteous from judgment becomes the basis for the **remnant** theme found throughout the prophets.

Perhaps because it is only human nature or perhaps because a formal literary motif has been created to frame these narratives, the person singled out by God now demurs and protests that he is unworthy or incapable of doing the job. For instance, Jeremiah claims that he is too young and does not know how to speak in public (1:6). God sweeps aside these excuses with assurances of support and the provision of special powers or signs. The latter aspect is more applicable to Moses than to the later prophets, who generally (with the exception of Elijah and Elisha) do not perform miracles.

Among the methods of dealing with the demurral is an empowering event. Isaiah, for instance, claims that he is not worthy to accept God's call or speak God's words because he has "unclean lips" (6:5). This means that his mortal lips could never be spiritually pure enough to speak holy words. The solution is for an angel to take a hot coal from the sacrificial brazier near the altar and symbolically cauterize Isaiah's lips. This is not a physical burning but a spiritual purification that occurs in a vision, not in reality. In this way the objection is removed and the prophet is empowered to speak God's message.

Once God has dispensed with the human's excuses, God discloses the prophet's mission. This charge ties the prophet to the original call to mission and the message to be delivered. It reinforces the reason why the prophet has been called to speak and defines the crisis that has made this mission necessary.

The Prophet's Compulsion

A special compulsion is associated with the call to be a prophet. It can be denied or delayed for a time, but ultimately it must be answered. For example, Jonah attempts to flee from his commission, but eventually comes to the realization that there is no escape and he must fulfill God's command to preach judgment to the Assyrian city of Nineveh (Jon. 1:13–17). The compulsion also includes the need to speak. Many call narratives include a reassurance that God will give the prophet the words to be spoken (Exod. 4:12; Jer. 1:7–9). Although a prophet may be reluctant to speak harsh words or condemn his own people, the divine compulsion to speak cannot be resisted (20:9).

Sometimes a prophet's speech is completely under God's control. Ezekiel, for example, is restrained from speaking any words of comfort or hope during the first portion of his ministry (3:25–27). After Jerusalem falls to Nebuchadnezzar's army in 587, Ezekiel is then released to speak a more reassuring message that promises an eventual end to the exile and a restoration of the covenant between Yahweh and his people.

The Prophet's Message

A prophet's message is always spoken in the name of God. A prophet never introduces his message with the words "thus says Amos" or "thus says Isaiah." Rather, the messenger formula that appears in the text is always, "Thus says the LORD [Yahweh]" (e.g., Mic. 2:3; Jer. 5:14). The message is thus the most important thing about the prophet, not the prophet himself or herself. This may be why prophets rarely mention specific names or dates that could draw the people away from the central core of the message. Certainly, there are some prophets, such as Balaam (Num. 22:4–6) and Elijah (1 Kings 18:17), who became famous in their own right, but this is based on the veracity of their message or their ability to speak for God.

Some prophets stand out as individuals in their society, but this is based in many cases on their doing something unusual or unexpected. Isaiah, who was a high-ranking member of the priestly community, parades through the streets naked like a prisoner of war. Imprisoned or humiliated on several occasions, Jeremiah cries out his personal frustration from his prison cell and the public stocks. Ezekiel performs street-theater pantomimes that are completely out of character for a priest. But no matter how odd they act or how flamboyant they may appear, what is at stake is ensuring that the people receive the message of God. Any outrageous acts they perform are designed to attract the people's attention to that message.

The Truthfulness of the Prophet's Message

For a prophet to gain credibility with the people, the substance of the message must come true. The Deuteronomic tradition regarding prophets in Deut. 13:1–4 cautions against prophets who call on the people to "follow other gods"; and 18:18–22 states that a true prophet is one who speaks in Yahweh's name alone and whose words come true. This is one reason prophets begin by declaring that they speak a message that comes from God. By doing this, they separate themselves from their words and thus cannot be charged with treason, sedition, or willful doomsaying. It is also why some prophets proclaim ambiguous messages that can be interpreted in more than one way. Of course, prophets may not even be aware of the full implications of the divine message being delivered. They are not omniscient themselves and can be surprised by events (2 Kings 4:27). Sometimes the full truth of a prophetic announcement will not be revealed until much later, and since God's actions cannot be limited, a certain amount of flexibility is built into many statements, allowing for different outcomes (e.g., Jeremiah's "temple sermon" in Jer. 7:1–15).

The greatest measure of trust and authority, however, comes to the prophet who takes the dangerous step of speaking about the present or the near future (e.g., Isaiah's "Immanuel prophecy" in Isa. 7:3–25). In doing this, the prophet must face the hostility of the people who will eventually experience the punishment expressed in the prophetic message. The prophet may even be incarcerated or undergo a trial by ordeal until it is determined whether the message has been fulfilled (e.g., Micaiah in 1 Kings 22:26–28).

Meanwhile, those who hear the prophetic message must decide whether to obey or reject prophetic instructions. If the message and the messenger are rejected, then a critical and potentially dangerous judgment has been made that the prophet is not a legitimate spokesperson for God. Complicating matters, occasionally two prophets speak contradictory messages, creating **cognitive**

dissonance, a condition in which the prophetic messages both appear to be true and can be tested only by actual events (Jer. 28).

Prophetic Vocabulary and Genres

It is only natural that prophets would speak in the language of the people they are addressing and would use images and vocabulary these people would find familiar and easy to understand (Ezek. 33:5–6). However, the Hebrew prophets operated over a period of about six hundred years, and the social and political situations changed drastically during these centuries. As the times changed, the prophets' audiences also changed, and so did the images and vocabulary that they employed.

Nevertheless, one way that a prophet identified himself or herself as a prophet was by using the images or language of a previous prophet. It is not uncommon for one prophet to make statements similar to those of earlier prophets or to have some portion of his or her career (very often the call narrative) parallel that of past prophets, especially Moses (Deut. 18:15). For instance, Isaiah's call story (6:1–4) contains a visual image of the earthquake and smoke familiar from Moses's Sinai theophany. Similarly, several prophets employ the oracle against the nations theme as part of their message (Amos, Isaiah, Jeremiah, and Ezekiel).

Of course, prophets introduced or emphasized particular phrases that became their identifying rhetorical marker. For example, Ezekiel frequently employs the recognition formula "then they shall know that I am the LORD" (7:27; 26:6; 36:11). Although this phrase is used in other prophetic texts (Isa. 52:6; Hosea 8:2; Joel 3:17), it seems to serve as a literary glue in Ezekiel, tying together his message and reinforcing his theme of God's self-disclosure in the events of Ezekiel's time.

The use of similar terminology by various prophets is seen in the phrase "all flesh," which appears most often in the latter chapters of Isaiah (40:5–6; 49:26; 66:16, 23–24), which date to the end of the exile (ca. 539). It is also found, however, in the writings of the exilic prophets Jeremiah (25:31; 32:27; 45:5) and Ezekiel (20:48; 21:4–5), as well as in the writings of the postexilic prophet Zechariah (2:13) and the apocalyptic book of Daniel (4:12). What seems clear is that this favorite phrase became stock-in-trade language for prophets from the period after 600.

Prophetic words often mimic the official language that monarchs use to officiate at a funeral, deliver a proclamation, ratify a treaty, promulgate law, conduct worship, or declare war. In every area of life where monarchs spoke, prophets challenged them in the name of Yahweh. The use of woe or **lament** oracles associates prophets with funerals (Ezek. 24:9–10). The parable and the proverb, with their association with wisdom (18:2–4), tie the prophets to the royal court and judicial situations (Isa. 5:1–7). The miracle story, with its emphasis on individual acts of assistance, is associated with village justice (e.g., Elisha's actions in 2 Kings 4:1–7; 6:1–7). A call narrative parallels royal diplomacy and accession to power (Jer. 1:4–10). The covenant lawsuit (Hosea 4:1–4), the oracle, or the juridical verdict ties the prophets to the gate court (1 Kings 22:10–17). And the oracles against the nations or execration rituals signal the prophet's prediction of war (Jer. 19; 46:13–26). Each type of prophetic speech is associated with the power of Yahweh alone to feed and protect the people.

What most clearly distinguishes the nature and style of a prophet is the historical context of his message. Elijah speaks directly to King Ahab, not to some future monarch of Israel. Isaiah's reference to the Syro-Ephraimitic war in Isa. 7:3–9 speaks to a specific historical event in the late eighth century. Haggai's pronouncement on the need to reconstruct the Jerusalem temple fits only into the immediate postexilic period and the rule of Governor Zerubbabel (between 520–515).

To be sure, the prophets as well as the narrator make references to the activities of previous prophets, but not usually by name (Jer. 26:17–19; Amos 2:11; Zech. 1:3–4). Instead there is an established tradition of citing prophetic speech—the continuity of the prophetic movement and of the message that the prophets bring from Yahweh—stretching back from their own day into the earliest history of the people.

Enacted Prophecies

Prophets were masters of both the silent and the sounded arts. Not only did they speak, they also performed symbolic actions. The combination of verbal and nonverbal forms of communication magnifies meaning. Symbolic actions may take the form of pantomime, an ancient and universal art of gesture, an expression of social interaction. Anthropologists, sociologists, and dramatists continue to identify a wide variety of pantomimes first celebrated in Stone Age cave paintings and found also in the magic, ritual, and dances of traditional societies. Technically, pantomime is theater without script. Performers in masks may even use words and music to accompany their gestures. But mime is primarily a spectacle, an art whose medium is movement and appeals to the sense of sight. Pantomime grew from a conviction in traditional cultures that only gesture, acrobatics, and dance can appropriately address human realities.

Prophets used three kinds of pantomimes: (1) single dramatic gestures, as when Jeremiah buries his clothes in the riverbank (Jer. 13:1–11); (2) austere practices or asceticism, as when Jeremiah refuses to marry and attend funerals or celebrations (16:1–13); or (3) identification with the silent actions or craft of another, as when Jeremiah, like a teacher, draws the attention of his audience to the potter at his wheel (18:2–4).

Use of Gestures

Ezek. 4:4–8   The initiation of speech is signaled by a pantomime or prophetic symbolic action. Ezekiel lays on his left side for 390 days and then on his right side for 40 days signaling the number of years of the kingdoms' exile.

Ezek. 4:7   Ezekiel is instructed to prophesy against Jerusalem with his "arm bared." Presumably, this means he raised his arm above his head causing his robe to slip off his arm. There is also a sense of employing a gesture of command typically used by military leaders (e.g., God's "outstretched arm" in Deut. 5:15; 7:19; 11:2; 26:8; 1 Kings 8:42; 2 Kings 17:36) or when God "bared his . . . arm" to indicate divine action against the nations (Isa. 52:10).

For the prophets, pantomime was not solely representational art. It was also, like the Native American Ghost Dance of 1890, an act or set of acts that was believed to be able to set events in motion. Prophetic symbolic acts could act as catalysts for social change. The message of change sometimes required overt action to throw off physical or cultural oppression or to restore a lost commitment to the covenant and its obligations.

Male and Female Prophets

Unlike the Israelite priesthood, which was exclusively male, both men and women functioned as prophets; no distinction seems to have been drawn between them as to their authority or authenticity. Thus Deborah's prophetic word to Barak is unquestioned, although the general does request the security of having her accompany the army into battle (Judg. 4:4–9). The prophet Huldah acts as an authenticator of a tradition associated with Moses when addressing the question of the scroll of law found in the temple in Josiah's time (2 Kings 22:14–20). This is in tune with the appearance of both male and female prophets elsewhere in the ancient Near East. Since it was understood that prophets had been chosen by a god to serve as his or her mouthpiece, a prophet's individual characteristics, including gender, had no bearing on the message. This is further evidence that prophets were not chosen for their self-importance, status, or personal abilities.

Modes of Prophetic Utterance

Prophetic speech was expressed in a variety of ways and uttered in several different styles. It was sometimes the result of a physical trance state (Ezek. 8:1; 11:1–5), occasionally induced by music and/or dancing (1 Sam. 10:5, 10; 2 Kings 3:15). Most often, however, prophecy was simply spoken as a report of a vision or dream (1 Kings 22:19–22) or as the words of God spoken to the prophet.

Prophetic words were attuned to genres from a variety of social situations. The woe or lament oracle cast the prophet in the role of a mourner (Ezek. 24:9–10). When the prophet operated within wisdom tradition, the message was given in the form of a parable or proverb (2 Sam. 12:1–15). In the case of a miracle story (2 Kings 4:1–7), the prophet operates as a divine representative and patron. In pronouncing a covenant lawsuit the prophet functions as a member of the divine assembly (1 Kings 22:10–17). The often elaborate oracles against the nations place the prophet in the position of a divinely appointed judge sent to pronounce a sentence on that nation (Jer. 48:46–47).

Except in the stories about Moses, miracle stories are found only in the tales about Elijah and Elisha. However, the miracles performed by these prophets were not so much authorizations of their power but rather indictments of the monarchs' abuse of their power and authority. Virtually all of these miracles are focused on some aspect of feeding and protecting oppressed people. In these instances, miracles demonstrated the easy manner in which Yahweh could feed and protect the people, while the monarchs were forced to make trade deals and treaties with other nations to try to feed and protect them. For example, the kings are forced to take widows' sons to fill their armies, endangering their lives, while Elisha channels God's power to raise the son of the widow of Zarephath back to life (1 Kings 17:17–24). While monarchs tax the meager resources of widows living on the brink of starvation, Elijah provides the widow with an endless supply of oil (2 Kings 4:1–7). And when a borrowed ax necessary to clear the land is lost, Elisha returns it so that the borrower will not face an insurmountable debt (6:1–7).

The Prophet's Social Role

On many occasions a prophet was forced to oppose the traditional views of the priestly community and the political agenda of the monarchy. In part this is reflective of the **egalitarian** ideal implicit in the covenant in which every person was equal under the law. That does not mean there is no social stratification, only that the terms of the covenant applied equally to all. Sometimes prophets are mentioned as part of the temple community (Isaiah and Ezekiel) or as court prophets (Nathan). Still, they seem always to have been able to stand apart from these institutions to criticize them and to point out where they have broken the covenant with God. In doing so, these "establishment prophets" created a following of disciples or a school of thought that preserved the message of the prophet and eventually organized it into a written, coherent document.

Occasionally a prophet such as Elijah or Elisha may appear to be totally autonomous and in fact peripheral to the mainstream of society. Even these apparently antiestablishment prophets, however, did not stand alone. They were part of and supported by a social group ("**sons of the prophet**") that functioned as a sort of underground network of material and spiritual assistance. This social support group would have provided meals and lodging for the prophet and would have helped him carry out his mission (2 Kings 9:1–10).

Within the political realm, the prophets often served as the conscience of the kings. It was their job to remind the monarch that he was not above the law and could be punished like any other Israelite for an infraction of the covenant (2 Sam. 12:1–15). Prophets also engaged in political acts. For instance, Elisha has one of his "sons" anoint Jehu as king (2 Kings 9:1–13), and Jeremiah counsels King Zedekiah to accept Yahweh's judgment and surrender Jerusalem to the besieging Babylonians (Jer. 21:1–10; 38:17–18).

Prophetic Immunity

Since the prophets were viewed as messengers of God, they were not supposed to be held liable for the message they spoke, and tradition dictates that they not be killed because of that message. That is the basis for Jeremiah's claim of **prophetic immunity**, telling his judges that he has spoken only the words given to him by God and that they would be shedding "innocent blood" if they carried out a death sentence on him (Jer. 26:12–15). Unfortunately, at least according to the **Chronicler**, prophetic pleas are not always effective in the face of political realities. Zechariah, a palace priest who leads the coup against Athaliah and places her grandson Joash on the throne in Jerusalem, later prophesies against Joash because of his idolatrous practices. The king orders Zechariah's execution but is cursed by the dying prophet, and God allows Joash to be defeated by the Syrians and murdered in his bed by his advisers (2 Chron. 24:15–25).

In more normal cases, if suspicion was raised that the person was not a true prophet, then the message was to be held up to scrutiny to see whether it came true (Deut. 18:22; Jer. 28:8–9). Suspicion of his credentials as a true prophet seems to be the reason for Uriah son of Shemaiah's execution. He speaks the same message as Jeremiah, but chooses to flee to Egypt rather than defend God's word and is subsequently captured and executed (26:20–23). Should the message prove false, then the prophet was subject to execution, either by the people or by God (26:12–19; 28:16–17).

Just because a prophet was spared from death, however, did not mean that he or she would not face public ridicule and physical punishment at the hands of dissenters. For instance, the high priest Amaziah publicly denounces Amos at Bethel for speaking without license within the precincts of the king's sanctuary (Amos 7:12–13). Elijah is threatened with execution by Jezebel and has to flee for his life (1 Kings 19:2–3). Jeremiah faces public censure (Jer. 36:21–26), is imprisoned (38:4–6), and is humiliated by being placed in the stocks (20:2).

Concern with the Present and Near Future

Because their job was to draw the people and the establishment back into a proper covenant relationship with Yahweh, prophets centered their message on the present and the near future. Sometimes their warnings were delivered prior to God's punishment, and sometimes their words served as an explanation why God had punished the people. Such an explanation is referred to as a **theodicy**, which offers reasons why God allows evil or destruction to occur. A theodicy also functions as an argument for continuing to serve a god who had allowed the people to be conquered and/or abused by another nation.

The major exception to the prophetic concern for the present and the near future is found in **apocalyptic** prophecy. By definition, apocalyptic utterance is concerned with end things (**eschatology**) and contains elements of tradition and history that are hidden intentionally in symbolic language. Zechariah and Joel are the best examples of apocalyptic prophets, and apocalyptic images are common in the book of Daniel, although Daniel is not technically a prophetic figure. The portions of these books that contain this type of literature are usually dated to the latter portion of Israelite history (200 and later). As a result, they employ many of the ideas and themes of earlier prophets. But they speak to a future time when the problems of the present are solved and God reigns over a restored nation (Zech. 8:1–8).

The Prophetic Theme of the Remnant

The theme of a righteous remnant is a common element in the prophetic literature. The theme reflects the belief that a righteous God cannot utterly destroy righteous persons without at least giving them a chance to survive. The story of Noah and the flood is an early example of this theme, although God speaks directly to Noah instead of employing a prophet (Gen. 6–9). In later Israelite history, however, the prophet serves as the bearer of God's message of retribution. Because of the failure of the people to obey the covenant, their punishment is certain, but a remnant may survive the coming destruction and rebuild the nation from the ashes. Ezekiel's vision of the "marking of the innocents" is one of the best examples of this message (Ezek. 9). His vision may be a parallel to the Passover account in Exod. 12:1–13, since divine messengers mark the foreheads of those persons who demonstrate a true repentance and sorrow over the sins of Jerusalem. When the rest of the population is executed and the city is destroyed, the ones who have been marked are to be spared and will serve as a remnant who will rebuild the nation.

The Reinterpretation and Compilation of Prophetic Literature

Prophetic speech has a long history of reiteration and reinterpretation. The prophets and the editors of the prophetic literature often employ themes and

---

Eden in the Prophets

Ezek. 36:33–36   In his description of God's promise to restore Israel, Ezekiel points to the exclamation by those who witness the transformation from desolation to fertility that "this land . . . has become like the garden of Eden."

Isa. 51:1–3   In a similar manner, the postexilic voice of Isaiah calls on the returned or returning exiles to be comforted in the Abrahamic tradition of which they are a part, for God's covenant promise of land and children will ensure that the "waste places" will become "like Eden."

Joel 2:3   In his depiction of the day of the Lord, Joel warns the people that what had once been a "land . . . like the garden of Eden" will be transformed as part of God's judgment into "a desolate wilderness."

---

imagery from earlier prophets, but also draw on the full tradition of Israelite storytelling to make their message clear. For example, several of the prophets use the story of the garden of Eden as a foil for lost opportunities or as a hope for an eventual idyllic restoration of the nation.

While we do not have a definitive picture of the process in which the words of each prophet were collected, written down, and edited, it is safe to say that it took place over many years and reflected shifting theological agendas as the fortunes of the nation changed. It seems likely that some of the prophets spoke their message to live audiences, but the compilation and editing of these words may well have taken place long afterward. In fact, there are only occasional references in the biblical text to prophecy actually being written down by a prophet or by one of his support group:

> Then the LORD said to me, Take a large tablet and write on it in common characters. (Isa. 8:1)

> > Go now, write it before them on a tablet,
> >   and inscribe it in a book,
> > so that it may be for the time to come
> >   as a witness forever. (Isa. 30:8)

> Thus says the LORD, the God of Israel: Write in a book all the words that I have spoken to you. (Jer. 30:2)

> Take a scroll and write on it all the words that I have spoken to you against Israel and Judah and all the nations. (Jer. 36:2)

> When they are ashamed of all that they have done, make known to them the plan of the temple . . . and write it down in their sight. (Ezek. 43:11)

Then the LORD answered me and said:
Write the vision;
  make it plain on tablets,
  so that a runner may read it. (Hab. 2:2)

The actual compilation of the prophetic materials and their editing in later periods must have been a complex and collaborative process. The difficulties this entails can be seen in the—to Western eyes—apparent disorganization and lack of chronological sequence found in books like Jeremiah and the somewhat jumbled presentation of major themes in Hosea. It is possible that some of these problems are due to the tumultuous upheavals faced by Israel and Judah during the eighth–sixth centuries. Another possibility may be that prophets with particularly long careers like Isaiah and Jeremiah actually spoke on many more occasions than are recorded in the biblical text, and what is eventually recorded is a synthesis of their themes rather than a dictated, word-for-word message. Decisions made by editors (members of the priestly and prophetic community) and redactors during the Persian period must have had an impact on the final version.

Whatever the actual process, these prophetic texts did survive. They were found in multiple copies in the scrolls produced by the Qumran community. The Septuagint Greek translation of the Hebrew text, while containing variations based in part on the translation process and on the versions available to the translators, became another source for the writers of the New Testament. The authors of the New Testament books and the works of later Christian theologians made use of the prophetic literature to clarify and provide proof texts for their doctrines. Because these are commentaries on the words of the Hebrew prophets, it is necessary to caution readers that they did not

New Testament Use of Old Testament Prophecies

Matt. 1:23   The Gospel of Matthew uses Isa. 7:14 as a proof text for the virgin birth of Jesus.

Matt. 2:5–6   The Gospel of Matthew quotes Mic. 5:2 as a proof text for Jesus being the **Messiah**, since he is born in Bethlehem and is destined to "rule in Israel."

Luke 4:18   In its portrayal of Jesus reading from the Isaiah scroll in the Nazareth synagogue, the Gospel of Luke dramatically quotes Isa. 61:1–2 and then has Jesus declare that the prophecy has now been fulfilled.

John 12:12–15   During Jesus's triumphant entrance into Jerusalem, the Gospel of John quotes Zech. 9:9 as a proof text that Jesus is fulfilling the prophecy that the "king" will ride upon a donkey.

necessarily concern themselves with the original intention or social context of a particular Hebrew prophet. Their interests, as one might expect, were directed to their own time and place, and their agenda was to provide a foundation, using ancient traditions, for their emerging religious movement. It would have been only natural for the Gospel writers, the apostle Paul, and other early Christian leaders to draw upon these ancient prophetic traditions to bolster their arguments for the messiahship of Jesus. Still, their call to return to obedience to the covenant and their assurance that God would provide relief in times of distress found a welcome audience in the periods after the destruction of the Jerusalem temple by the Romans.

3

Premonarchic Prophetic Activity

While the majority of the Hebrew prophets operate during the monarchic and postexilic periods, prophetic figures appear in the biblical narrative prior to Saul and David. The two most prominent of these figures are Moses and Balaam. Little is known about their social world, and in any case the accounts that describe them date to a much later period. Little attempt is made by the biblical writers/editors to flesh out either the thirteenth-century Egyptian setting for Moses or the twelfth-century culture of Moab in the Balaam narrative. The principal purpose in both of these stories is crisis management, and the action involves a human chosen to serve as a conduit for divine power. It is clearly more important to the theology of the writers to demonstrate **Yahweh's** supremacy over other gods. What later readers may learn about life in Egypt, the Sinai, or Transjordan during the late second millennium is not really germane to this purpose.

Moses

A simple reading of the text demonstrates that Moses is much more than a prophet. His leadership of the Israelite tribes is all-encompassing, and he functions in both secular and priestly capacities. He serves as a judge hearing the cases of the people (Exod. 18:13), and he also officiates at public sacrificial offerings (24:5–6). Because of his special standing with the people and with Yahweh, he becomes closely associated with the tent of meeting, a portable sacred precinct that is otherwise restricted only to the members of the priestly community (40:30–32).

What may be most useful to our discussion of prophetic activity is the account of Moses's **call narrative**, which provides the basic **framework** for the call of several later prophets (especially Isaiah) and sets a tone for **theophanies** elsewhere in the biblical narrative. His call (3:1–4:17) may be outlined in four stages:

1. The theophany in which Yahweh first speaks to Moses occurs in conjunction with a "burning bush" that is not consumed. This miraculous phenomenon on Mount Sinai demonstrates Yahweh's mastery over creation, provides a setting for interaction between the deity and the chosen mortal, and transforms that ground into sacred space (3:5). Of course, the narrative also plays on human curiosity, and the audience must have been amused when Moses cannot resist turning aside from his own activities to investigate this marvelous sight. By definition, no divine call occurs without a divine manifestation of some sort. The theophany includes an identification of the deity involved and the reason for the deity's decision to appear at this particular place and time.

2. The human reacts with fear to the theophany and immediately offers a demurral, or excuse, why he or she should not be the one to perform the assigned task. Again, the audience is entertained by Moses's excuses, which are particularly creative. In each case, God rejects the excuse or provides a solution. For example, when Moses says he is nobody important (true, but not a sufficient reason for excusing him), God's response is "I will be with you," and that is sufficient (3:11–12). Moses continues to delay making a decision by asking God's name (a clear indication of the polytheistic world in which Moses lives). Yahweh responds with a theological pun based on the verbal root of the divine name ("I AM sent you"). In this way, God makes the point that "he is" and other gods "are not." Moses then asks for some means of proving that he has official standing as a representative of this particular God. Yahweh gives him the power to perform a series of signs, a means of getting the people's attention and perhaps convincing them that Moses really can do what he claims. And finally, almost in desperation, Moses declares that he has no training or ability to speak before audiences, much less the god-king pharaoh of Egypt. This final demurral provides the opening for the Priestly editor of these materials to introduce Moses's brother Aaron into the narrative, a man who will become the first high priest of the Israelites (28:1–5).

3. Once Moses has run out of excuses, God then provides resolution to the conversation and sets a precedent for future call narratives. The deity dismisses all of the mortal's excuses by saying that he or she will have

Yahweh's words and power working for the newly appointed prophet. Therefore the newly appointed prophet is not to be afraid (Jer. 1:8; Ezek. 2:6).

4. At this point no further argument is possible, and as God lays out the mission of the prophet, the only response can be, "Here am I; send me" (Isa. 6:8).

Once he returns to Egypt, Moses's prophetic activity is demonstrated in the contest with Egypt's pharaoh and in the sequence of ten plagues. The account of the ten plagues is cast in the form of a literary framework that systematizes Moses's conflict with Pharaoh and demonstrates clearly to the Egyptians the power of Yahweh (Exod. 7:5). Each time Pharaoh refuses to allow the Israelites to go into the desert to worship Yahweh, Moses predicts the coming of a plague. Occasionally Aaron is the more active participant (8:16–17), but the stepped sequence remains basically the same. When Pharaoh is forced to acknowledge that he and his magicians cannot end a particular plague, Moses then predicts the end of that calamity. God's manipulation of Pharaoh, hardening his heart in each sequence of the cycle, functions as a didactic exercise for the benefit of the Israelites (7:14–12:51). It repeatedly reminds them who really is God in this story.

Similar examples of Moses's intercessory role occur in the narratives of the wilderness wandering, when the people "murmur" over a lack of food or water (16:1–8). The vast majority of Moses's attention, however, is given over to administrative (18:13) and military affairs (17:8–15) during the Sinai and wilderness treks. In effect, he is forced to share responsibility with the tribal elders (18:13–27), and a sign of how these men share more than executive power is found in the narrative in Num. 11:24–30. When Moses realizes he

---

Plague Sequence

- Moses petitions Pharaoh to allow the Israelites to worship Yahweh for three days in the desert.
- Yahweh "hardens Pharaoh's heart," and the Egyptian god-king refuses to cooperate.
- Moses predicts a plague and it is enacted at God's command when Moses or Aaron is instructed to "stretch out your hand."
- Unable to stop the plague, Pharaoh pleads with Moses to pray to Yahweh to end the plague.
- After the plague ends, Yahweh "hardens Pharaoh's heart" again, and the king again refuses to allow the Israelites to go worship. That in turn brings the sequence full circle to start again with the next plague.

must delegate some of his authority, the elders are assembled before the tent of meeting and God's presence is manifested among them. The impression is created that God takes a portion of the divine spirit that had been placed in Moses and places it in each of the **seventy elders** (compare the removal of one of Adam's ribs to create Eve in Gen. 2:21–22). As a result, these men are overcome by the power of God's spirit (compare Saul in 1 Sam. 10:5, 10–11), and they all begin to prophesy. This demonstrates to the people that some of God's power has been placed within their leaders and they can therefore rely on them, like they do on Moses, for advice and the solution to their problems.

Further evidence of the importance of Moses as the originator of prophetic precedents can be found in the echoes that occur in later prophetic speech and behavior:

Episode in Moses's Life	Examples in Later Prophets
call narrative (Exod. 3:1–4:17)	• Isaiah (Isa. 6) • Jeremiah (Jer. 1:4–18) • Ezekiel (Ezek. 1:1–3:11)
contest-between-gods **motif**: plague sequence (Exod. 7–12)	• Balaam's curses and blessings (Num. 22) • Gideon pulls down Baal's altar (Judg. 6:25–32) • Elijah's contest on Mount Carmel (1 Kings 18)
intercessory prayer: wilderness period murmuring (Num. 11:1–3; 14:13–19)	• Samuel prays prior to battle with Philistines (1 Sam. 7:8–9) • unnamed prophet prays for Jeroboam's hand (1 Kings 13:6) • Elisha prays for the Shunammite's son (2 Kings 4:33)
dialogue with God: Moses's complaint (Num. 11:10–15)	• Samuel disputes naming king (1 Sam. 8:6–22) • Jeremiah's complaint (Jer. 20:7–18) • Habakkuk's complaint (Hab. 1)
public disputes: Korah's revolt (Num. 16:1–35)	• unnamed prophet confronts Jeroboam (1 Kings 13:1–10) • Amos's reply to Amaziah (Amos 7:11) • Jeremiah's trial (Jer. 26:7–19)
tradition-history: Moses's obituary (Deut. 34:10–12)	• Samuel's farewell address (1 Sam. 12) • Elijah's ascent and return (2 Kings 2:11; Mal. 4:5) • Jeremiah's seventy years of exile (Dan. 9:2)

Balaam

The other significant prophetic figure in the premonarchic period is Balaam. A non-Israelite seer, apparently he had gained a reputation as a true prophet, someone whose predictions in the name of a god came true. Outside the Bible, his name and at least one example of his prophetic ability are recorded in an eighth-century Aramaic inscription found at Deir Alla in the eastern

Universalism

In their portrayal of Yahweh as supreme among the gods, the biblical writers periodically inject the theme of universalism into the narratives. In these narratives, a non-Israelite character makes a broad statement of faith identifying Yahweh as the most powerful or the only true god in all the earth. The character makes this declaration because she has come to know what Yahweh has done for the Israelites (as in the case of Rahab in Josh. 2:9–10) or because he has had a personal experience of Yahweh's power (Naaman in 2 Kings 5:15). Although the theme of Yahweh's universally manifest power eventually develops into the concept of monotheism or an exclusive belief that Yahweh is the only God, this concept will not be fully fleshed out until late in Israelite history, perhaps not until after 400.

Jordan valley: "This is the story of Balaam, son of Beor and a seer. At night the **divine assembly** appeared to Balaam, son of Beor. He dreamed he heard El pronounce a death sentence on his city" ("Stories of Balaam," *OTPar* 132).

His reputation as a seer is the basis for an attempt by the king of Moab to use Balaam's powers to curse the invading Israelites (Num. 22–24). Balak describes Balaam as so attuned to the gods that both his blessings and his curses are always effective (22:6). As is so often demonstrated in the wilderness narrative (11:2; 21:7), the prophet, as a god's intermediary or representative, is believed to be capable of interceding for good or ill with the god(s). In the process, however, both Balaam and Balak are given a lesson on the power of God to control the message of a prophet (compare Ezek. 3:25–27). As Balaam says repeatedly in his professional disclaimer, prophets may be asked to do something, but if they are true to their calling, they can speak only the words given to them by God: "Do I have the power to say just anything? The word God puts in my mouth, that is what I must say" (Num. 22:38).

Although the narrative also makes Balaam the butt of a divine joke (the talking donkey in 22:22–35), it depicts him in this instance as a prophet of Yahweh and is fairly sympathetic to him (similar positive language occurs in Mic. 6:5). Balaam employs sacrificial rituals to obtain God's answer, but he is not simply a diviner; in fact, he abandons his usual procedure of invoking a god or seeking an omen through **divination**. Having perceived that Yahweh's intention is to bless the Israelites, he leaves himself open to direct revelation from God. At that point, he becomes empowered to speak God's blessing on the Israelites.

Later traditions treat Balaam as an unwilling pawn or villain whose curse is transformed into a blessing by the God of the Israelites (Deut. 23:5; Josh. 24:9–10; Neh. 13:2). In fact, other accounts describe how the Israelites killed Balaam during their war against the Midianites, identifying him as a diviner

(Num. 31:8; Josh. 13:21–22). Perhaps the more negative appraisal of Balaam in these texts is due to the biblical writers' desire to champion only Israelite prophets and to separate them from diviners and seers (2 Pet. 2:15 and Rev. 2:14 also have this negative view). The **universalism** theme that runs throughout much of the biblical text is present in both the positive and the negative portrayals of Balaam. In both versions, Yahweh is proved to be a powerful deity without any divine rival and one capable of speaking through foreign prophets.

4

Early Monarchic Prophets

Despite the "mixed crowd" that left Egypt (Exod. 12:38), Israel is portrayed as a fairly unified people during the formative period of the exodus, conquest, and settlement. The leadership of Moses and Joshua, while faced with repeated challenges (Num. 11:1–15; 16:1–50; 21:1–9), generally held sway over the people and tied them together until the Promised Land was in their grasp. This is at least the story told by the writers and editors of Exodus, Numbers, Deuteronomy, and Joshua. The social, religious, and political chaos that dominates the tales in the book of Judges, however, suggests that there actually was little unanimity during the early years of Israel's settlement in the land. The political and social evolution of the nation required the people to learn to cope with their new land, the challenges of the environment, and the difficulties associated with being a fringe culture within a larger social domain. Eventually, the realities of what is necessary to cope and survive as an identifiable people will lead to the elevation of strong national leaders as chiefs and eventually as monarchs.

Samuel

Given the ancient Israelite belief in a cyclical universe, it is not surprising that the reader of the biblical narrative will be continually presented with a succession of figures who share Moses-like characteristics. During the period of transition between the judges and the beginning of the monarchy, this figure is Samuel. Like Elijah in a later period, his life and career shares many items paralleling Moses:

1. *Miraculous circumstances at birth*. Moses barely survives Pharaoh's order to exterminate the Hebrew male infants (Exod. 2:1–10). Samuel is born after his mother, Hannah, had been barren for years and becomes pregnant only through divine intervention (1 Sam. 1:1–20).
2. *Call*. Despite Samuel's call occurring when he is a child (1 Sam. 3), it involves a distinctive **theophany**, an amusing byplay of mistaken identity on the part of Eli, and an acceptance of the task by what would otherwise be considered an unlikely candidate.
3. *Military success*. Like Moses, Samuel leads the Israelites to victory against their enemies. For both Moses and Samuel, this victory is accomplished entirely with the aid of **Yahweh**, the **Divine Warrior** (1 Sam. 7:7–11; Exod. 17:8–13).
4. *Judge over the people*. Like Moses, Samuel formally sits in judgment on the legal complaints of the Israelites as he moves from village to village in a judicial circuit (1 Sam. 7:15–17; Exod. 18:13). During the period of the judges, Deborah also functions in both a prophetic and a judicial capacity. Unlike Samuel, however, Deborah's story centers on a single episode and does not describe her career in any detail (Judg. 4–5).

In addition to these characteristics, which resemble Moses's leadership, Samuel also functions as a transitional figure representing both the anarchic period of the judges and the emergent period of chiefdoms and kings. That Samuel is not a Levite and yet functions as a priest suggests that membership in the priesthood is not yet a Levitical monopoly at this time. Of course, given his miraculous birth story and his later reputation as a seer, Samuel transcends normal social labels. As both judge and seer, he can be consulted on any matter of concern to the people, whether public or private, secular or religious. The rather chaotic situation of the people during this transitional period in fact may require that Samuel perform a variety of roles. There is, for example, neither a central government nor a central shrine where governors or priests can serve all of the tribes. Even Samuel exerts his authority over only a small area in the central region of Palestine's hill country—a circuit of cities ranging from the cultic sites at Bethel, Gilgal, and Mizpah to his own hometown of Ramah. Still, with the possible exception of Deborah, Samuel's nominal authority stretches over a larger range of territory than any of the other judges were able to control, and this suggests that the political situation was beginning to shift toward greater cooperation between the tribes.

Despite the political and social difficulties that he faced, Samuel provides a model of authority that had not existed since Joshua. Getting the people to look to a central authority figure was crucial as the tribes emerged from their fiercely held local autonomy to forge a chiefdom led by Saul and his supporters. It was no small thing for the tribes to relinquish their individual control over their warriors and allow a combined army to be commanded by an individual who did not belong to their own tribe or clan. Such a situation is admirably portrayed in the ancient Song of Deborah, which condemns several tribes who refused to join forces even during a time of great crisis (Judg. 5:13–18). Perhaps because he is widely regarded as a divine intermediary rather than a political figure, Samuel facilitates the transition to statehood. When the tribes of Israel face a crisis that requires the cooperation of more than two or three tribes, they can turn more freely to the prophet Samuel as their mediator and facilitator.

It is indeed Samuel's reputation as a seer that brings the young Saul to him (1 Sam. 9:9). Although the meeting is ostensibly about a private matter of lost animals, it also inaugurates an entirely new political and religious arrangement in Israel. That meeting also inaugurates a new role for prophets, who hereafter will be involved in the selection of kings and also will serve as their chief critics on many occasions.

In this early period of state formation, the roles and responsibilities of both kings and prophets had to be carefully worked out; and, not surprisingly, the process of defining these separate roles involved considerable conflict over rights and responsibilities. Of course, what we have is the Deuteronomist's portrayal of the prophet-king relationship, but that does not mean it is entirely dependent or reflective of the sixth-century editor's (or editors') perspective. Perhaps to make it as clear to the audience as possible, the growing storm is described in a series of narratives beginning with Samuel's anointing of Saul with oil (10:1), which is significant in at least two ways: (1) it not only designates Saul as God's choice but also reminds the king of the importance of the prophet who has anointed him; and (2) because olive oil was involved in nearly every aspect of daily life (cooking, cosmetics, lamp oil, medicine), it serves as a perfect symbol of the many responsibilities of the monarch to maintain and nurture the economic welfare of his people.

Once Saul is acknowledged as their king by the tribal leaders, he quickly discovers that his word is not absolute and that he must continue to bow not only to God's command but also to the directives of God's representative, Samuel. It must have galled the man chosen by God to lead the nation to be limited in any way. After all, he had been shown to contain an element of God's spirit when he "danced with the prophets" and prophesied himself (10:10–13; compare the **seventy elders** in Num. 11:24–30), so he naturally would have considered that no constraint should be placed on his actions when he thought he knew what needed to be done. The narrative emphatically demonstrates, however, that the king is not above either the law or God's representative (see Nathan's use of the king's call to justice **motif** when David committed adultery).

The prime example of the evident tension between Samuel and Saul occurs in a series of episodes in which Saul repeatedly fails to demonstrate the attributes of a faithful servant of God (1 Sam. 13–15). In the first instance, Saul must act in his role as military chief while being reminded that cultic practices belong to the priestly community alone. The issue is whether Saul will carry out this role in obedience to Yahweh, Israel's Divine Warrior, or whether he will act on his own initiative. The drama is played out as Saul waits for Samuel at Gilgal. As he waits the requisite seven days for the prophet, the Philistines gather in strength, and the frightened Israelite warriors begin to slip away (13:5–7). When Samuel does not appear, Saul takes matters into his own hands and offers a sacrifice to God before going into battle with the Philistines. Perhaps his sacrifice was a way of calling on God for help, or perhaps it was to determine if Yahweh would be with him in battle. Neither reason adequately accounts for his actions, though, because he had been instructed to wait for Samuel to arrive. Samuel reminds Saul that patience is not a luxury for military or political leaders; rather, it is a necessity for those who would trust in God. By exceeding his instructions, Saul has not only usurped Samuel's role as diviner, he has also proved his lack of faith in God's ability to help Israel (13:8–14). The episode also gives the storyteller the opportunity to insert a prediction that Saul's dynasty will be eclipsed by "a man after his [God's] own heart" (13:14), a transparent reference to David.

When Samuel gives him another chance to demonstrate his loyalty to Yahweh, Saul fails again. In the name of Yahweh, Samuel calls on Saul to conduct a *herem*, or holy war, against the Amalekites, a perennial enemy of the Israelites since Moses's time (Exod. 17:8–16; Deut. 25:17–19). In effect, Samuel instructs Saul to continue the war of conquest begun by Joshua, since the *herem* is a form of ethnic cleansing that will rid Israel of a persistent enemy and a cultural threat. The king slaughters the Amalekites in battle, but he does not completely obey Samuel. Instead he takes rich spoils back with him to his capital to demonstrate his prowess. This is a clear example of the effort of the fledgling monarchy to add to its power base through public display much like Roman generals and emperors did when they held triumphal parades in Rome to showcase not only their military victory but also the wealth that comes through conquest.

The situation as portrayed is ripe for confrontation, and Samuel does not disappoint. His righteous indignation and pointed doomsaying are a forerunner of similar prophetic speech during the divided monarchy when the prophets are often the only articulated voice of social and political criticism (Jer. 22:13–23; Hosea 8:4–6; Amos 2:6–16). Saul tries to excuse himself by claiming that the people took a portion of the spoil as a sacrifice to God. This cannot, however, justify his failure to obey the divine command for total destruction. Samuel responds with a piece of dripping sarcasm that must have humiliated the proud king in his moment of triumph: "What then is this bleating of sheep in my ears, and the lowing of cattle that I hear? . . . The LORD anointed you king over Israel. And the LORD sent you on a mission. . . . Why then did you not obey the voice of the LORD?" (1 Sam. 15:14, 17–19).

The simple answer is that Saul has disobeyed again, and this pattern of disobedience, shaped in literary terms as a "disqualification story," now provides the justification for God's decision to reconsider the hereditary claim of Saul's family to the throne of Israel. Some of this narrative obviously has been reworked to suit the political needs of the Davidic dynasty, since Samuel's announcement that God "has torn the kingdom of Israel from you this very day" (15:28) adds authority and legitimacy to David's claim to the monarchy. The statement in 15:22–23, which is less obviously tinged with Davidic political interests, articulates a general theological principle:

> Has the Lord as great delight in burnt offerings and sacrifices,
>   as in obeying the voice of the Lord?
> Surely, to obey is better than sacrifice,
>   and to heed than the fat of rams.

This statement of what is expected of all kings becomes a ready cliché in later prophetic speech (e.g., Hosea 6:6; Mic. 6:6–8). In this confrontation between two powerful figures, the prophet as Yahweh's representative must win out over the king. God can anoint someone to be king, but this ruler must in turn provide an example of both leadership and obedience to the nation and to God. Otherwise the prophet will be waiting in the wings to condemn the monarch and/or choose a new king at God's command. With the establishment of the hereditary Davidic monarchy and the granting of the "everlasting covenant" to the house of David (2 Sam. 7:1–17), a variation in this theme occurs for the kings of the southern kingdom of Judah, but the threat of divine displacement remains intact for the kings of the northern kingdom of Israel (2 Kings 9:1–13).

In the case of Saul's misdeeds, God instructs Samuel to seek out a more suitable candidate to replace the house of Saul on the throne (1 Sam. 16:1–13). The comical narrative describing how Samuel eventually anoints David points up that prophets are human and therefore capable of error and also continues the sequence of stories in which the younger son rises to a position of authority (e.g., Jacob in Gen. 25:19–34; Solomon in 1 Kings 1). Samuel is very impressed with Jesse's older sons but eventually must ask the old man if he has any other sons, since God reminds the prophet that appearance is not everything and that God "looks on the heart" of the candidate (1 Sam. 16:7). David, the youngest son, will then take Saul's place as the "LORD's anointed" and will spend many years growing into a job he cannot ascend to until Saul's death. The entire narrative is part of the "**apology** of David," which disqualifies Saul's descendants from inheriting Saul's throne and promotes the establishment of the Davidic monarchy.

One final prophetic role played by Samuel occurs after his death. In the final days of his rule, Saul is completely cut off from God. Samuel is dead, no other prophetic or priestly voice has taken Samuel's place, and most poignantly, God no longer speaks directly to Saul (contrast 10:10–11; 19:19–24). Faced with imminent battle against the militarily superior Philistines, Saul breaks his own command and goes to consult the Witch of Endor and asks her to conjure up the ghost of Samuel so he may ask him what to do (28:3–25). Samuel's response is predictable both from the standpoint of a prophet and as the voice of the editor who wishes to reiterate the legitimacy of the Davidic claim to the throne. He simply repeats in summary fashion all of his previous statements, condemning Saul for his disobedient actions and reminding him that God "has torn the kingdom out of your hand, and given it to your neighbor, David" (28:17). The ghostly prophet then predicts the king's demise along with his sons. This narrative makes clear that prophets are not gods to be consulted through mediums and wizards. They function only as spokespersons for God and do not take the initiative to speak in their own name.

Nathan

In the face of Saul's failures to effectively defend the Israelite territories from the Philistines and to hold the tribal groups together as an effective national entity, David must spend a great deal of effort solidifying his position against potential tribal fragmentation and demonstrating his ability to win victories. After the death of Saul's son Ishbaal (2 Sam. 4), the tribal elders come to David's stronghold in Hebron and acknowledge him as their king (5:1–5). David then takes immediate steps to establish himself as a strong military leader against the Philistines and shrewdly captures the politically neutral site of Jerusalem and makes it his royal capital (5:6–25). The crowning symbolic step taken by the new monarch is to transport and house the **ark of the covenant** in Jerusalem (6:1–15). This act ties the secular and sacred authority to that place forever after and also associates it with his dynasty. In the middle of this consolidation of royal power, the prophet Nathan steps forward to both build up and tear down David's royal ego.

Unlike Samuel, who operated independently of political institutions, the prophet Nathan is depicted as a member of David's royal court. In fact, Nathan is intimately attached to David as one of his advisers and presumably also functions as a diviner for the court. One might expect that, as such, he would be a political loyalist. That certainly seems to be the case when he announces that God intends to establish an everlasting covenant with David and his descendants. The context of the oracle is David's desire to build a "house" or temple for Yahweh, an act designed to further enhance Jerusalem as his royal capital. While Nathan's initial response is positive (7:3), this is quickly transformed by a subsequent oracle into what could be considered a rejection of David's efforts to confine Yahweh to a house or "king's temple." Instead a divine promise is made to establish an everlasting dynasty for David. By playing on the meaning of the word *house*, Nathan proclaims that David may not build a house or temple for God; instead it will be God who will build a house or dynasty for David (7:8–17).

God's promise of an everlasting dynasty establishes a covenant relationship with David that not only legitimizes David's authority to succeed Saul on the throne, it also sanctions a hereditary monarchy and divine right to rule in

---

Hesed in Political Context

The Hebrew word ***hesed*** is translated "loving kindness, unfailing love, everlasting love," and starting in Exodus it is used as a divine quality explaining God's willingness to assist and care for the Israelites (Exod. 15:13; 34:6–7) and as the basis for Yahweh's forgiveness of an imperfect nation (Num. 14:18–19; Deut. 7:12). Once the monarchy is established, the term is extended to include the loyalty of subjects and allies (2 Sam. 2:5–7; 3:8) and, most important, the relationship between God and the Davidic rulers of Israel. That same relationship is then translated in the prophetic literature as a promise of a future "just king" and a return for the nation to its relationship to God:

> Moreover the Lord declares to you that the Lord will make you a house.... I will not take my steadfast love [*hesed*] from him.... Your house and your kingdom shall be made sure forever before me; your throne shall be established forever. (2 Sam. 7:11–16)

> He is a tower of salvation for his king,
>   and shows steadfast love to his anointed,
>   to David and his descendants forever. (2 Sam. 22:51)

> When the oppressor is no more, ...
> then a throne shall be established in steadfast love
>   in the tent of David,
>   and on it shall sit in faithfulness
> a ruler who seeks justice
>   and is swift to do what is right. (Isa. 16:4–5)

> Come to me;
>   ... so you may live.
> I will make with you an everlasting covenant,
>   my steadfast, sure love for David. (Isa. 55:3)

perpetuity. Such a divine promise does not, however, give the kings of David's line a blank check to use their power in any way they please. Nathan's oracle affirms that kings, just like the people, must still obey God's commands and the stipulations of the covenant. Individual Davidic kings can and will be punished for their sins; nevertheless, God will remain loyal to the promise made to David to establish his dynasty, never taking away the "steadfast love" upon which it is founded. Thus the oracle concludes with the observation that what happened to Saul and his family will not happen to David's (7:15; 1 Chron. 17:13).

This new relationship between God and the king also has an impact on the relationship between the prophet and the king. When David sins by engaging in a clandestine, adulterous affair with Bathsheba and then arranges for the death of her husband, Uriah, to cover up what is normally a capital crime (2 Sam. 11), it is Nathan who announces God's judgment of David. To do this in an indirect manner, Nathan employs a **juridical parable** that ultimately forces David to acknowledge his guilt and pronounce his own punishment:

> There were two men in a certain city, the one rich and the other poor. The rich man had very many flocks and herds; but the poor man had nothing but one little ewe lamb, which he had bought. He brought it up, and it grew up with him and with his children; it used to eat of his meager fare, and drink from his cup, and lie in his bosom, and it was like a daughter to him. Now there came a traveler to the rich man, and he was loath to take one of his own flocks or herd to prepare for the wayfarer who had come to him, but he took the poor man's lamb, and prepared that for the guest who had come to him. (2 Sam. 12:1–4)

This transparent parable shows a power difference between the men, based on wealth and social standing. The poor man has a single possession other than his family that he values. The rich man violates the laws of hospitality by taking the lamb from the poor man instead of taking an animal from his own flock. All of these statements are an obvious indictment of the king, as they graphically illustrate what David has done by taking Uriah's wife, Bathsheba. Thus Nathan can charge David without naming him until David has passed judgment on the "rich man" (12:5–7).

Adultery is a capital crime (Deut. 22:22), but under Israelite law a conviction requires two witnesses (19:15). In this case God is the only witness, and since it is the king who has committed the crime, recompense is geared to a political punishment that fits the crime. Nathan's parable and the shame attached to the revelation of his act forces David to acknowledge his behavior, to confess, and repent (2 Sam. 12:12–13). Although his dynasty will not be abolished as Saul's was, the child of adultery will die (12:14), and David will have to face the anguish of rebellion and dissension within his own house (12:10–11). Since David has acknowledged Nathan's authority in the prophecy of God's intention to grant his dynasty an "everlasting covenant"

(7:8–17), he must now accept the prophet's authority to rebuke him over his sin of adultery.

Nathan's use of the parable of the ewe lamb is an example of the **Deuteronomistic Historian**'s motif of the king's call to justice (also 1 Kings 21:17–29). According to the protocol of this motif, when the king violates the covenant it becomes necessary for a prophet or other divine representative to confront him. When the shamed king confesses and repents, the punishment that he would otherwise receive according to the law is passed in some manner to the next generation.

This literary motif depicts the prophet administering justice on the highest-ranking member of Israelite society and demonstrates that the king is not above the law. In Nathan's case the use of the parable presents a test case and in turn requires that the king acknowledge that Yahweh can discern what might otherwise be hidden to human investigators. Thus the prophet serves as the champion of the covenant as well as the voice of God sitting in judgment.

Ahijah

The political realities associated with a fledgling state and the strong forces of fragmentation so often present in tribal societies made it almost inevitable that the kingdom of David would not remain intact for long. The picture portrayed in the text of the glorious reign of Solomon, his construction of the Jerusalem temple, and his efforts to build the prestige and the economy through foreign alliances suggest that the Israelites were moving forward toward true statehood (1 Kings 6–10). However, the inherent problem with new hereditary monarchies is that they are overly dependent upon the abilities and personality of the heir to the throne. Solomon's successor, Rehoboam, is a weakling who does not grasp the political tensions among the tribal elders created by his father's political efforts. That plus the concerns expressed by the Deuteronomistic Historian over Solomon's accommodation to the gods of his many foreign wives (11:1–13) creates a perfect storm that will rip the new nation apart and demonstrate once again the role of the prophet as the representative of God who will designate divine choice of a new ruler.

A great deal of effort had gone into creating an apology, or justification, for David's assumption of power. Along those same lines Solomon is portrayed as a wise king who could create general prosperity throughout the land (1 Kings 3). However, the reality of Israel's political divisions becomes evident in the reaction to Solomon's policy of diplomatic marriages. Having many wives was not the issue, since that was expected of monarchs who used royal marriages as a way of establishing political and economic alliances. It was the construction of shrines to the gods of his foreign wives that required divine reaction and stern admonition from the prophet Ahijah (11:9–13). The covenant that had been made with David was not to be set aside, but as part of Solomon's punishment, his son Rehoboam would lose control over all but the southern portion of the kingdom.

Ahijah's task in this political drama is modeled after that of Samuel in 1 Sam. 16:1–13, when he was directed by God to search for Saul's successor and subsequent rival. Since God has determined that the nation will be divided and a new king must be found for the northern nation, Ahijah seeks out Jeroboam, a member of Solomon's bureaucracy and therefore a man with some administrative experience (1 Kings 11:28). Instead of anointing him, however, Ahijah performs a very different symbolic act. Grasping Jeroboam's new garment, Ahijah tears it into twelve pieces. He instructs Jeroboam to take ten of these strips of cloth as his assurance that he will rule the ten northern tribes of Israel. Only one tribe is to be retained by Solomon's son Rehoboam as a sign of the continuation of the Davidic covenant (11:29–37). This symbolic gesture parallels or perhaps mimics Saul's division of his oxen into twelve pieces when he exercises his role as chief and calls on the people to lift the siege of Jabesh-gilead (1 Sam. 11:5–7). Ahijah's actions also function as an unusual example of an investiture ceremony in which an individual is armed with authority by being given the symbols and robe of his office.

Jeroboam's Sin (1 Kings 12:26–32)

- Rival cultic centers are created at Dan and Bethel—at the extreme northern and southern ends of the kingdom—in order to replace Jerusalem as the primary shrine to which Israelites are expected to bring tithes and offerings.
- Golden calves are installed in these two shrines to substitute for the ark of the covenant and to meld Baal worship with Israelite practice—perhaps reflective of the Israelites not yet being monotheists.
- Local **high places** (*bamot*) are tolerated in villages, allowing the people to maintain their traditional worship practices, but also allowing for the injection of Canaanite rituals and gods—and thus generating Jeroboam's popularity with the people outside the major cities.
- Non-Levites are appointed by the king to serve as his loyal cadre of priests, thus ensuring greater loyalty to the new king, but not always to the law and the covenant. Their training and their desire to protect their jobs become a major source of conflict with Yahweh's prophets.
- A revised religious calendar for the major pilgrimage festivals is established to better coordinate with the growing season and harvest in the northern kingdom—a move recognizing the differences in growing season and climate, but violating the stipulations of the cultic calendar associated with sacrifice in Jerusalem.

Dan and Bethel as Cultic Sites

Gen. 12:8   Abram builds an altar at Bethel, calls on the Lord's name, and stakes out the Promised Land.

Gen. 31:13   God is self-identified as "God of Bethel," referencing Jacob's pillar and vow made there, and commands Jacob to leave Laban's household and land and return to the "land of your birth."

Judg. 18:14–31   The migrating tribe of Dan steals Micah's idol and transports it to Laish (renamed Dan), where it is installed with a Levite priest to officiate before it.

Judg. 20:18   Israelite tribes, preparing to attack Benjamin at Gibeah, first go to Bethel to inquire of the Lord "which of us shall go up first."

Ahijah's oracle establishes two separate tracks to the monarchy. The Davidic covenant provides for the divinely sanctioned, hereditary monarchy in the southern kingdom. According to this agreement a continuous line of Davidic kings in Judah will last until the fall of Jerusalem in 587. The Davidic line will not be a trouble-free dynasty, but only two monarchs will be assassinated, and there will be no break or change of ruling families. The relationship between God and the kings in the north, however, reverts to the "monarch on trial" arrangement employed during Saul's rule. Each northern king will be presented with the obligation to uphold the terms of the covenant, and each will be expected to obey it without wavering. Thus God says to Jeroboam: "If you will listen to all that I command you, walk in my ways, and do what is right in my sight by keeping my statutes and my commandments, as David my servant did, I will be with you, and will build you an enduring house, as I built for David, and I will give Israel to you" (1 Kings 11:38).

According to the Judean narrators of 1–2 Kings, the kings of Israel were never able to meet this strict standard of behavior. Jeroboam himself sets the tone for misrule by committing what these writers term the **sins of Jeroboam**. These writers maintain that Jeroboam sinned because, in his effort to create a separate political identity for the northern kingdom, he initiated a series of steps designed to focus attention on his own administration and cultic centers and away from the sovereignty of Yahweh. Their judgment of the **apostasy** of the northern kings will be echoed in the challenging words of many of the prophets as well.

Although these Judean writers label Jeroboam's actions as sin, we can also understand them as shrewd strategies designed to create political identity and autonomy for the northern kingdom. For example, the sanctuaries at Dan and Bethel are built on sites long associated with cultic activity and were intended to prevent the Israelites from traveling to Jerusalem (1 Kings

12:28–33). Still, Jeroboam's politically motivated decrees become the criteria used by the biblical writers to judge the actions of all future kings. Thus in the account created by the Deuteronomistic Historian in Samuel–Kings, a just king is one who obeys the covenant like his "ancestor David" (2 Kings 18:1–8), and a bad king is one who continues the sins of Jeroboam (14:3–4, 23–24). Later prophets will also take the kings of Israel to task for continuing the sin of Jeroboam (Hosea 8:4–5).

Naturally, after such a list of horrendous monarchic sins, Ahijah will be obliged to condemn Jeroboam, just as Samuel had to reject Saul. The curse laid on the house of Jeroboam occurs when the king's wife disguises herself (compare the disguised Saul and the Witch of Endor in 1 Sam. 28:8) and goes to the prophet on behalf of her ill son. Nearly blind in his old age Ahijah is warned by God of her coming, and he uses the opportunity to detail Jeroboam's refusal to keep God's covenant, literally "thrusting Yahweh behind his back," in favor of other gods (1 Kings 14:9). As a result, and worst of all for any royal family, just like Saul's, they will be denied the chance to establish themselves as dynasts in Israel (14:6–14). They will be so dishonored that only this sick child will be allowed proper burial (14:11–13; compare Elijah's curse in 21:21–24). Thereafter the succession to the throne in the northern kingdom is to be governed more by military power than by legal rights. As a practical matter, succession by assassination becomes the rule rather than the exception.

The Unnamed Man of God from Judah

One additional narrative related to the Deuteronomistic Historian's assessment of Jeroboam's initial acts as king of the northern kingdom involves an unnamed "man of God" from Judah. This nameless prophet challenges the new king's authority during the ceremony inaugurating the king's newly built royal shrine at Bethel. If this story truly meshed with the chronological scheme of the sixth-century Deuteronomistic History, one would have expected that Ahijah would have been the one to stand before the triumphant king at Bethel and condemn him for his hubris. Since the narrative also contains the prophecy of the coming of Josiah and the destruction of Bethel's altar in the late seventh century (1 Kings 13:2–3), however, it is quite likely that this story represents a separate, later tradition than the Ahijah narrative. The episode suggests that Jeroboam's sins begin when he establishes an illegitimate shrine, separate from Jerusalem. They are then shown to have long-term consequences that are finally rectified, according to this embedded prophecy, by a future "just king" who will cleanse the site of that sin and, at least temporarily, restore Davidic rule over the area.

The narrative also illustrates once again the manner in which royal and prophetic authority can come into conflict. In this scene Jeroboam is dedicating his royal shrine at Bethel and promoting his leadership over the newly created nation of Israel. In the middle of what should be a triumphant moment for the new king, he is interrupted by the unnamed prophet from Judah. Initially in his public pronouncement, the prophet completely ignores Jeroboam and directs his curse against Bethel and its altar. By deliberately snubbing Jeroboam the impression is made that God has already revoked Jeroboam's authority to rule. Justifiably upset over the disruption of the ceremony and wishing to restore his control over the situation, Jeroboam "stretche[s] out his arm" to order the man's arrest. The king's gesture points out the culprit to be seized and contains a familiar movement associated with command (Josh. 8:19; 2 Sam. 24:16) or action (Exod. 3:20; Job 1:11). In this instance Jeroboam's dismissive gesture is matched by the prophet's or God's reaction when the offending hand is caused to wither. Thus the intent of the commanding gesture is nullified and the authority of the king is further diminished when he is forced to lower himself and ask the prophet to intercede with God to heal his hand (1 Kings 13:6; compare Pharaoh in the plague sequence in Exod. 5–11). After being healed, the king's authority and his effort to recapture control of the situation are further eroded when the prophet refuses Jeroboam's offer of hospitality. By doing so, the prophet reverts to his original stance of ignoring the king's presence and power.

The curious story in the second half of the narrative (1 Kings 13:11–32) is another demonstration that no one, not even a prophet, may disobey God's command without being punished (also Num. 20:1–13). The man of God has been given firm instructions not to turn aside or return home by the same path (1 Kings 13:17). However, an "old prophet" of Bethel assures him that he has received an angelic message giving the other man license to stop for a meal (13:18). The apparent confusion at this mixed message from what he must have assumed to be a reliable source creates a situation that can be termed **cognitive dissonance**. In other words, two seemingly truthful statements stand in direct conflict and will require a test to determine the real truth. In this case, truth is revealed by the lion's attack and the Bethel prophet's remorse (13:24–32). The moral of the story, as in many of the tales in which prophets confront kings, is that strict obedience to God's command is the highest imperative in life.

5

Elijah and Elisha

In the period immediately after the division of the kingdom (ca. 930), no strong prophetic figure emerges. As we saw above, two prophets condemn Jeroboam in separate incidents (1 Kings 11:9–13; 13:1–10); but these are apparently isolated events that do not represent a systematic effort at reform, and no subsequent episodes involving these prophets give us a sense of their careers. Not until the ninth century will prophets once again appear who are able to launch an effective challenge to the power of the king and the religious establishment in the northern kingdom. These remarkable prophets are Elijah and Elisha.

It is not possible to say much with any certainty about this shadowy time in Israelite history. The biblical narrative is heavily edited and provides only enough information to suggest the difficulties faced by the two small kingdoms. What little is known from other sources comes from the records of King Shalmaneser III of Assyria (858–824). On his "Monolith Inscription," Shalmaneser records his official version of the Battle of Qarqar on the Orontes River in Syria in 853. Among the petty rulers mustered against him is King Ahab of Israel, who is said to have supplied two thousand chariots and ten thousand soldiers—the largest contingent of any of the allied states. Such a prominent place among the allies and such large numbers suggest that Ahab was among the leaders of the coalition and a relatively powerful and influential ruler.

However, that is not the biblical picture of Ahab. In 1 Kings 18–22 he and his Phoenician wife, Jezebel, are portrayed as ruthless villains and enemies of **Yahweh**. Furthermore, Ahab's role as a powerful local ruler is repeatedly

57

diminished, since in these narratives he is completely dominated by his strong-willed, foreign wife. In fact, the storyteller blames Jezebel for most of Ahab's failures. While such a diplomatic marriage would have established a logical political alliance between Israel and Phoenicia, the biblical writers, as they did in condemning Solomon's foreign wives (11:1–8), present it as an invasion by the forces of Baal religion. Jezebel's name even becomes a negative label synonymous with wickedness and infidelity despite her seeming to be an ardent advocate for her religion, a faithful wife, and a strong supporter of her husband and children. For the biblical writer, however, she is condemned for maliciously hunting down the prophets and worshipers of Yahweh, killing all she can find. Apparently abetting her actions, Ahab does nothing to stop her campaign of religious purification in Israel.

Elijah Cycle

Elijah and Elisha are the larger-than-life heroes of this extended narrative, and much of what they do is designed to champion Yahweh worship and gain authority and recognition for Yahweh's prophets. In the process, they are portrayed as individuals capable of performing miracles, and their actions for good and their combating evil are magnified in the text. Elijah, whose name means "My God is Yahweh," bursts on the scene without an initial call story or even an introductory statement beyond his affiliation with the Tishbites of Gilead. Perhaps his mysterious origins help the narrator to focus on Elijah's role as social critic and champion of Yahweh worship. After all, he must confront the immense powers of the state and the Baal priesthood single-handedly. He does this in spectacular fashion, first predicting a three-year drought, to be followed by a famine throughout the land of Israel (1 Kings 17:1). This strategy is a perfect gambit because Jezebel's god, Baal, is believed to be a god of storms and fertility. Thus Elijah's prophecy directly calls into question Baal's power and asserts that Yahweh alone controls the rains and harvests. The theme of this prophet and all others is thereby firmly set forth in the question, who really is God?

Having pronounced a near death penalty on the farmers of Israel and having presented a challenge to Ahab's legitimate rule, Elijah spends the three years of the drought east of the Jordan River and at Zarephath in Phoenicia (17:2–24). By performing life-giving miracles during this time in Jezebel's home country, he demonstrates the power of his God, whose **covenant** promise was to provide land and children. In contrast to the denial of life-giving rain in Israel, Elijah, Yahweh's representative, provides food to a starving widow and her son. Then, after the son has apparently died, he revives the son. Elijah's actions stand in stark contrast to those of Ahab and Jezebel, who take away life with their purge of Yahweh worshipers and who, by their introduction of the worship of Baal, are the cause of the famine in the land. The point made is that those who serve Yahweh receive the benefits of the covenant, and these benefits can be shared by those who acknowledge the authority of Yahweh's prophet.

Contest on Mount Carmel

When the initial testing period is completed and at a point when the economy of Israel must have been in near collapse, God instructs Elijah to return to Israel and challenge Ahab to a contest that will dramatically and publicly demonstrate Yahweh's power and Baal's total impotence (1 Kings 18). Not since Moses's time has there been such a direct, public confrontation between a king and a prophet. In fact, Moses's obituary decrying the nonappearance of another prophet "like Moses" (Deut. 34:10–12) may now be set aside in favor of this new miracle worker. But while Moses challenged a foreign god-king, the pharaoh of Egypt, Elijah's confrontation is with an Israelite king and a foreign god.

Consideration of where to stage the contest takes into account several factors. First, the proposed site for the trial is Mount Carmel, a promontory that overlooks the Mediterranean coast and serves as a perfect platform from which to watch for storms coming in from the sea. Second, the mountain had previously served as a cultic site since Elijah rebuilds the Yahweh altar "that had been thrown down" (1 Kings 18:30). Finally, as at Mount Sinai (Exod. 19:10–25) the people are called to assemble before a mountain (1 Kings 18:19) where they can witness God's power being manifested. Such attention to the value of sacred space, as well as the utilitarian possibilities of a **high place**, clearly points to an understanding of the significance of spatial factors by storyteller, prophet, and audience.

In approaching the story of the contest on Mount Carmel it is necessary to take into account the ways in which space or specific designations for space are intentionally manipulated or transformed. For instance, the term "all the land" (Josh. 11:16; Deut. 19:8) may be used for "the possession of Yahweh" and thus be considered "sacred space," but it also is a geographic reality with specific dimensions—"from Dan to Beer-sheba" (2 Sam. 3:10)—giving it political and economic implications. On a smaller scale, humans, as social beings, decorate their space both physically with personal items that set an aesthetic tone and symbolically through cultural markers or communal understandings.

In the contest on Mount Carmel, physical or firstspace (a mountain that overlooks the Mediterranean Sea) is magnified in importance by its transformation into sacred space through cultic rituals and sacrifice (allowing it to take on dimensions of thirdspace). It also obtains a political dimension since it provides the stage for a magnificent public display of divine power that has the potential to either enhance the king's power or radically diminish it in the

Spatial Concepts in Ancient Israel

The current discussion of critical spatiality theory uses the following terms:

firstspace   equals concrete items that can be mapped and that we determine to be geophysical realities.

secondspace   is imagined space, in other words, ideas about what space consists of and potentially can be used for.

thirdspace   can be thought of as "lived space," including the social interaction that takes place within that discrete space.

fourthspace   is remembered space that comprises memories of how space has previously been used and the ways in which those memories help to determine how space is subsequently classified or used.

There is value in employing this **framework** for understanding how space is lived and perceived in the ancient world by different elements of society. By applying these concepts, it becomes possible to classify how space is associated with events, legal formulations, architectural design, political boundaries, and personal ambitions. One way of deciphering the spatial understanding of the ancient Israelites is to examine the ways in which space is both defined and manipulated by persons and events. This process can be as simple as identifying the physical places where the Israelites work, worship, transact business, practice and execute legal decisions, and gather for important announcements. These mundane social practices take on different meanings, purposes, or intentions depending on where in space and time they occur and who is performing the action in question. Thus the content or substance of the act (farming, speech, religious ritual, and transaction) derives meaning from (1) the rank, authority, or status of the person involved and (2) the physical and symbolic space (including time, place, occasion, or setting) involved. Remembered space or associations with space can also be evoked for personal or political purposes (e.g., Saul's coronation at Gilgal in 1 Sam. 11:14–15; compare Joshua's role as war chief at Gilgal in Josh. 4).

minds of the people (secondspace). Subsequently, whenever the story of the contest is told, the sacred character of the mountain is once again brought to mind along with Elijah's and Yahweh's triumph there (fourthspace). With agreement by both parties, the rules of their contest seem quite simple. Both Elijah and the 450 prophets of Baal will construct an altar to their god. The Baal prophets and then Elijah in turn are to call upon their god to accept the sacrificial bull. The gods will indicate their acceptance of the sacrifice by casting down divine fire upon the altar and bringing rain to end the drought. The suspense, as well as the comic nature of this story, is heightened when Elijah lets the opposition go first. Their daylong pleading with Baal goes unanswered despite their "limping" dance and ritual bloodletting (1 Kings 18:26–28). These acts may be part of a mourning ritual or a form of penitence (Deut. 14:1), but more likely are designed to invoke the power of a storm god during the summer months, when he would ordinarily be absent in the underworld. A very amused Elijah taunts their failed performance and ridicules their nonresponsive god: "Cry aloud! Surely he is a god; either he is meditating, or he has wandered away, or he is on a journey, or perhaps he is asleep and must be awakened" (1 Kings 18:27).

Elijah's taunt takes its cue from Mesopotamian epic literature. In both the tales of Atrahasis and the story of Enki and Ninmah, a sleeping deity must be awakened in order to deal with a growing calamity. In addition, the idea that the deity is sleeping may have been part of the ritual of awakening associated with the rains that ended summer droughts each year. The necessity to perform this ritual also stands in contrast to the description of God in Ps. 121:4, who "neither slumber[s] nor sleep[s]."

Elijah takes his turn next and performs a series of symbolic acts designed to restore the people's confidence in Yahweh as the God of Israel (1 Kings 18:30–40). First, he gathers the people around him and rebuilds the platform of a ruined altar that had previously been dedicated to Yahweh (similar to Gideon's actions in Judg. 6:28–32). He then takes twelve stones representing the twelve tribes of Israel and uses them to build an altar in Yahweh's name (compare Josh. 4:1–9). Finally, he digs a trench around the altar and has water poured over the sacrificial bull and wood three times, thus filling the trench and saturating the fuel for the sacrifice. This last step symbolizes the bounty of the coming rain and, in addition, demonstrates that no chance spark can ignite his sacrifice.

Then at a time specifically appointed during the day for sacrifices and oblations (1 Kings 18:29), Elijah calls upon Yahweh to demonstrate that the "God of Abraham, Isaac, and Israel" is "God in Israel" and that Elijah is his prophet. This parallels the account of Moses's confrontation with Pharaoh and suggests just how closely the biblical writers patterned the Elijah cycle after the Moses narratives (Exod. 9:13–14). Yahweh's response is immediate and provides a precedent that separates Yahweh worship from that of the Canaanite gods. No elaborate or stylized ritual acts or self-mutilation are necessary. Plus with such a quick response there is no opportunity for Baal's priests to taunt Elijah or God. Sacrifice, altar, and water are all consumed by divine fire from heaven in a spectacular demonstration of power.

Such a decisive act elicits two strong emotions on the part of Elijah's audience. First, in the face of a clear **theophanic** manifestation, they are appropriately afraid, and this causes them to make a collective statement of abject submission: "The LORD indeed is God!" (1 Kings 18:39; compare Rahab's statement in Josh. 2:11). Then, perhaps as an emotional release, the people become fiercely angry at being deceived by the adherents of Baal. Responding to Elijah's command, they massacre the prophets of Baal (1 Kings 18:40), perhaps in reflection of the Deuteronomic command to slay false prophets (Deut. 13:1–5). Finally, after Elijah's servant performs a sevenfold ritual of observation of the elements, it begins to rain and the final test of Yahweh's power is completed (1 Kings 18:41–46).

Elijah's Theophany on Mount Horeb

Even though Elijah has won the contest on Mount Carmel and demonstrated the superiority of Yahweh's power over Baal's, Jezebel remains a formidable opponent. When she threatens to kill Elijah, he runs away in fear for his life (19:2). That Elijah has operated to this point as a social outsider now works against him. As a Gileadite from the area east of the Jordan River, he has no ties to any group or person other than a servant, and apparently he has no strong clan ties or political power base in Israel. His flight may reflect this lack of crucial support or simply the cooling of the people's emotions, which allows Jezebel to once again take command of the situation.

Since so much of the Elijah narrative appears to have been modeled after the events of Moses's life, however, Elijah's flight may be patterned to resemble Moses's initial flight from Egypt (Exod. 2:11–15; also Exod. 12). Just as Moses fled Egypt after killing an Egyptian and journeyed to Mount Sinai, so also Elijah journeys to Mount Horeb (since Mount Sinai is called Mount Horeb in these narratives, the destination of Moses and Elijah is the same). While he is in the wilderness, Elijah must rely on God to feed him, just as the Israelites did. He survives his journey to Mount Horeb only because of divine intervention; an angel provides bread and water (1 Kings 19:4–8; compare the provision of manna in Exod. 16).

When Elijah arrives at Mount Horeb, he receives his formal call as a prophet, which is absent from the earlier narrative. The theophanic call is staged like other divine encounters with fugitives (e.g., Hagar in Gen. 16:7–12). God asks him, "What are you doing here, Elijah?" (1 Kings 19:9). In response to what is essentially an indictment for inappropriate behavior, a fugitive generally produces an excuse or a justification (e.g., Adam and Eve in Gen. 3:8–13), and Elijah does both. He explains that he has been working zealously for Yahweh without a body of supporters. Now he has taken flight so that there will be at least one voice left to defend God.

The ensuing theophany is quite mystifying. Elijah experiences strong winds, earthquake, and fire (1 Kings 19:11–12). All of these, plus a thunderous voice, are typical manifestations of Yahweh's power frequently found in biblical accounts of theophanies (Exod. 19:16–19; 20:18; Job 37:1–5). But in this case the narrator takes a different tack in describing God's presence. None of these traditional forms of power—earthquake, wind, or fire—contains the spirit of God. Instead the prophet perceives the presence of Yahweh only in the silence that follows these manifestations (1 Kings 19:12–13). What the narrator may be trying to do is draw a clear distinction between Yahweh and Baal, a storm god whose theophanies would also be characterized by earthquake, wind, and fire. It is also possible that the theophany has been reshaped by a later editor whose theology has moved beyond simple natural events as signs for God and who now wishes to show that Yahweh's presence is both universal and internal.

In any case, Elijah clearly understands that he is being addressed by God, and he wraps his face in his mantle to shield it from the power and glory of God's presence (as does Moses in Exod. 3:6). At the entrance to his mountain cave, he is asked once again by Yahweh, "What are you doing here?" (1 Kings 19:13). The refrain embedded in the text—the exact same response comes from Elijah in 19:10 and 19:14—suggests that this story may have been regularly reenacted by the Israelites. It has the feel of a dramatic performance and sets the audience up for Yahweh's threefold charge to the prophet. The three acts he is to perform are designed to transform Israel religiously and politically (19:15–16): (1) anoint Hazael as the new king of Aram (Syria), (2) anoint Jehu as the new king over Israel, and (3) anoint Elisha as his prophetic successor.

Elijah performs only the third task and leaves the first two for Elisha, whom he designates as his successor by **casting his mantle** over Elisha's shoulders. This is one of many examples in which clothing functions as both a symbolic object and a social marker in the biblical narrative. Since nationality, gender, age, and social condition (e.g., widowhood) are signaled by particular garments, it is only natural that the prophets would have taken advantage of this ubiquitous prop in their spoken and **enacted prophecies**. Thus in much the same way that Moses uses his staff to open the Red Sea (Exod. 14:16), Elijah (and later Elisha) uses Elijah's outer garment (mantle) as an object of power to open

---

Use of Clothing as a Social Symbol in Prophetic Literature

1 Kings 11:29–30   Ahijah removes Jeroboam's new linen robe and tears it into twelve pieces to signify the division of the kingdom and Jeroboam's claim to rule ten of the twelve tribal districts.

2 Kings 2:13–14   Elisha retrieves Elijah's mantle after his master is taken by God, and like Elijah he uses it to open up the waters of the Jordan River and thereby demonstrates he is the prophet's true successor.

Isa. 20:2   Isaiah graphically displays the danger faced by Judah by stripping off his clothing and walking about naked like a prisoner of war or a slave.

Jer. 13:1–11   Jeremiah removes his "linen belt" and buries it in the Euphrates riverbank as a signal that Judah's danger will come from that direction and indicating that the people, like his piece of clothing, will be exiled in Mesopotamia on God's command.

up the Jordan River (2 Kings 2:8, 14). As the story of Elisha's calling continues, he requests and receives permission to say good-bye to his parents (contrast Luke 9:61–62), and then he disappears from the narrative until 2 Kings 2.

Naboth's Vineyard and the King's Call to Justice

The cycle of Elijah stories resumes in 1 Kings 21 with the story of Naboth's vineyard. This narrative is the classic example of the **motif** of the king's call to justice, which addresses two questions: What are the primary qualities of a just king? What recourse do the people have when a king chooses to abuse his power?

When King Ahab expresses a desire to add Naboth's fine vineyard to his own adjoining property, Naboth resists the king's offer and exercises his right to refuse to either sell or exchange his land for another field. His case is based on the principle that ownership and inheritance of the land is tied to Yahweh's covenantal promise. According to this tradition, each Israelite tribe, clan, and household received a portion of the land following the conquest (Josh. 13–19). Therefore, forced land transactions or the concept of eminent domain stand outside the sovereign powers of the king (Lev. 25:23; Num. 36:7). Naboth declares that he will not deprive his sons of their inheritance in the covenant community, and therefore he will not release ownership of his household's covenantal bequest. Faced with this tradition of ownership, Ahab has no recourse under law and must accept his failure, however grudgingly, in this case.

Jezebel has no such legal qualms when it comes to the exercise of royal powers. The narrator highlights the differences between Phoenician and Israelite royalty by showing that she freely acts to obtain the land for her husband through deceit and force. The queen hires two false witnesses (matching the number of witnesses required for a capital case; Num. 35:30) and has Naboth charged with treason and blasphemy (Exod. 22:28). When Naboth is executed (along with his family; 2 Kings 9:26), the land is left without an heir, and Ahab is then able to claim it as part of the royal domain (1 Kings 21:8–16).

The justice motif dominates the conclusion of the narrative. Ahab, who clearly does not mourn the death of his subject, is intentionally stepping off his newly acquired property. He is enjoying the thrill of walking off the distance between each boundary marker on the parcel of land. In this way he officially and symbolically takes possession of the property (Amos 2:6 condemns those who foreclose on land by forcing farmers into debt slavery for the price of a "pair of sandals"). Elijah uses the vineyard as the backdrop for his confrontation with the king. In this way Naboth's violated legal rights and the violated land, polluted by Ahab's proprietary steps, are linked.

As was the case when Ahijah curses Jeroboam's family (1 Kings 14:1–18), Elijah condemns Ahab's family to a terrible fate. Not only will they suffer the loss of the throne to another ruling family, they will also be utterly destroyed and suffer the dishonor of being left unburied with their abandoned corpses consumed by animals like so much garbage (21:17–24; compare 14:7–14; Jer. 8:1–2). The king is terrified by Elijah's curse and performs an act of contrition so complete that even Yahweh remarks on it: "Have you seen how Ahab has humbled himself before me?" (1 Kings 21:29). In the face of the king's abject repentance, it would be difficult to carry out God's sentence immediately against him. As a result, God is portrayed as both a just and merciful deity, capable of relenting in the face of true repentance (compare Joel 2:14; Jon. 3:9). The narrative ends with God declaring that the sentence will pass to Ahab's descendants, who presumably will continue to violate the covenant with God and thus are deserving of their punishment.

Micaiah and the Two Kings

In contrast to Ahab's reprieve described in 1 Kings 21, the story in 1 Kings 22 provides evidence of the occasional rough edges left by the redaction of these episodes. The curious story of Ahab's confrontation with the prophet Micaiah in 1 Kings 22 also describes Ahab's death in battle. Interestingly, the episode described contains all of the chilling aspects of Elijah's curse (21:19–24), including the motif of being consumed by animals while dogs lick up Ahab's blood. Since 1 Kings 21 concluded with the statement that God would not bring the disaster "in his days," these two chapters seem contradictory. The apparent contradiction reflects a common solution employed by editors/redactors, who evidently were well acquainted with conflicting traditions about the kings of Israel. Rather than resolve the inconsistencies by omitting or harmonizing this second narrative, they chose to include both stories. The narrators were therefore able to make two different theological points. The first story illustrates God's mercy to those who truly repent, and the second demonstrates that no king is above the law and may not ignore the words of God's true prophet.

Micaiah is introduced in 22:8 as a prophet who "never prophesies anything favorable" about Ahab (a similar opinion of Elijah appears in 18:17). The situation that brings him into public conflict with the king is actually a common one. Before going into battle, the kings consult either priests or prophets to determine if the **Divine Warrior** will aid them in gaining a victory (1 Sam. 13:12). Ahab's ally, King Jehoshaphat of Judah, however, is not content to consult Ahab's four hundred court prophets, who are part of Ahab's court and could be expected to reinforce policies or decisions made by their employer. Jehoshaphat may also be a reluctant ally in this story since the lands in question border Israel, not Judah. Therefore he asks that a more neutral or authoritative prophetic voice be heard, and Ahab, needing Judah's assistance, has no choice but to grant the request.

As a result, the prophet Micaiah is ordered to appear before the kings to deliver his message. Hoping to obtain a favorable response, Ahab attempts to take command of the scene and does everything he can to intimidate Micaiah. His efforts involve the use of the physical symbols of his royal office (two kings seated in their robes and on their thrones), which are conspicuously positioned at the gate of the nation's capital city, which happens to have been built upon the site of a threshing floor. The use of significant space associated with business and legal proceedings ties the event to the role of the king as protector of the people and chief magistrate. To add to the spectacle, Ahab's four hundred prophets are also capering about before the kings, prophesying their assurances of success (1 Kings 22:10–12).

In the face of such an intimidating scene, it is no wonder that Micaiah initially just echoes the words of Ahab's prophets. What is then curious is that after manipulating these elements of significant space and systematically placing his agents to create as powerful a setting as possible, Ahab, in his exasperation over Micaiah's initial response, steps out of his authoritarian role as king long enough to cajole the prophet into telling him the true message given to him by God. Despite the staging of the event, the king really does not want Micaiah to simply parrot the sycophant message of the court prophets, who were assuring the king of a military victory. In other words, Ahab, in his desperation to know the truth, condescends to speak directly to someone he despises in order to learn God's intentions for the coming battle.

Given the green light by the king, this apparently unaffiliated prophet at last voices a radically different message from that of Ahab's court prophets. He describes the forces of Israel "scattered . . . like sheep that have no shepherd" (22:17); his vision thus implies that Israel will lose the battle and Ahab will die. When Ahab challenges his prophecy, Micaiah reveals an even more remarkable vision. He describes Yahweh enthroned and surrounded by the **divine assembly**. In this courtly vision, the deity asks one of the members of the assembly to place a "lying spirit" into Ahab's prophets in order to convince them to entice him into a battle in which he will be killed (22:19–23). In this way, Micaiah can freely disagree with the court prophets while giving them a plausible alibi why they are speaking falsely.

Of course, Ahab, who has a political position to uphold, does not accept Micaiah's message without question. Still, he also recognizes that the lone prophet has bravely faced up to the ridicule of the king and the court prophets and has transcended the power of a vast array of symbols of power to stand by his prophecy. It is a dilemma since the kings are faced with the problem of whom to believe on the eve of a military engagement. Together the court prophets' message of encouragement and Micaiah's negative one create a situation that is termed **cognitive dissonance**. The truth of their opposing messages can be determined only by the outcome of the battle. Ahab tries

Symbols of Power

Now the *king* of Israel and King Jehoshaphat of Judah were sitting on their *thrones*, arrayed in their *robes*, at the *threshing floor* at the entrance of the *gate* of *Samaria*; all the *prophets* were prophesying before them. (1 Kings 22:10–11, emphasis added)

- Two kings represent the temporal power of two sovereign nations.
- The thrones of office symbolize their power and status.
- Their robes of offices mark them as kings and invest them with the authority to command the people (1 Sam. 24:4–5).
- A threshing floor is associated with harvest, distribution of grain, and dispensing justice in the village setting (Ruth 3:3–14; 2 Sam. 24:18–24).
- In the urban culture, the city gate is a place for business, the transaction of legal matters, and a staging area for military activities and royal pronouncements (Gen. 19:1; Deut. 21:19; Josh. 20:4; 2 Sam. 10:8; 19:8).
- Samaria is the capital city of Israel and the symbol of its political leadership over other cities (1 Kings 16:24).
- The four hundred court prophets of Ahab have already predicted victory for the kings, and their overwhelming numbers at this audience reinforce their authority and confidence in their message (compare the 450 prophets of Baal in 1 Kings 18:19).

putting his own spin on the message. He also tries to tip the odds in his favor by imprisoning Micaiah and then disguising himself as a common soldier. This gambit fails, of course, and after he is fatally wounded during the engagement, dogs lap up Ahab's lifeblood as it drips from the floor of his chariot (22:29–38). Despite the assurance at the end of the episode in 21:29, the words of Elijah's curse, as it was originally spoken, are fulfilled (21:19), and the true prophet's authority is further enhanced.

Political and Prophetic Transitions and the Elisha Cycle

Completing this cycle of Elijah stories is a short episode in which the prophet continues to condemn the next generation of Ahab's family for trusting in every god except Yahweh (2 Kings 1:3–16). King Amaziah's decision to consult Baal-zebub of Ekron about his recovery from a fall is typical of the times (8:7–8). In a polytheistic society, any god or divine representative who has a reputation for healing is worth consulting (compare 2 Kings 5), but this is not appropriate for a member of Yahweh's covenant community. Later prophets will repeat Elijah's complaint against the unfaithful king:

Now if people say to you, "Consult the ghosts and the familiar spirits that chirp and mutter; should not a people consult their gods, the dead on behalf of the living, for teaching and for instruction?" Surely, those who speak like this will have no dawn! (Isa. 8:19–20)

> My people consult a piece of wood,
>   and their divining rod gives them oracles. (Hosea 4:12)

A parallel theme, which also serves as a mini-version of the contest between gods that had taken place on Mount Carmel in 1 Kings 18, is tied to the judgment of Ahab's son Amaziah for his idolatry: the necessity of showing respect to a prophet as the messenger of God. The king's frustrated attempts to arrest Elijah result in the destruction of two squadrons of his soldiers at the word of the prophet (2 Kings 1:9–12). Only when the third military commander falls on his knees and humbly approaches the prophet does Elijah consent to speak to him and prophesy for the king (1:13–16). The narrative thus sets a precedent in future dealings between king and prophet by linking respect for the prophet with respect for God. Furthermore, the prediction that the king will die reinforces the Deuteronomic principle that a king who usurps undue powers and becomes a covenant breaker brings destruction upon himself (Deut. 17:14–20).

The story of Elijah's translation to heaven completes his cycle of stories and marks him one last time as the true successor to Moses (2 Kings 2:1–14). Elijah departs as mysteriously as he arrived, leaving Elisha to carry on his work. The traditions that surround Elijah and his being one of only two persons in the Old Testament/Hebrew Bible who does not die have made him unique (the other person is Enoch; see Gen. 5:24). His special status within Jewish tradition is found when he reappears with Moses in the story of Jesus's transfiguration in Matthew 17:3–4. In later Judaism he becomes the symbol of the coming **Messiah** (Mal. 4:5–6), and an empty chair and a glass of wine are always left for him at the Passover celebration in expectation of his return.

Following Elijah's spectacular departure, Elisha immediately takes up his master's mantle and assumes his responsibilities as the champion of Yahweh and a vocal critic of Israel's monarchy. However, there is a more personal character to the stories involving Elisha. In many of these tales, he manifests his authority as Yahweh's prophet by helping distressed members of Israelite society or his own group of supporters, the **sons of the prophet** or their dependents. There is less real narrative flow in the Elisha cycle than in the Elijah material, and this is probably because the editors simply grouped the stories together without concern for chronology or story line. Elisha seems to perform one miracle after another, and in each case there seems to be an effort to demonstrate the value of service to Yahweh. In only a few of the stories does the prophet confront kings and priests; instead he is frequently portrayed as helping or encouraging the people of the land. Since the narrators usually focused

The Israelite Egalitarian Ideal

Yahweh chose Israel from among all the other nations and made the covenant promise to every Israelite. Yahweh is described as "God of gods and Lord of lords . . . who is not partial and takes no bribe, who executes justice for the orphan and the widow, and who loves the strangers, providing them food and clothing" (Deut. 10:17–18). Although status, wealth, and authority differences existed among the people, they all were expected to care for one another's needs, just as their God, Yahweh, did. In addition, all were to be treated equally under the law. Many of the prophets champion this ideal as the means of obeying the covenant with Yahweh while reminding the powerful of their obligations:

> Your princes are rebels
> and companions of thieves.
> Everyone loves a bribe
> and runs after gifts.
> They do not defend the orphan,
> and the widow's cause does not come before them. (Isa. 1:23)

If you truly act justly one with another, if you do not oppress the alien, the orphan, and the widow, or shed innocent blood in this place, and if you do not go after other gods to your own hurt, then I will dwell with you in this place, in the land that I gave of old to your ancestors forever and ever. (Jer. 7:5–7)

Thus says the Lord of hosts: Render true judgments, show kindness and mercy to one another; do not oppress the widow, the orphan, the alien, or the poor; and do not devise evil in your hearts against one another. (Zech. 7:9–10)

primarily on the misdeeds of the kings, their inclusion of the Elisha stories is a bit unusual and may be based on a desire to highlight Yahweh's concern for the faithful and less powerful in society. The covenant and its benefits for the people of Israel are also tied to an **egalitarian** ideal that transcends social barriers by offering justice to all of the people.

The narrator's depiction of Elisha's efforts to reward and protect his supporters is designed to show that Yahweh and his prophets will care for the faithful and the weak. Elijah's intercession for the barren Shunammite couple, his provision of a miraculously magnified meal (4:42–44; compare Matt. 14:14–21), and the retrieval of a valuable tool (2 Kings 6:1–7) all speak to this concern for the common people. Such isolated expressions of power, meeting the needs of a few people at a time, become the model for many of the healing and provisioning miracles of Jesus in the New Testament (Matt. 15:32–38; John 9:1–12).

Elisha's Political Role

The story of the campaign against Moab combines the traditional role of God's representative traveling with the army (Judg. 4:4–10; 1 Sam. 7:7–11) with the role of a condemning prophet (2 Kings 3). In this episode Elisha travels with the combined armies of Jehoram son of Ahab and King Jehoshaphat of Judah as they attempt to bring a rebellious Moab back into their political control. It was not uncommon for priests and prophets to accompany the army. Their role would be to interpret omens or seek divine intercession before and during a battle (e.g., Deborah in Judg. 4:8–9). When the expedition's ill-conceived line of march takes the combined forces south into arid country that cannot support the needs of the army, the prophet is called on to save them. Elisha is reluctant to act on behalf of an Israelite king and son of Ahab, but because the righteous King Jehoshaphat is also present, he feels a moral obligation to provide assistance. The prophet calls for a musician and subsequently enters a trance state. In his **ecstatic** prophecy, he predicts that the dry wadi bed will be filled with life-giving water from rain upstream and that the expedition will ultimately be successful (2 Kings 3:13–20).

In one of those rare cases where an event is depicted in both the biblical account and an extrabiblical document, the Moabite version of the battle appears on the Stele of Mesha. This monumental inscription was written at the command of King Mesha of Moab, the same king mentioned in 3:4. Interestingly, this royal inscription describes a complete victory for Moab. Neither the prophet Elisha nor Mesha's desperate sacrifice of his son on the walls of the besieged capital city (3:26–27) are mentioned in the Moabite version of the campaign: "I defeated the son of Omri and drove Israel out of our land forever. Omri and his son ruled the Madaba plains for forty years, but Chemosh dwells there in my time" ("Annals of Mesha," *OTPar* 168).

Comparing the Moabite version of the war with the account in 2 Kings 3 makes clear that preserving the facts of the battle is not the primary concern of the biblical writers. Instead the agenda of the narrators is to focus on the difference between good kings and bad kings. Since the division of the kingdom, the narrators chose to evaluate the monarchs of both Judah and Israel by comparing them with Jeroboam. If they had "walked in the way of Jeroboam" (1 Kings 15:34; 16:19), they were considered evil kings who brought destruction to the land and deserved no aid from God or the prophets. By contrast, God's covenant promise ensured that Yahweh would come to the aid of righteous kings, who were more like David.

In the remaining narratives in which Elisha deals with political matters, he acts as a catalyst for accomplishing the tasks that Elijah had received earlier at Mount Horeb (19:15–18). He travels to Syria (Aram) and informs Hazael, a Syrian general, that he will become the new king of that country (2 Kings 8:7–15). Of course, the prophet also shows his pain over this transition of power and the necessity of delivering this message. Weeping, he tells the ecstatic general, "I know the evil that you will do to the people of Israel" (8:12). Later, Elisha sends one of the sons of the prophet to anoint the Israelite general Jehu as Yahweh's chosen king (9:1–10; compare 1 Sam. 16:1–13; 1 Kings 11:28–31). The result of these actions is civil conflict and multiple royal murders. Hazael uses Elisha's information to advance his own political ambitions. He suffocates King Ben-hadad and takes his place as the ruler of Syria (2 Kings 8:15). Jehu's anointing precipitates a civil war and the deaths of the reigning kings in both Israel and Judah. The conflict in Israel concludes with a general purge of all of Ahab's official family (both kin and supporters; 10:1–31). The story reaches its climax when Jezebel publicly attempts to thwart Jehu's efforts on her own by labeling Jehu a "Zimri," a man who betrays his king, as the rebel enters the gates of Jezreel (9:31; compare 1 Kings 16:15–20). Jehu easily deflects her attempt to malign him by crying out, "Who is on my side?" Jehu's question forces the people to choose between him and the house of Ahab. They choose him and Jezebel is thrown from a balcony window while he rides triumphantly into the city (2 Kings 9:30–37). This final act of royal murder fulfills Elijah's curse on Ahab's family, with Jezebel's corpse consumed by dogs (1 Kings 21:20–24).

As Jehu gained support as Israel's new king, he took many steps to eliminate members of Ahab's family and worshipers of Baal. He called upon the political leaders within the nation (elders and members of the royal household) to recognize the shift in power by executing the seventy "sons of Ahab" and transporting their heads to him at Jezreel. The baskets containing their heads are neatly stacked on either side of the city gate—once again a symbolic use

Labeling Techniques

Labeling is a social mechanism that can be used to honor or shame an individual or group. For a label to be effective, it must be culturally recognizable. For example, in the United States, the name "Benedict Arnold" would be ancient Israel's equivalent of "Zimri" as the label for a traitor. In both cases, historical circumstances have created the validity of the label. Accepted labels become permanent and the basis for the labeled individual's identity thereafter. That is fine for those with positive labels. If someone is labeled as a generous person, people will seek him or her out for favor or assistance (Prov. 19:6). However, those labeled hot-tempered are to be avoided because they "stir up strife" (15:18). Labels can be accepted or rejected. To reject or deflect a label, one must either change one's behavior or appearance or provide a convincing argument that transforms public opinion. For instance, someone who has become a leper can have that label removed through the certification of the examining priest (Lev. 13:9–17). In the end, a label's power is dependent on whether the public or the audience considers it to be a true assessment of a person's character.

of significant space (2 Kings 10:1–27). The political purge is given legitimacy by citing Elijah's prophecy of the demise of Ahab's house (10:10). Then through a ruse, Jehu eliminates all the Baal prophets and worshipers. He asks them to assemble for a "great sacrifice" and has them all killed by his soldiers (10:18–27). Such a bloodletting is countenanced as a sign of Jehu's faithfulness to Yahweh, but he does not escape the negative label applied by the **Deuteronomistic Historian**, which notes that he "did not turn aside from the **sins of Jeroboam**" (10:28–29).

Despite his rise to power in Israel, Jehu's tiny kingdom almost immediately begins to feel the encroaching pressure of the westward spread of Assyrian **hegemony**. Although the biblical account does not mention this, the Black Obelisk of Shalmaneser III (841) includes the terms of a vassal treaty between Assyria and Israel and portrays Jehu bowing down before the majesty of the Assyrian ruler while offering tribute to that sovereign.

One additional narrative in the Elisha cycle that hinges on political matters highlights the **universalism** theme and argues once again for Yahweh as the source of life and health. This theme demonstrates Yahweh's power through the words and actions of non-Israelite characters (e.g., Balaam in Num. 22–24; Nebuchadnezzar in Dan. 2:46–47). In 2 Kings 5 a Syrian general, made desperate by his need to be cured of leprosy, travels to Israel to seek a cure and ends up making a firm declaration of Yahweh's universal power.

Naaman is a high-ranking military commander afflicted with leprosy. Such an affliction would have separated him from close contact with the royal court, prevented him from leading the army, and endangered any possibility of maintaining his high social status in the king's service. Naturally, he sought a cure, but when all these local remedies fail, Naaman at last takes the advice of his wife's Israelite slave girl and makes preparations to travel to Israel to consult Elisha. He must engage in some difficult political maneuvering to gain safe passage into Israel, which is considered enemy territory, but eventually he comes to Elisha's house (5:5–9). However, he never gets to see the prophet face-to-face. Instead Elisha's servant, Gehazi, relays instructions to the general. As far as the general is concerned, this is neither proper social etiquette nor an impressive demonstration of prophetic power. Believing that he has been snubbed or made fun of, Naaman nearly storms off in anger. His servants, however, convince him to attempt the cure suggested by the prophet, and so he finally consents to dip himself seven times in the Jordan River.

Miraculously cured of his leprosy, Naaman rushes back to reward Elisha for giving him his life back. In his enthusiasm, he boldly declares, "Now I know there is no God in all the earth except in Israel" (5:15). The narrative thus fulfills the characteristics of the universalism theme described above. Although the thankful general presses Elisha to accept a gift for his services, the prophet refuses any payment since this would be considered profiting from a divine gift. It is possible that Elisha's refusal is based on his attempt to differentiate himself from priests or professional healers or miracle workers, who performed their cures for a fee. The prophet wants it clearly understood that the healing power came from Yahweh, not the prophet, and was a demonstration of God's power, extended even to persons outside the covenant.

The general then asks Elisha for a future consideration. As part of his role as adviser to the Syrian king, Naaman is expected to participate in an annual religious ritual honoring their god Rimmon. He assures the prophet that this will in no way conflict with his new devotion to Yahweh, and he proves this by requesting two loads of Israelite soil to take back with him to Syria (5:17). His request for Israelite soil reflects the belief that gods are localized within the lands in which they are worshiped. By taking soil back to Syria, Naaman believes he is physically extending the presence of Yahweh into his own country (compare Abraham's introducing Yahweh worship to Canaan by building altars at each of his stopping points; Gen. 12:7–8). While not granting him dispensation for his actions in the Rimmon temple, Elisha at least does not condemn the general and tells him to "go in peace."

Although Elisha dies a physical death, his end is as curious as that of his master, Elijah, and this is reflected in the mysterious power associated with his tomb and his physical remains. Apparently, the site of Elisha's burial is forgotten over time. Finding a ready-made tomb, a burial party reopens the chamber, intending to push aside the remains of all previous burials. As they prepare to lower a corpse into the tomb's shaft, a band of raiders interrupts the mourners and they simply abandon the body in order to escape. When the body falls onto Elisha's bones, the corpse is revived, and the man jumps from the tomb and runs after his frightened friends (2 Kings 13:20–21). Just as Elijah's mantle had functioned as an object of power during the prophet's career, so too did Elisha's bones. In the future, however, the words, not the relics, of the prophets will demonstrate the power of God.

6

The Major and Minor Prophets

We now turn our attention to the canonical section of the Old Testament/Hebrew Bible that contains the works of the prophets (Hebrew *nebi'im*). The biblical **canon** places the three Major Prophets (Isaiah, Jeremiah, and Ezekiel) first, followed by a collection of twelve Minor Prophets (Hosea–Malachi), sometimes referred to as the Book of the Twelve. The designations "major" and "minor" have to do with book size and, to an extent, their overall impact. The first thing to note about these prophetic works, both major and minor, is that they are not placed in chronological order. If they had been, then Amos would be first, since it deals with the first half of the eighth century. They also vary immensely in size, ranging from Obadiah's twenty-one verses to Isaiah's sixty-six chapters. These works generally center on the reason God has chosen to call a prophet to deliver a divine message, usually one of warning and remonstrance and judgment. Only Jonah is framed in terms of a story about a prophet. Most of the books have a **superscription** that provides a little background on the prophet and his historical setting: "The word of the LORD that came to Hosea son of Beeri, in the days of Kings Uzziah, Jotham, Ahaz, and Hezekiah of Judah, and in the days of King Jeroboam son of Joash of Israel" (Hosea 1:1).

In terms of style and **genre**, the prophetic books have variations as well as common themes. All contain oracles, or statements of divine pronouncement spoken in the name of **Yahweh**, and most include poetic sections, prose narrative, dialogue, song, and **wisdom** sayings. The length and artistic character of their messages vary, and that is probably a reflection of their level of education and perhaps the length of time that they function as prophets. All of them rely on the necessity of obedience to the **covenant** with Yahweh as the hallmark of Israel's and Judah's relationship with God and the basis upon which the nations and their people are to be judged.

Obviously, the specific historical setting of each prophet will have a bearing on how they describe that relationship. For instance, the books of Isaiah (10:5) and Hosea (4:12–14) express great concern about the people's idolatrous practices, the foolish political alliances of the kings, and God's decision to punish them using the Assyrian war machine as a divine vehicle of destruction. Another factor that distinguishes the message and person of the prophets is their own social setting. Amos, for example, is a farmer from a small village in Judah, who is unlikely to be personally familiar with urban centers of either Israel or Judah. In contrast, Isaiah and Ezekiel are urban dwellers and members of the high-ranking priestly community and are probably familiar to the elders and even kings of Judah. Because of these social differences, the sophistication of their individual messages varies, and in some cases their backgrounds dominate the types of examples or metaphors they employ: Amos tends to use agricultural images, while Ezekiel focuses on matters of ritual and individual purity in many of his **enacted prophecies**.

Social justice is a common theme in the prophetic literature. It reflects a real concern with the society's lack of interest in and abuse of the weaker elements in their culture (idealized as "orphans, widows, and strangers"). Ancillary to the cry for justice at all levels of society is a concern that the people have become tied to ritual practices that lack either personal faith or understanding. Thus Amos criticizes the rich and powerful for exploiting the poor as a means of increasing their wealth and authority (8:4–6), and he proclaims that Israel's fall and eventual exile are a just punishment for such regularized violations of traditional and economic practices (6:1–8; 8:7–12). Similarly, Jeremiah (5:26–27) describes "scoundrels" who gather up the "goods of others" "like fowlers" in their traps and by their self-serving treachery "they have become great and rich."

Finally, it should be understood that the writings of the prophets have been edited into their current form. While they may in fact represent a portion of the actual words or at least the basics of the delivered messages of these prophetic figures, there are also additions by later editors designed to emphasize a particular theological point or clarify for their audience a historical or political allusion. For example, Jer. 33:14–26 pairs the restoration of a Davidic king, a "righteous Branch," with the presence of the Levitical priesthood in maintaining the sacrificial cult when the nation is restored. Since much of Jeremiah is extremely critical of the priestly community (e.g., 6:13–15; 8:8–13), it is more likely that Jer. 33 is the product of Levitical editors in the postexilic period (compare Zech. 12:12–13). A simpler example of the editing process is found in the final verse of Hosea: a "wisdom **colophon**" with its concluding admonition to readers to walk in "the ways of the LORD" (14:9; compare Deut. 8:6) has been added by a later hand. Given that Hosea's message is a final plea prior to the destruction of Israel by Assyria, the wisdom saying is appropriate for a later audience more likely to learn from the example of Israel's unfaithfulness.

In the following chapters, I have arranged the prophetic books in chronological order, starting in the eighth century. Attention will be given to their historical setting and the way in which their message may have resonated with the original audience. The book of Daniel, which is not part of the prophetic canon, has been included here as an example of late postexilic **apocalyptic** literature comparable to that found in Zech. 9–14.

7

The Book of Amos

At the time that Amos was called to become a prophet, he was living in a small village named Tekoa in the Judean highlands, just south of Jerusalem. It is hard to imagine a more out-of-the-way or unlikely place for a prophet to be called to serve God's purposes. World events and the acts of kings must have seemed very far away from Tekoa, a village of perhaps 150 people, and yet these same events will conspire to draw him into the public arena. Amos's mission is to leave his own land and travel north to the kingdom of Israel, a country ruled at the time by Jeroboam II (786–746). Both Israel and Judah were enjoying a brief period of peace and prosperity—the result of the capture of Damascus, the capital of Syria, by King Shalmaneser III of Assyria in 802. The elimination of Israel's chief economic and military rival gave the rulers of the northern kingdom, at least temporarily, more latitude in making treaties and in dealing with neighboring countries. Israelite merchants also enjoyed this period of freedom to trade in previously restricted areas and new markets and thus were able to increase their fortunes. Of course, this is only a respite before the Assyrian kings once again begin to expand their **hegemony** into all of Syria-Palestine. In fact, by the end of the eighth century, an exhausted Israel will be conquered, its capital city destroyed, and much of its populace deported and scattered within the vast Assyrian domain (2 Kings 17:1–23). Amos's task will be to warn the Israelites of this coming disaster and to show them how to prevent their own cultural extinction before it is too late.

Chronologically, Amos is the first of the eighth-century prophets and the first of the so-called classical prophets, whose messages appear in books bearing their names. Since he is a farmer living in the small Judean village ten miles south of Jerusalem, his world has been limited to a relatively small area. He is skilled in a variety of tasks associated with life on a small farm (Amos 7:14), but he is not a Levite and does not appear to have had any formal education beyond what would have been available in the village. Despite this, God calls him to serve as a prophet and, more important, a prophet to the people of the northern kingdom of Israel. Only Jonah among the Hebrew prophets will be given a similar task when he is told to go to the Assyrian capital of Nineveh (Jonah 1:2). Amos's original social setting and the physical location where he will deliver his message will set the tone for many of the images in his prophetic speech and his very strident attitude.

It is unlikely that Amos had ever traveled more than a few miles from his village. He probably had gone to Jerusalem to celebrate the major religious festivals, but it is doubtful that he had been to Israel. That he must now travel

Terms Used for the Northern Kingdom

The Hebrew prophets use several different names for the northern kingdom. Of course, the ancient audience would have been aware of this and may well have appreciated the subtlety involved in the choice of a particular name for this country.

Israel the official political term for the northern kingdom after the division of the united monarchy and prior to the fall of its capital, Samaria, to the Assyrians in 721 (1 Kings 12:20–2 Kings 17:23). After 721 "Israel" is once again employed as a collective term by the prophets for all Israelites in the land (Ps. 81:8; Isa. 43:1; Mal. 1:1).

Joseph the Joseph tribes (identified with his twin sons Manasseh and **Ephraim**) are collectively identified by some prophets with the northern kingdom (Ezek. 37:16; Amos 5:6; Obad. 18). This name draws attention to the importance of the Joseph tribes in the political structure of the northern kingdom.

Ephraim one of the twin sons of Joseph, his name is often equated with the northern kingdom, and this probably is based on the dominance of this tribe over the other northern tribes during the monarchy (Isa. 7:8; Hosea 9:8).

Jacob the ancestor whose sons become the founders of the twelve tribes of Israel (Gen. 29:31–30:24) is occasionally equated with the ten tribes that compose the northern kingdom, just as the southern kingdom is referred to as Judah, Jacob's son. These names are also associated with the geographical and political divisions of the land (Isa. 2:5–6; 10:20; Mic. 2:12). After 721 the names "Jacob" and "Israel" refer to all Israelites (Ps. 14:7; Nah. 2:2; Mal. 3:6).

Samaria the capital of the northern kingdom, Samaria is occasionally synonymous with the nation itself (Isa. 36:19; Obad. 19).

to that neighboring kingdom and specifically to one of its major cultic centers would have made his work even more difficult. Although he would have spoken basically the same language, his clothing, mannerisms, and attitudes cause him to stand out and, as we will see, make him an object of ridicule in some circles.

The first thing that becomes clear, when reading the book of Amos, is that he is a very angry prophet. He freely and in great detail condemns the people of Israel for their social injustices and their unorthodox worship practices. By the end of his time there, the prophet appears relieved that he has delivered his message and can return home, leaving his Israelite audience to their fate. In this sense, he is emotionally disconnected from his audience and may therefore feel more at liberty to condemn them. He shows very little compassion and offers them only a bare-based, very strict adherence to the **covenant** as a guide to deliverance. He does speak briefly of the possibility of redemption for the righteous, calling on the Israelites to "seek the LORD and live" (5:6, 14–15). Even so, he only hints at the possibility that the Lord may "be gracious to the **remnant** of Joseph" (5:15). To further reinforce his message from the viewpoint of a Judean, the prophet warns Israel against having any confidence whatsoever in its shrines at Bethel and Dan or in the monarchy founded by Jeroboam (4:4; 6:8; compare Jer. 7:15).

The harsh memories of the division of the kingdom that took place at the end of the ninth century and of King Jeroboam's sins serve as a transparent backdrop to Amos's message (1 Kings 12:25–33). Amos appears to be all too aware of the measures taken by King Jeroboam I to separate his new nation from its southern neighbor. The new king of Israel had recognized that his people would continue to look to Jerusalem as their religious center and as the place where major sacrifices were to be made. Thus Jeroboam initiated a series of religious reforms to provide alternative worship centers for his people and turn their allegiance to his regime. Although these reforms made good political sense at the time, they became the basis for the subsequent criticism of Israel and of those kings who continued to promote the **sins of Jeroboam**. Now over a century later, Amos, a man of Judah, stands before an audience of Israelites at Bethel and challenges them to repent and reject not only Jeroboam's sin but also the royal shrine that serves as a focal point and an economic engine among them.

The harshness of Amos's message, when he condemns Israel's adherence to the practices initiated by Jeroboam, suggests that he does not really believe that the nation and its people will repent and thus survive the coming destruction. He even refers to the Israelites as a "remnant" *before* foreign invaders actually stripped the nation of its resources and people (Amos 5:15). Given this prediction of such a gloomy future, Amos does not waste words on deaf ears. He simply tells them all they need to know in order to save their lives and then leaves it to them to act on this frank, no-nonsense advice.

Since he is a stranger without previous introduction or a following at Bethel, Amos wisely begins his work with a rhetorical strategy designed to draw an audience (1:3–2:8). He figuratively sketches out a grand tour of Israel's neighbors, starting with Damascus (Syria) in the northeast and then turning south to Gaza in Philistia. He denounces Israel's economic partners and each of the neighboring states: Tyre (Phoenicia), Edom, Ammon, Moab, even Judah. As each neighboring country is mentioned, Amos condemns these longtime political rivals for their various transgressions and draws on the energy of the crowd, who must have been delighted by the promises of divine retribution against their enemies.

Amos's Geographic Strategy

Nation	Location	Crime	Punishment
Damascus (Syria)	northeast of Israel	devastate Gilead	fall of Damascus and exile of its ruler and people
Gaza, Ashdod, Ashkelon, Ekron (Philistia)	southwest of Israel along coastal plain	raid villages and send slaves to Edom	cities destroyed and rulers overthrown
Tyre (Phoenicia)	northwest of Israel on Phoenician coast	send slaves to Edom and break treaties	fiery destruction of city and strongholds
Edom	southeast of Israel in Transjordan	continual raiding and warfare	Teman and strongholds of Bozrah destroyed
Ammon	east of Israel in Transjordan	military atrocities against Gilead	Rabbah destroyed and king exiled
Moab	east of Israel in Transjordan	desecrate graves of kings of Edom	strongholds of Kerioth destroyed; king and officials killed
Judah	southern kingdom	covenant violations	strongholds of Jerusalem destroyed
Israel	northern kingdom	bribery, injustice toward poor, cultic prostitution, idol worship, abuse of Nazirites, silencing of prophets	denied strength to resist surrounding armies; Samaria falls and Bethel's altar destroyed; exile of survivors

In each case, Amos begins his prophetic harangue with the formula "for three transgressions of ——, and for four, I will not revoke the punishment." This $x + 1$ rhetorical device is something that his audience could chant along with him as it is repeated. After each refrain, Amos then recites the rather formulaic transgressions of the target kingdom and announces God's sure punishment upon them. In some cases, these crimes are quite gruesome (1:13; 2:1), suggesting that the troops were unleashed to commit acts that ordinarily would not be countenanced under the standards of international law. One can easily imagine that the growing crowd would have cheered and urged Amos to continue—at least until he reached his intended goal, the condemnation of Israel itself. It is not recorded whether they melted away when Amos began his list of charges against Israel, but after what they had heard about other nations, they surely knew what the prophet had in store for them.

Perhaps hardest to hear in his litany of charges will be the claim that the people of Israel have "commanded the prophets, saying, 'You shall not prophesy'" (2:12). They have consciously chosen not to heed or hear God's fair warnings. In a series of rational queries (3:3–6), Amos reminds them that "God does nothing, without revealing his secret to his servants the prophets" (3:7; see 4:6–13 for additional signs of God's discontent). The sound of the roaring lion becomes the note driving fear into their hearts and a signal of the assembling nations who will carry out God's punishment on an unfaithful nation (3:8–15).

Social Injustice Theme

Turning at last to the point of his virtual geographic tour, Amos voices a biting critique of Israel that begins at 2:6 and centers on violations of the very basics of social justice and points to corruption of the next generation as well. Amos condemns Israel's repeated social injustices and challenges the business practices of those "who trample the head of the poor into the dust of the earth" (2:7). In fact, this catchphrase is practically Amos's theme song. It is repeated in 5:11 and 8:4, and each time Amos makes it clear that the wealthy have chosen to take advantage of the poor and the weak, actions that are in direct violation of the **egalitarian** ideal and the fundamentals of the covenant with **Yahweh**.

Amos uses concrete imagery to capture the horror of these crimes against the disadvantaged. He condemns the legal abuse of bribing judges, describing it as "sell[ing] the righteous for silver" (2:6). Other probably legal but unethical strategies for dealing with the repayment of debt also provoke Amos's ire. For example, he ridicules the practice of selling persons into debt slavery for defaulting on very small loans as selling "the needy for a pair of sandals" (2:6). Furthermore, the unauthorized use of "garments taken in pledge" for bedding while seeking a vision from a foreign god (2:8) is tantamount to stealing from the poor and certainly violates the covenant's demand to worship only Yahweh. It is likely that Amos is drawing on real-life situations echoed throughout ancient Near Eastern **wisdom literature** and in petitions found in the Psalms (e.g., Ps. 56). For example, another peasant farmer, this one from Middle Kingdom Egypt (2134–1786), spoke of the responsibility of the wealthy and the powerful to provide justice and fair treatment to the poor

and the weak: "You are the chief steward, you are my lord. . . . You father
the orphan, you husband the widow. . . . [But] those who distribute the grain
put more in their own ration. Those authorized to give full measures short
their people. Lawmakers approve of robbery" ("A Farmer and the Courts in
Egypt," *OTPar* 232–35).

In like manner, the twelfth-century Egyptian sage Amen-em-ope included in
his list of admonitions that the wise is not to "take bribes from the powerful
and oppress the poor for their sake" (*OTPar* 300; compare Ps. 15:5).

Since Amos was very familiar with hard work and the difficulties faced
by those who struggle day to day to survive, Amos knew that justice was not
always readily available to day laborers or bond servants, who owned no land,
operated no businesses, and had only the clothes on their backs to serve as
a guarantee that they would do a full day's work. One such man in the late
seventh century had a scribe write a letter to the governor pleading for his
legal rights in much the same way that Amos championed the debt slaves in
his time: "Your servant was harvesting. . . . The work went as usual and your
servant completed the harvesting and storing of my quota of grain. . . . Despite
the fact . . . Hoshaiahu, son of Shobai, kept your servant's cloak. . . . Please
order my supervisor to return my cloak either in fulfillment of the law or as
an act of mercy" ("Yavne Yam Letter," *OTPar* 355–56).

Both this letter and Amos's oracle call on the authorities to adhere to the
legal principle found in Exod. 22:26–27. Sometimes the only source of identity that the poor possessed to show that they were not slaves was their outer
garment. Recognizing the basic human desire to hold onto this thin shred of
dignity, the law forbade the field owner or foreman from abusing them and
leaving them to shiver through the night without their cloaks. Although they
had only this garment to serve as collateral and as a pledge that they would
work an honest day's labor, workers were to be treated with respect and not
reduced to the shameful indignity of naked slaves.

Amos holds back none of his indignation as he describes the indifferent
stance of the wealthy toward the poor. **Archaeological** evidence from eighth-
century settlements in Israel and Judah suggests that the monarchy and its
supporters exercised increasing control over the economy. Royal herds were
increased (2 Chron. 26:10), and large tracts of land were systematically
enclosed and farmed to produce ever greater quantities of grain, olive oil,
and wine (Isa. 5:8). Although these efforts supported increased trade and
the influx of luxury and manufactured goods, many of the small landowners were driven off their property and into the employ of the state or the
uncertain life of day laborers. Their suffering is then increased by unjust
business practices in which merchants use false balances ("make the ephah
small and the shekel great"; Amos 8:5) and sell bags of contaminated grain
to increase their own profits at the expense of those who must buy from
them (8:6).

Given their disregard for the needs of the poor, it is no wonder that Amos describes the wives of the greedy merchants and leaders of Samaria as sleek "cows of Bashan" (4:1), who fatten themselves indulgently on other people's grain and then call out for even more (compare 6:4–7). When the city of Samaria falls, he predicts that they will be dragged through the breaches in the walls and their impaled bodies flung as a final indignity into a dung heap (4:1–3). The rich, who have flaunted their prosperity by maintaining two fine houses, one each for the summer and winter seasons (compare Ahab's two palaces at Jezreel and Samaria in 1 Kings 21:1), and have decorated them with ivory to display their wealth, will see them torn down and abandoned (Amos 3:15).

Hypocrisy Theme

Amos also addresses the theme of religious hypocrisy that he finds in Israel. He asserts that the people's worship is useless and hollow because it is conducted in rote fashion without a foundation of true faith or devotion (2:7). The prophet also reflects on the greedy merchants who cannot even wait for the **sabbath** or other religious holidays to end so that they can resume their crooked business practices (8:5; compare similar abuses in Neh. 13:15–18). Their avarice obviously far outweighs their piety.

It is not surprising that the prophet is so bitter. He cannot understand how the people amid their prosperity can fail to recognize that it is God who gives them their wealth. As a small farmer, intimately acquainted with the delicate balance between survival and disaster tied to seasonal rains, it amazes him that these people do not understand the signs of God's displeasure (Amos 4:6–10). Disasters such as famine ("cleanness of teeth"), selective droughts ("one field would be rained upon" and another left to wither; compare Hag. 1:10–11), "blight and mildew," and locusts and pestilence (compare Ps. 78:46) were all intended to remind the people of their obligations to God. They celebrate festivals and call solemn assemblies in the name of Yahweh, but they do not create the just society that God, the source of their covenantal blessings, desires for the people:

> I hate, I despise your festivals,
>   and I take no delight in your solemn assemblies.
> Even though you offer me your burnt offerings and grain offerings,
>   I will not accept them. . . .
> But let justice roll down like waters,
>   and righteousness like an everflowing stream. (Amos 5:21–24)

Tying ritual and justice together, Amos indicates that the wealthy and powerful who stage and gain status from the festivals and sacrificial offerings have failed to provide justice or demonstrate righteousness (his list of charges is given in 2:6–12). Now Yahweh, the primal source of justice and righteousness, like the uncontrollable waters of river or perennial stream, will sweep away their power like a house of cards. Amos's words echo the prophetic admonition of Samuel, who declared that "to obey is better than sacrifice" (1 Sam. 15:22), and thereby remind the people that the conditions of the covenant have not changed and that they are not free to operate as if God took no notice of their actions. In a later period, Isaiah, Jeremiah, and Malachi will follow Amos's lead in condemning the hollow worship and unacceptable sacrificial offerings of the people of Judah:

> Bringing offerings is futile;
>> incense is an abomination to me.
> New moon and sabbath and calling of convocation—
>> I cannot endure solemn assemblies with iniquity. (Isa. 1:13)

> Of what use to me is frankincense that comes from Sheba,
>> or sweet cane from a distant land?
> Your burnt offerings are not acceptable,
>> nor are your sacrifices pleasing to me. (Jer. 6:20)

> Oh, that someone among you would shut the temple doors, so that you would not kindle fire on my altar in vain! I have no pleasure in you, says the LORD of hosts, and I will not accept an offering from your hands. (Mal. 1:10)

Amos also focuses his venom on the rival temple at Bethel, which was established as a **high place** by Jeroboam I when the kingdom initially was divided. He sarcastically "encourages" the people to come to Bethel to make their offerings and tithes there and to have the amounts of their offerings published for all to hear (Amos 4:4–5; compare Mark 12:41–44). Then he tells them that Yahweh has completely rejected Israel's worship as unacceptable and as so much useless "noise" (Amos 5:21–24). He tells them that those who seek God instead of Bethel will see that city devoured by fire "with no one to quench it" (5:4–7; compare the unnamed prophet's statement in 1 Kings 13:2–3).

Eventually the authorities can stand no more of this confrontational prophet's incendiary words. Amaziah, the high priest of Bethel, writes to King Jeroboam II and also publicly charges Amos with making both treasonous and blasphemous statements. He ridicules Amos and sarcastically calls him a "seer" (Amos 7:12), a term that usually implies special prophetic abilities and perhaps may be applied to diviners (compare 1 Sam. 9:9). Amaziah is likely attempting to exercise his official powers to control speech and behavior within the sacred precincts of the temple at Bethel (compare Eli in 1:14). To be sure, he does not wish to recognize Amos's right to speak as a prophet of Yahweh and his verbal attack is designed to extinguish any legitimacy that Amos may have achieved among the people. In a similar incident, the Jerusalem priest

Zephaniah is charged with a similar responsibility during Jeremiah's day. He is given authority to "control any madman who plays the prophet" (Jer. 29:26).

Amos, of course, rejects the non-Levitical priest's claim that he has no right to speak in the "king's sanctuary" (Amos 7:10–12), an interesting phrase since it should be termed "Yahweh's sanctuary." Since he has been labeled as unqualified and unauthorized to speak here, Amos stands on his rights as someone called to perform this service for Yahweh. His account of his call to serve is quite simple but adequate enough to set aside Amaziah's charges: "The LORD took me from following the flock, and the LORD said to me, 'Go, prophesy to my people Israel'" (7:15). While his account does not compare in style to the elaborate **call narratives** in Isaiah and Jeremiah, it contains just as much power, since it describes the way that God intruded into his life. Amos did not ask for this assignment, and he proudly declares that he is not a "prophet's son" (7:14), someone who had gained his status through inheritance or schooling. Instead God thrust this burden upon him to proclaim the coming crisis to these people on the brink of a disaster that will engulf them.

Unlike Amaziah, who owes his position to the king's patronage, Amos has no credentials granted by the establishment. When Amos tells Amaziah, "I am no prophet, nor a prophet's son" (7:14), he is reasserting the position that true prophets are free agents working directly for Yahweh and do not require any certification other than the truth of their message. In the process he also justifies his divine mission to Bethel, a place identified as a primary source of Israel's disobedience to the covenant.

Although Amos leaves little hope for the nation of Israel in his statements, there is a brief use of the remnant theme in Amos 5. In his typically succinct manner, he simply tells the people to "seek the LORD and live" (5:4, 6) so that Yahweh will have an excuse to relent and lessen their punishment. But unlike similar incidents in which God chooses to relent or repent a previous decision (2 Sam. 24:16; Jer. 26:19), Amos's statement seems to offer only a brief glimmer of hope. In his consistently stern style, Amos paints a picture that even the complacent leaders "who are at ease in Zion" and "who feel secure on Mount Samaria" should take to heart (Amos 6:1). They have only to look at the destruction brought on neighboring kingdoms (6:2) to realize that God is capable of "raising up against you a nation" that will rain destruction on them as well (6:14). The only break in an otherwise gloomy picture is found in 9:11–15, which describes the restoration of the Davidic kingdom and a return of the land's prosperity. Since this glimpse of a brighter future is more appropriate to the message of the prophets of the late monarchy (Jer. 30:18–22; Ezek. 39:21–29) and the exile (Isa. 43:19–21), it is possibly a later addition to the book of Amos.

Amos warns the people not to look forward to the "day of the LORD" (Amos 5:18–20), for it will bring them judgment, not greater prosperity or positive intervention by God. In doing this he reminds the people that they do not control God's actions, nor should they expect certain outcomes, especially when they are in violation of the terms of the covenant. Assumptions or false expectations bring nasty surprises like the man who "rested a hand against the wall, and was bitten by a snake" (5:19).

This very earthy prophet often draws on his life experiences as a farmer and herdsman and uses the pastoral images and wisdom sayings of his country background to make his point. For instance, his questions are designed to evoke commonsense responses and remind the people of their illogical actions: "Do horses run on rocks? Does one plow the sea with oxen?" (6:12). At another point he describes the people of Israel as "summer fruit," or figs (8:2; compare Hosea 9:10). They are sweet and full of initial promise but quick to decay and become worthless. Such a familiar image, taken directly from his daily life as a farmer and clearly recognizable to his audience, surely must have struck an ominous chord with some of them as the Assyrian specter of power moved inexorably westward into Syria-Palestine.

8

The Book of Hosea

U nlike his eighth-century contemporary Amos, the prophet Hosea has both the luxury and the burden of speaking to his own people. Although his message is often harsh, he does offer the hope that reconciliation with **Yahweh** is still possible if the people will only repent and return to their allegiance to the **covenant**. Because Hosea speaks at the end of an era for Israel, there is a clear sense of desperation in his pleas for the people to change their ways. The long reign of Jeroboam II (786–746) is about to come to an end, and his successors are weaklings, fighting among themselves. Under the leadership of Tiglath-pileser III (744–727), Assyria has emerged as an international power and is steadily expanding its hegemonic influences farther west. During this period Israel will come under the control of Assyria first as a client state and then as a bound vassal with heavy annual tribute payments. In the end, Assyria will destroy Israel in 721 because of its repeated revolts against Assyrian domination. In this period of extreme crisis for his nation, Hosea almost ignores the Assyrian threat and instead concentrates on what he perceives to be the root causes of Israel's problems: idolatry and squandering the land's covenantal potential.

Israel's Idolatry: The Marriage Metaphor

The marriage metaphor employed in the first part of the book shows the prophet's first-person reflections on his marital experience (Hosea 3) and gives

89

a third-person account that introduces God's revelations to Hosea and contains a fuller discussion of the struggles faced by marriage with an unfaithful wife (Hosea 1–2). While it is unclear which account is older, they are related by a common theme and complement each other. Both accounts contain the prophet's condemnation of idolatry and serve as **enacted prophecies** that involve his marriage to a woman named Gomer, whose infidelities are reflective of God's covenantal "marriage" to Israel. This marriage metaphor serves, in a graphic sense, to demonstrate that Gomer's willful adultery is to be equated with Israel's worship of other gods. Hosea's dysfunctional marriage displays not only his own marital difficulties but Yahweh's often stormy relationship with Israel. Gomer's promiscuity symbolizes Israel's blatant idolatry with the gods of Canaan. Hosea, in turn, represents in fact and in metaphorical personification the long-suffering husband/God who laments his wife's/Israel's actions, looks for ways to deal with the situation, and eventually determines to dissolve the covenant between them.

These first three chapters also raise two intriguing questions. First, was Hosea a Levite? If so, then in the northern kingdom he would have been unable to function as a priest, since the **sin of Jeroboam** would have excluded him from the working priesthood. It also would have colored his attitude toward the non-Levitical priests who served in Israel's shrines and the kings who supported them. Second, was Gomer a prostitute before Hosea married her? If so, then the tension between his prophetic role and his priestly background would be heightened, since a Levite was forbidden by law to marry a prostitute (Lev. 21:14–15). However, if she became unfaithful only after they were married, then the metaphorical equation between Gomer and Israel is more appropriate. The resolute faith of Abraham, who had first received the covenant promise from God (Gen. 12:1–3), is transformed by the sins of later generations, and God repeatedly laments that Israel is a "stiff-necked people" (Exod. 32:9; 33:5; 34:9) who repeatedly "turn to other gods" (Hosea 3:1). There is no consensus among scholars on either issue. Certainly, it is not necessary for Hosea to have been a Levite or for Gomer to be either a prostitute or simply promiscuous prior to their marriage for the metaphor to work. However, the social and religious context in which he speaks suggests that he is an advocate, if not a member, of the Levitical community.

Broadening the image of Hosea's troubled marriage to Gomer is the birth of three children to the couple. Each child is given a symbolic name, which functions as another form of enacted prophecy (compare Isa. 8:1–3). It is possible that the symbolic names are simply part of the metaphor and have no substance in reality. However, if they were actually given to the children, then whenever the child's name is spoken, the prophecy is brought to mind and its power is reinforced among the prophet's Israelite audience.

Jezreel, Hosea's first son (Hosea 1:4), is named for the strategic east-west corridor between Megiddo and Beth-shean where Jehu defeated Ahab's son, took the throne of Israel by force, and established his own ruling dynasty (2 Kings 9:15–26). Since Jehu had done this at the instigation of the prophet Elisha (9:1–3), the child's name implies that the reigning king, a descendant of Jehu, owes his power to Yahweh's intervention. Because this is the case, his power can just as easily be taken away by a dissatisfied God. The Jezreel valley is the most fertile area of Israel; thus Yahweh's threats to "take back my grain . . . and my wine in its season" (Hosea 2:9) suggest an approaching famine and resulting economic disruption, as well as the potential for political unrest and civil conflict. The child's name sounds a warning to those currently heading the government that the benefits of the covenant relationship are about to be withdrawn and the king's authority will be taken away (13:11).

The name of the second child (1:6), Lo-ruhamah ("Not Pitied"), condemns the social injustice so prevalent in Hosea's time. Like Amos, the prophet Hosea angrily indicts those who unthinkingly worsen the plight of the poor and the weak in society (4:2; 7:1–3; 10:13; 12:7–8). The child's name suggests that when Yahweh brings the nation to judgment there will be no pity on an unjust Israel (2:4).

The name of the third child (1:9), Lo-ammi ("Not My People"), revokes Israel's identity as the people of Yahweh. It is hard to imagine a more terrible denial of Israel's privileged status (13:14–16 speaks of the devastation to come). The people have prided themselves as God's chosen nation and had assumed that Yahweh would always be there to protect them. The covenant had assured the Israelites that Yahweh would provide them with land and children (compare 2:8–9). But because they had been unfaithful to Yahweh and had ascribed their abundant harvests to Baal, they had defaulted on their obligation to uphold the covenant (2:13). As a result, when in their desperation they finally seek the Lord, "they will not find him" (5:6). The name may also have a secondary meaning, since it suggests that Hosea suspected the child was not actually his, given his wife's unfaithfulness.

In the face of Gomer's infidelity and the shame she has brought on his household, Hosea has no choice but to confront her. One can compare Hosea's actions with the legal injunction in Num. 5:31, which deals with cases of suspected adultery. A husband who has been incensed by a "spirit of jealousy" because he suspects that his wife has been unfaithful to him must bring her before a priest for a trial by ordeal. While Hosea does not employ this legal strategy, he does ask the children (now presumably old enough to understand the situation) to reason with her and to plead that she abandon her infidelities (Hosea 2:2).

When reason fails, Hosea exercises his power as head of the household and severely punishes Gomer. First, he secludes her in order to separate her from her lovers (2:6), and he strips her of her finery in an effort to demonstrate that he is the source of her possessions and well-being (2:3; compare Ezek. 16:37–39). Ultimately, he drives her from his home and formally divorces her

---

Benefits of the Covenant Agreement

If you heed these ordinances, by diligently observing them, the Lᴏʀᴅ your God will maintain with you the covenant loyalty that he swore to your ancestors; he will love you, bless you, and multiply you; he will bless the fruit of your womb and the fruit of your ground, your grain and your wine and your oil, the increase of your cattle and the issue of your flock, in the land that he swore to your ancestors to give you. (Deut. 7:12–13)

(Hosea 2:9–12; compare Mal. 2:15–16). The divorce is symbolized by his withdrawing the traditional gifts granted by the head of the household to his wife: grain, wine, and all other products that were Gomer's due if she had been a wife in good standing (compare Exod. 21:10). Just as these actions signal the end of Hosea's marriage, they also indicate the end of Israel's covenant with Yahweh. There is no question that Yahweh will not continue to provide the fruits of the covenant when Israel has turned to other gods.

While Hosea has the right under Israelite law to divorce Gomer for adultery, he would shame himself and his household by abusing her in public. The elements of the marriage metaphor could thus lead to a dangerous reading of the text. Hosea's treatment of his wife and his children (Hosea 2:4–5) has sometimes been used to justify similar actions in modern relationships. This is a perversion of the biblical narrative and of the intent of the passage. Hosea 1–3 is not a story about the absolute submission of wives to their husbands, nor does it give license to husbands to brutalize their wives for real or imagined transgressions. The symbolism refers to the actions that God intends to take against the unfaithful nation of Israel—famine, exile, and slavery.

Despite their religious infidelities, Yahweh seeks to restore and forgive the nation, and this is again reflected in the marriage metaphor. Hosea agrees to take Gomer back if she renounces her other lovers forever and acknowledges that only he is her lord (2:14–20). Hosea's actions mirror Yahweh's, who will take Israel back if it renounces its Baals/lovers. When Gomer returns, Hosea acknowledges that their children, whom he rejected as "children of whoredom" in 2:4, are legally his heirs (compare Code of Hammurabi 170–71). The children's symbolic names, which had served as a warning to the nation, are now reversed as fertility returns to the land and God establishes a new covenant with Israel (2:21–23). In the more compact description of his marriage in Hosea 3, on her return to his household the prophet adds a further test of his wife's ability to remain chaste. He demands that she accept a celibate role, not "play[ing] the whore" or even having intercourse with him (3:3). The period of celibacy in the metaphor signifies the time to come when Israel will be "without king or prince, without sacrifice or pillar, without ephod or teraphim" (3:4) and reliant alone on its relationship with Yahweh. "If the father of a household who has children by his wife and by his slave, adopts the slave's children, then his household shall be divided evenly between the children of both, after his wife's firstborn son has received the preferential share" ("Code of Hammurabi 170," *OTPar* 112).

Hosea's allusion to the Valley of Achor (2:15) underscores what is at stake in Yahweh's offer of reconciliation. This was the place in the conquest narrative where Achan and his family had been stoned to death for his violation of the *herem* ("holy war") following the Battle of Jericho. By stealing from the loot captured at Jericho that had been dedicated to God, Achan had defiled all of the Israelites, not just himself (Josh. 7:22–26). Consequently, the fate of the entire nation was at stake, and the conquest could not continue until Achan acknowledged his guilt and accepted his punishment. He and his entire household, matching the command to destroy all the people and property, are stoned, absolving Israel of its guilt. The allusion to Achor in relation to Gomer's sin indicates that God in his mercy could restore the covenant only if Israel truly became faithful to Yahweh once again. But that restoration is dependent on Israel's submission to Yahweh's authority and renunciation of all other lovers/gods.

Additional Expressions of the Idolatry Theme

Although much of the rest of the book of Hosea is not as focused on a single theme, the prophet continually returns to the issue of idolatry and its detrimental effect on the nation. Israel's rampant idolatry and the **syncretistic** cultic practices of Israel's shrines and priesthood are chronicled in Hosea's repeated condemnations: "With their silver and gold they made idols for their own destruction" (8:4). Their mixed rituals consciously include sacrifices to Yahweh as well as other gods. While this is understandable within the general context of Canaan and the polytheism of their neighbors, it does not satisfy the basic requirements of the covenant with Yahweh. Thus a desire to placate and obtain the favor of as many deities as possible is simply a form of religious adultery and cannot be tolerated. As a result their offerings will be rejected by Yahweh, who demands their exclusive worship: "Though they offer choice sacrifices, though they eat flesh, the LORD does not accept them" (8:13).

To further illustrate his point, Hosea describes the useless practice of consulting "a piece of wood" and using divining rods to determine the will of the gods (4:12; compare Isa. 42:17). They "sacrifice on the tops of mountains, and make offerings upon the hills," a clear reference to the **high places** that the sin of Jeroboam had perpetuated in the land (Hosea 4:13; compare Jer. 2:20). Also referring to Jeroboam's political and religious reforms that had endorsed idolatrous behavior, Hosea announces that "the calf of Samaria shall be broken in pieces" (Hosea 8:5–6; compare Mic. 1:7).

Hosea also associates Israel's worship of the Baals with their misuse of the land. This is manifested in a countryside that is in mourning, with "all who live in it languish[ing]," including the animals, birds, and fish (Hosea 4:3). Some powerful and wealthy individuals were apparently taking advantage of the weakening economy to buy up plots of land, either by cheating their neighbors out of their property or by using the courts to their own advantage (compare 1 Kings 21). Since the covenant promised land to each Israelite household, Hosea regards this misuse as a clear violation of the covenant (Deut. 19:14). He accuses them of becoming so corrupt that they dare to "remove the landmark," the sacred boundary stones that marked landownership (Hosea 5:10; see Prov. 23:10). Hosea assures them that these actions will draw down upon the nation the full force of God's wrath (compare Isa. 5:8).

Another recurrent expression employed by Hosea to denounce Israel's idolatry and foolish attitudes is his use of the wind metaphor. Although the people seem to be carried away, literally "wrapped up" in their delight and celebrations associated with their worship of idols by the "wings" of the wind, it will instead transport them to the place of their due punishment (Hosea 4:19; compare Ps. 35:5; Isa. 57:13). Although they attempt to sow their fields with the assistance of the prevailing wind, they will actually "reap the whirlwind" and not benefit from the expected harvest (Hosea 8:7; compare Isa. 26:18). On a practical and political scale, this image means that instead of gaining greater prosperity for the nation by making vassal treaties with Assyria and Egypt (Hosea 12:1), they will be afflicted by the dry "east wind," which serves God's purpose to oppress and shrink their resources. The "winds" of the superpowers that only serve their purpose will end up "strip[ping] his [Ephraim's] treasury" as Israel attempts to submit its increasingly heavy tribute payments (13:15).

Boundary Markers

Do not topple the markers on the boundaries of a field, your conscience will destroy you. To please the pharaoh, observe the borders of your neighbors' fields. ("Teachings of Amen-em-ope," *OTPar* 296)

Cursed be anyone who moves a neighbor's boundary marker. (Deut. 27:17)

> Do not remove the ancient landmark
>   that your ancestors set up. (Prov. 22:28)

> Do not remove an ancient landmark
>   or encroach on the fields of orphans. (Prov. 23:10)

Wind Metaphors

The east wind or sirocco that blows in off the desert is a scorching blast and therefore a suitable metaphor for Israel's political and economic troubles as well as for Yahweh's manifest power. A hot wind that carries no moisture or humidity contributes to the difficulties faced by Israel's farmers and literally parches their throats and dries their skin as it blows (Isa. 17:13; Jer. 4:11; Ezek. 17:10). Since Yahweh is the lord of creation, both rain and winds are under his control (Amos 4:7, 13), and the prophets often use these elemental forces to describe both blessing (Isa. 49:10) and bane for a people dependent on their harvests to survive.

Isa. 11:15 "The LORD will utterly destroy the tongue of the sea of Egypt, and will wave his hand over the River with his scorching wind."

Isa. 27:8 In a "day of the LORD" prophecy, Isaiah includes the "fierce blast of . . . the east wind" as one of God's weapons.

Jer. 13:24 Using an agricultural image, Jeremiah describes how the people will be scattered into exile "like chaff driven by the wind from the desert."

Jer. 18:17 Because the people have forgotten God in their stubborn idolatry, God will "scatter them before the enemy" as if by "the wind from the east."

Ezek. 17:10 "When it [the vine] is transplanted, will it thrive? When the east wind strikes it, will it not utterly wither, wither on the bed where it grew?"

Knowledge of God Theme

Yet another major theme developed in the book of Hosea is the knowledge of God. For Hosea this theme is the key to a true understanding of the covenant and of God's relationship with the people. However, once again Jeroboam's sin becomes a stumbling block for the people. As the prophet attempts to reason out the inexplicable decision on the part of the people to "play the whore" (4:14), Hosea points to the nation's two leadership groups: monarchy and priesthood. In their greed for power, they "feed on the sin" of the people (4:8), allowing them to forget God's law and rejoicing at wickedness (7:3). Despite their responsibility to lead and instruct the nation, they have failed to provide the people with the knowledge they need to be obedient to the terms of the covenant (4:1–6; 5:1). As a result "there is no faithfulness or loyalty, and no knowledge of God in the land" (4:1). Given that circumstance, God finds it necessary to proclaim a lawsuit against Israel, indicting them for their iniquities and pronouncing judgment upon them for their sins (compare Mic. 1:2–7).

By acting in ignorance of what is expected of them under the covenant, the Israelites' sacrifices and offerings are unacceptable because they do not set aside their devotion to other gods: "For I desire steadfast love and not sacrifice, the knowledge of God rather than burnt offerings" (Hosea 6:6; compare

Hesed in Covenantal Context

The term that Hosea uses in 6:6 as a parallel to "knowledge" is "steadfast love." The Hebrew word *hesed* is variously translated "love, loyalty, abiding love, steadfast love, everlasting love, mercy." This technical legal term is found most often in treaty language and especially in passages in which the covenant is spelled out for the people. In this case, *hesed* is the basis on which God chose to establish the covenant with Abraham and his descendants, and reciprocally *hesed* is expected of the people of the covenant. *Hesed*

- is used in the context of a request by Abraham's servant that God adhere to a treaty obligation to make Abraham the father of many nations (Gen. 24:12, 14, 27);
- appears in the Ten Commandments as part of Yahweh's commitment to the covenant promise (Exod. 20:6);
- is the basis of Moses's intercession for the people in the wilderness: "Forgive the iniquity of this people according to the greatness of your steadfast love, just as you have pardoned this people, from Egypt even until now" (Num. 14:19);
- is an expression of faithfulness on the part of those who would keep the covenant: "who love me and keep my commandments" (Deut. 5:10);
- functions as part of the **covenant renewal ceremony** staged by Joshua to celebrate the conquest of the land and to renew the Israelites' commitment to serve Yahweh: "to love the LORD your God, to walk in all his ways, to keep his commandments" (Josh. 22:5); and
- is the term God uses to reassure the people of divine compliance with the terms of the covenant: "I act with steadfast love, justice, and righteousness" (Jer. 9:24); and "he is gracious and merciful, slow to anger, and abounding in steadfast love" (Joel 2:13).

Samuel in 1 Sam. 15:22). For this reason, the people will be abandoned by God "until they acknowledge their guilt and seek my [God's] face" (Hosea 5:15). In like manner, "it shall be like people, like priest" (4:9): the priests who are responsible for the lamentably ignorant condition of the people will face a similar fate. Furthermore, since their illegitimate kings have failed to call upon Yahweh exclusively (7:7), they will be swept away and swallowed up by the very nations with whom they sought to bargain as treaty partners (8:8–10; 10:7).

Hosea's use of treaty language is reminiscent of Samuel's condemnation of Saul for failing to keep God's commandments (1 Sam. 15:22). The difference, however, is that the people lack the knowledge they need to be able to obey (Hosea 4:6). They literally "do not know the LORD" (5:4). Their destruction has become inevitable and even more lamentable because their leaders have failed to instruct them in the terms of the covenant, for "a people without understanding comes to ruin" (4:14). Like Gomer, who has been a bad example and a poor teacher for her children, the kings and priests of Israel teach only accommodation with foreign cultures, and they fail to instruct the people of the necessity for strict adherence to Yahweh worship (5:1–4).

The increasingly desperate political situation facing Israel at the end of the eighth century makes it certain that the growing conflict between Egypt and Assyria will draw their vassal states into the maelstrom. For many of these small kingdoms, including Israel, they cannot hide or really protect themselves from the ravaging armies of the superpowers. Hosea's frustration with this situation can be seen in his ridicule of Israel's leaders, referring to them as "silly and without sense" as they court both superpowers while assuming they can find safety in playing both sides (7:11). He assures them that the resources they have squandered on palaces and walled fortresses will be consumed in the flames kindled by their conquerors (10:14). Instead of listening to the words of God's prophets and recognizing their legitimate role as sentinels placed there to warn the nation, they call each prophet "a fool" or a "man of the spirit," a raving madman (9:7–8). As a result, God will teach them the full extent of their miscalculations by allowing these foreign powers to ravage Israel and take away their precious idols and temple treasures as spoil (10:3–8).

Still, Hosea is speaking to his own people, and he cannot leave them to be destroyed without warning them of the coming destruction. He calls on them one last time to "sow for yourselves righteousness" so that they may "reap steadfast love": if they seek God, "he may come and rain righteousness upon you" (10:12). This reassurance is coupled with the firm promise that, though Yahweh will indeed punish them, their punishment will be like that of a parent who finds it necessary to correct a wayward child (11:1–7). This parenting theme is built on the assumption that the parent/God loves the child and therefore is willing to put forth the effort to instruct as well as punish Israel. Such an attitude rings true to every parent who knows the frustrations of guiding a child through to adulthood:

> The more I called them,
>   the more they went from me. . . .
> Yet it was I who taught **Ephraim** to walk,
>   I took them up in my arms;
>   but they did not know that I healed them. (11:2–3)

In Hosea's voice Yahweh cries out, "How can I give you up, Ephraim?" (11:8), while acknowledging that Israel's return to the land will come only after they have been punished for their deceitful behavior (12:2). Once they have discovered that "Assyria shall not save us" (14:3), Yahweh may redeem them. Before this can happen, however, they must return in faithfulness to Yahweh

(14:4–7), just as Gomer had to pledge faithfulness to Hosea. They and their plundered land can be healed and restored, but first they must regain their lost knowledge of Yahweh's power and the covenant. If they truly recognize the danger, they will follow the prophet's advice to "hold fast to love and justice, and wait continually for your God" (12:6; compare Mic. 6:8).

9

The Book of Isaiah

I saiah is the longest and structurally the most complex of the prophetic books in the Hebrew Bible. Its chapters reflect at least three separate time periods: ca. 740–697, 539–535, and 515–500. Among scholars, the traditionally accepted sections of the book, Isa. 1–39, 40–55, and 56–66, correspond to these three time periods. The prophet Isaiah is mentioned by name only sixteen times throughout the entire book, suggesting a deliberate effort on the part of the editors to depersonalize the text and giving the message of **Yahweh** more prominence than the prophet who delivers it. That is certainly the case in the latter two segments of the book, which were written well past the time of the original Isaiah and thus do not depend upon his public pronouncements or his personal presence. Each section of Isaiah will be dealt with in chronological order at appropriate places in this book.

In this chapter I discuss First Isaiah, or Isaiah of Jerusalem, who dates to the late eighth and early seventh centuries. Unlike either of his contemporaries, Amos or Hosea, he seems to be of high social status and to have free access to the king. He speaks authoritatively, and given the situation for other prophets there appears to be surprisingly little official opposition to his harsh oracles. Of course, his message is not always welcome, and it is sometimes ignored or given little attention. There are also occasions when Isaiah engages in direct confrontation with the king and even extreme physical displays to get his message across. His activities in this regard may reflect either his low expectations of gaining the attention of his audience (whether kings or commoners) or the desperate situation faced by the nation at the time.

Although the text is not explicit on this point, he may well have been a member of the religious establishment, with an authoritative priestly role in the Jerusalem temple. Isaiah's message is that of a well-educated man committed to the Davidic monarchy, the Jerusalem temple, and Jerusalem/Zion itself as the place where God has caused his name to dwell (compare Deut. 12:11 and Isa. 12:6; 18:7). Even so, as a prophet he condemns individual Davidic kings, the temple community, and the inhabitants of Judah and Jerusalem for their failure to keep the **covenant** with Yahweh (28:1–8). They will have to face the consequences of their covenant violations. By the end of Isaiah's career, the northern kingdom of Israel will cease to exist (2 Kings 17:5–6; 18:9–12) and the land of Judah will become an Assyrian vassal with much of its countryside devastated by invading armies (18:13–16).

Isaiah's Call

The account of Isaiah's call does not appear until the sixth chapter, which seems strange to modern readers, who quite naturally expect that a book about Isaiah's message and career would begin with his call to become a prophet. Whatever the reason the later editors had for placing the story at this point in the book, the account of Isaiah's call is as familiar to modern Western readers as any other part of the Old Testament because Handel used elements of it as the opening text for his *Messiah*. The specifics of the call help us to date it, since Isaiah tells us that it happened in the year King Uzziah died (740). The mention of seraphim in 6:2 is likely based on the design of the **ark of the covenant**, which had crossed wings on the lid representing angels upholding the throne of God (Exod. 25:17–22; also 1 Kings 6:23–28). Because of this imagery, it is possible that Isaiah experienced his vision while he was within the inner precincts of the Jerusalem temple.

In Isaiah's vision, the various manifestations of power all exhibit Yahweh's control over creation (compare Elijah's vision in 1 Kings 19:11–12). An earthquake shakes the pivots of the doors, symbolizing the presence of a force no door can shut out or restrain. A cloaking smoke then fills the temple and adds an element of tension and mystery to the scene, which is also found in Moses's **theophany** at Mount Sinai (Exod. 19:16–18). Also familiar from Moses's theophanic experience is Isaiah's attempt to deny his call. When he is confronted with the challenge of prophetic service, Isaiah protests that his lips are mortal flesh and therefore "unclean," or ritually impure, and thus he cannot speak the holy words of Yahweh. If Isaiah was a member of the priestly community, he would have been particularly concerned about matters of **ritual purity** and conscious of the great distance between the mortal and divine realms.

Simply stating the obvious, however, does not serve as an acceptable excuse to decline God's call. A quick remedy comes in this vision as an angel uses a pair of tongs to take a burning coal from the altar. Applied to his lips, the coal spiritually cauterizes Isaiah's mouth with this holy fire. This form of divine cleansing empowers him to speak the words God will give him (Isa. 6:6–7). Once his self-imposed impediment has been removed, he hears the voice of God asking, "Who will go for us?" and Isaiah can only respond, "Here am I; Send me!" (6:8; compare 1 Sam. 3:1–14).

Like other prophets, Isaiah's commission will not be an easy one. The political realities of the last three decades of the eighth century contain the mounting threat of the Assyrian invasion. Both Israel and Judah will feel the brunt of these incursions, which made for desperate times and scrambling after solutions that were beyond the capacity of the kings of these minor kingdoms. It is not surprising, therefore, that when Isaiah is commanded to speak he is warned that people will neither hear nor understand (Isa. 6:9–10; compare Zech. 7:11–12). The nation has rejected all previous warnings (Amos 2:12; Hosea 6:5), and now Yahweh intends to allow Assyria to destroy their cities and take their people into exile (Isa. 6:11–13; also 5:24; compare Amos 5:10–13). Despite this inevitable punishment, Isaiah is assured that a **remnant** will survive and will in the future serve as a "holy seed" to grow out of the "stump" of the nation (Isa. 6:13).

One aspect of Isaiah's call echoed throughout his prophetic message is his use of the term "holy." Isaiah employs it as the opposite of "human." But human behavior could become holy, just as Isaiah's lips are empowered to speak holy words. The people in turn could model themselves after the "Holy One of Israel," whose covenant and laws provide the direction for ethical behavior (5:16, 19). This term for God becomes a catchphrase in each section of the book of Isaiah (41:14; 60:9, 14) and is constantly repeated to emphasize the need of the people to "lean on the LORD, the Holy One of Israel" (10:20) so that when they have been purified they will naturally turn their eyes and "look to the Holy One of Israel" (17:7; also 29:19, 23).

It is only natural, therefore, that in this prophet's message the familiar themes of social justice, the obligation to aid and not oppress the weak, and the obligation to worship only Yahweh become the keys to holiness and compliance with the covenant. These themes, of course, are not unique to Isaiah. Injunctions against profaning Yahweh's holy name are found throughout the prophets (e.g., Jer. 34:16; Amos 2:7; Ezek. 36:22–32). Warnings against oppressing the weak form a regular staple in prophetic speech (e.g., Jer. 7:5–7; Ezek. 18:12; Zech. 7:9–10).

Oracles of Warning

Two examples of Isaiah's message illustrate the manner in which he announces judgment and offers the people a choice. In Isa. 1:10–23 the prophet first plays upon the familiar tradition of the destruction of the wicked cities of Sodom and Gomorrah (Gen. 19). Because of the sinful nature of these places, which caused their destruction by God, the prophets appear to be able to evoke fear and shame simply by voicing their names (Jer. 23:14; Amos 4:11). With that as his opening salvo, Isaiah then turns to Yahweh's past interaction with the people and their failure to uphold their covenantal obligations. Like Amos 5:21–24, Isaiah condemns their worship practices as nothing but empty rituals. He assures the people that Yahweh will refuse to listen to prayers that are not heartfelt or to accept meaningless or flawed offerings. Instead he calls for a culture known for maintaining a high level of social justice—what the covenant had stipulated as the basic requirement for a full life with God. He assures them that Yahweh has given the people a choice. If they are willing to cleanse themselves of the innocent blood that they have shed in oppressing the poor and the weak (Isa. 1:16–17), then redemption is possible. If they do not choose the way of righteousness, however, war and destruction are implicitly threatened, "for the mouth of the LORD has spoken" (1:20).

In his Song of the Vineyard (5:1–7), Isaiah uses a **juridical parable** to collectively indict the kings and the people of Judah (compare 2 Sam. 12:1–14). The setting for the song is the gathering of celebrants at the harvest festival. The grape harvest is such a fundamental expression of the land's fertility that it became a familiar metaphor of prosperity and divine blessing in the biblical tradition (2 Kings 18:31; Isa. 16:8–10; Zech. 3:10). Isaiah takes full advantage of the people's anticipated joy and high expectations as they labor at the winepress. But as is typical of many prophets, he turns what should have been a song of joy into a cry against injustice (Jer. 8:18–21; Joel 1:11–12). In painstaking detail, the prophet sketches out Yahweh's formal case against the people and the justification for their punishment.

The Song of the Vineyard depicts Yahweh as an owner who constructs and then lavishly tends his hillside vineyard and quite naturally expects his labors to bear fruit. It is useful to read this song as a contrast to Deuteronomy's depiction of the bounty of the Promised Land. There the people are said to inherit a region already tamed by previous inhabitants, who have already hewn cisterns from the soft limestone hillsides and whose vineyards and olive groves are well established (Deut. 6:11). The Israelites do not even have to work to get the water for their crops as they did in Egypt, where farming depended on labor-intensive irrigation. Instead seasonal rains loosen the ground for planting and encourage plant growth (11:10–12).

By contrast, the song in Isaiah is more realistic in its description of the arduous process of preparing and working a hillside vineyard in the Judean countryside. For it to be a success, hard and heavy labor are a necessity. The first step is the construction of terraces that encircle the hill and provide a series of platforms upon which to plant fruit trees and vines. The terraces are designed to minimize erosion and take full advantage of the seasonal rains while hoarding as much of the moisture as possible in the ground. They also provide sufficient farming space to meet the needs of small villages and perhaps even provide a surplus in good years. Terracing also ensures that the vines will benefit from the moisture stored in the soil during the critical winter months, when new leaves appear and the shoots and root system begin to grow. Like other crops, grapevines can be damaged by too little water, by over-irrigation, or by watering too late in the season.

By the time of Isaiah in the late eighth century, terraces were being installed on slopes that long ago had been harvested of their lumber and had become badly eroded. To counteract the damage, farmers engaged in the heavy labor necessary to build retaining walls and bring in new topsoil from elsewhere to fill the terraces. Isaiah 5:1–7 probably describes the reconstruction of such a terrace as Yahweh digs the soil, clears the stones, and plants the vines. When Isaiah describes the vineyard as lying on "a very fertile hill" (5:1), it is because a great deal of backbreaking labor has made it so.

Once the land has been prepared, the choice vine cuttings are planted (compare Jer. 2:21). This act serves in the prophetic literature as a sign of Yahweh's establishment of the covenant with Israel (Isa. 6:13 and Jer. 31:27–28 contain allegorical references to "holy seed" or the sowing of a field). Just having the opportunity to develop such a vineyard is described as the sign of a peaceful and prosperous sedentary existence (2 Kings 18:31). It compares with the uncertainties of the nomadic life of the landless, who do not have the luxury of waiting years for the vines to mature and begin producing fruit (Jer. 35:6–10). Drawing on this covenantal metaphor of planting a vineyard, Ezek. 17:5–6 describes the setting of seedlings in fertile and well-watered ground, where roots could find strong purchase and leaves and vines could stretch across the ground luxuriantly.

Planting the cuttings is only the first step. The farmer must keep the vineyard free of moisture-sapping weeds, briars, and thorns. In some cases, the farmer could use a plow to keep the weeds under control, but narrow areas would have to be hoed regularly by hand (Isa. 7:25) during the growing season. Then, during the first six years of growth (Lev. 25:3), the farmer would prune the maturing vines (Isa. 2:4) in the winter months to remove a portion of the previous season's growth (4 Macc. 1:29). This pruning would enhance the growth of the remaining grape clusters (2 Esd. 16:43). Additional pruning in the early summer months (May and June according to the Gezer Calendar; OTPar 156) would remove unproductive tendrils and dead vegetation (Isa. 18:5; John 15:2).

The wise farmer also took measures to protect vines and fruit from foraging by small animals (Song 2:15) and travelers (Prov. 24:30–31). Accordingly, the owner of the vineyard in Isa. 5 constructs both a hedge and a stone wall to guard the vineyard and its maturing fruit from harm. He also builds a watchtower to shelter the laborers and to serve as a lookout for marauding bands of animals or humans. Probably not every farmer could afford to go to such lengths to protect his fields, but in Isaiah's song, in which Yahweh is the owner, all of the various means of protection are put in place. Thus the prophetic image is a divine owner who makes every effort to create a fertile field, lays out the choicest cuttings, and then provides protection from all outside dangers.

Isaiah's song also mentions the installation of a wine vat, which would have been carved out of the soft limestone of the hillside. Like the threshing floor, the wine vat was a communal facility that benefited the entire village (Hosea 9:2). It would not be necessary for every farmer to carve out his own vat, but every laborer would be expected to participate in treading grapes at harvest time. As one team of workers exhausted itself, another would take its place until all of the ripe grapes set aside for wine production had been crushed into pulp. The workers kept themselves energized and in rhythm by singing or chanting (Isa. 16:10), accompanied by music performed by their wives and daughters (Judg. 21:20–21) and perhaps with the keen anticipation of the fruits of their labor. Egyptian depictions of treaders show that their efforts are synchronized to the beat of batons or clappers.

The harvesting of the grapes from mature vines would take place in late summer, when new growth had stopped and the bark darkened (Num. 13:20). At this point, the grapes were tasted to determine when they were ready to be taken to the winepress. This would be the stage at which the owner or his overseer could judge the quality of the grapes (Isa. 5:2). If the grapes were sour, such as those mentioned in Ezekiel's proverb (Ezek. 18:2), they might have been picked too early and thus not yet produced enough sugar to make them sweet.

But the grapes in Yahweh's vineyard are sour for another reason. Isaiah says that the vineyard produced "wild grapes," not unripe ones. Jeremiah also uses the metaphor of a reliable stock of grapes that has inexplicably been transformed into a "putrid" or "foreign" variety (Jer. 2:21). Jeremiah's wordplay points to influences beyond the normal control of the vintner. Clearly the vine is at fault. So also in Isaiah: this vine is acting unnaturally. Its normal cycle has been interrupted, and its fruit has never adequately ripened. What remains is worthless, lacking in any nourishing value, and totally unfit for its intended use. The labor that went into the construction of the terraced vineyard and its cultivation can yield nothing if the vines have gone bad. All that can be expected, given these conditions, is an abandoned field where "no songs are sung, no shouts are raised; no treader treads out wine in the presses" (Isa. 16:10). In the juridical summation, Yahweh concludes, "What more was there to do for my vineyard that I have not done in it?" (5:4). God's rhetorical question also functions as part of the testimony in a divine lawsuit against the nation and provides the basis for a full indictment of their iniquities.

Such evil cannot be borne, for the land is precious and the time expended by the owner and the laborers can never be recovered. And so, Isaiah's song concludes with a harsh divine punishment. God renounces all interest or concern in any future dealings with this vineyard. Its terraces, walls, soil, and vines are to be thrown down and left in a state that can be compared only to the condition of ruined cities abandoned by their gods (e.g., the Sumerian "Laments for Ur"). With the terraces destroyed, the soil will erode away, and what remains will nurture only thorns and weeds. Wild animals will prowl through this once-civilized place. The final insult comes when Yahweh withholds the rains (compare 1 Kings 17:1; Jer. 14:1–6; Hag. 1:11). The resulting drought spells disaster for both land and people and is generally taken in ancient Near Eastern literature to be a sign of divine displeasure: "The dust storm leaves the city and the Temple of Nanna in ruins. . . . The walls are breached and corpses block the gates. . . . Where crowds once celebrated festivals, bodies lay in every street, corpses piled on every road" ("Laments for Ur," *OTPar* 253).

At the end of the song, Israel and Judah are identified as the worthless vine (Isa. 5:7). What has made Yahweh's "vines" go bad are the people's unjust practices and the shedding of innocent blood. These injustices are chronicled for all to see and include depriving the poor of their lands by creating huge estates (5:8), a practice known as latifundialization (Mic. 2:2 is another example). They are also charged with drunkenness and self-indulgent living (Isa. 5:11–12), public deception by the leaders (5:18–21), and bribery (5:23). The divine judgment against them will result in the total devastation of their most valuable possession—the land (Jer. 2:4–8; Hosea 2:3). It will be transformed into a ruined place, just as the vineyard was laid waste (Lam. 2:13). Furthermore, the nation will be left open to the assaults of other people (Isa. 5:26–30), and the "chosen" who "are wise in [their] own eyes" (5:21) will go into exile because of their lack of knowledge (5:13; compare Hosea 4:1–2).

Isaiah may have understood this destruction as preparation for a new beginning (Isa. 1:24–28). Massive destructive events, such as floods and earthquakes, were often understood as preparation for the creation of a new, cleansed world (Joel 3:14–18). If this is the case, the complete destruction of the vineyard signals the end of the old world of the monarchy and unfaithfulness to the covenant. Once every trace of the old and corrupt world is removed, the stage is set for a new beginning. In this new creation, the new "vines" will escape the fate of the first vineyard because they will have been cleansed of the internal corruption that led to destruction in the first place.

It is also appropriate to think of Isaiah's Song of the Vineyard as a juridical parable couched in the agricultural terms that would have been very familiar to the prophet's audience. Just as the prophet Nathan forced David to convict himself with the parable of the ewe lamb, Isaiah summons the inhabitants of Jerusalem and Judah to listen to the song and "judge" between Yahweh and his vineyard. Only after the verdict is decreed do they learn that *they* are the vineyard and that *their* actions will lead to their destruction. This theme of reversal is found most prominently in Judges (17:6 prefaces the story of a

Levite who serves Micah's private shrine and idol) and in ancient Near Eastern literature such as the horrific "Visions of Neferti" from the First Intermediate Period in Egypt (ca. 2181–2055). The punishment also reflects penalties for violating covenants that were well known from Israel's repeated political dealings with the Assyrians.

Political Message

Many of Isaiah's major pronouncements are tied to specific historical events. During the final years of the eighth century, the nation was in the throes of Assyria's westward expansion. Ever since 800, Assyria had been extending its **hegemony** into Syria-Palestine through military engagements and political strong-arm tactics. As a result, all of the smaller nations of that region were forced into vassalage and compelled to pay tribute and provide soldiers and supplies for the Assyrian war machine. This led to an almost continuous series of revolts by the smaller states, usually during the transition of power when a new Assyrian king came to the throne. Although these revolts were brutally suppressed, they continued to occur on a regular basis. Israel, like the other kingdoms, participated in several attempts to throw off the Assyrian political yoke. By the last decades of the eighth century, however, the fate of the troublesome northern kingdom was sealed. In 721 Israel was conquered and its people taken into exile by the forces of King Sargon II of Assyria (2 Kings 17:5–6). The invading Assyrian armies also devastated the southern kingdom of Judah, and King Sennacherib laid siege to Jerusalem in 701. These were truly desperate times. Despite his repeated use of the phrase "fear not" (Isa. 7:4; 10:24; 37:6), it is unlikely Isaiah's message brought much solace to Judah's beleaguered kings.

Also during the 730s, the Egyptians repeatedly encouraged the small vassal states of Syria-Palestine to revolt against Assyria. This was a typical ploy by rival superpowers that were more than willing to use the discontent of the smaller border states to weaken their opponent in order to further their own political ambitions. Evidence of that discontent is seen when most of the rest of the Syro-Palestinian states, Israel, and Syria formed an alliance against Assyria. A similar strategy had been successful in the past; for example, Ahab joined with other states in the mid-ninth century to prevent the Assyrians from controlling their region (see "Annals of Shalmaneser III" in *OTPar* 179). By the end of the eighth century, however, Assyrian power had grown much stronger. Moreover, their ruthless use of various psychological warfare techniques, such as massacring whole cities and mutilating prisoners, gave them a decided edge in any conflict (Hosea 13:16; Amos 1:13).

Because he feared Assyrian reprisal and did not see any marked advantage in joining the rebellious states, King Ahaz of Judah refuses to join the newly formed coalition headed by Israel and Syria. The result is what is known as the Syro-Ephraimitic war. Israel and Syria ally themselves against Judah and initiate hostilities designed to place a more cooperative leader on Judah's throne. The crisis that Ahaz and his advisers must face is complex. On the one hand, as an Assyrian colony, Judah has a treaty obligation to put down any rebellion against Assyria. On the other hand, as a covenant partner of Israel, Judah has a legal responsibility to support Israel's struggle for freedom. Regardless of whether Judah decides to support Assyria or Israel, it faces dire consequences. If Judah does not join their struggle against Assyria, Israel and Syria will invade and Ahaz may be dethroned. But if Judah joins in their struggle, Assyria most certainly will punish Judah and its king!

Ahaz's council of advisers cannot reach a decision. Given the dangerous prospects associated with either path, they vacillate in their opinions and shake "as the trees of the forest shake before the wind" (Isa. 7:2). Perhaps to clear his head, the king temporarily closes their deliberations and orders a tour to inspect Jerusalem's defenses. He realizes that regardless of which decision Judah makes, there will be an invasion, and Jerusalem must prepare for a long siege. Ahaz's tour takes him outside the city walls and away from all but his immediate entourage. The crucial scene in this drama is set at one of the city's most strategic sites: "at the end of the conduit of the upper pool on the highway to the Fuller's Field" (7:3; the parallel use of this same site for the Rabshakeh's speech occurs in 36:2). This strategic spot is associated with one of the important industries of the city and also represents a crucial link to the city's water supply. It represents the physical life of the inhabitants in this time of crisis and is therefore an appropriate place for the prophet to confront the king with a question of life or death.

The setting also provides Isaiah with the chance to lobby the king and members of his entourage. The prophet first proposes that Judah remain nonaligned in this conflict since their reliance should be on Yahweh's role as the **Divine Warrior** and Lord of the covenant. This echoes the statement in Hosea 12:1 condemning Israel for its foreign alliances with both Assyria and Egypt, a dangerous game that in Isaiah's lifetime has resulted in the total destruction of the northern kingdom and the exile of its people.

A key assumption in Isaiah's argument to remain nonaligned is the tradition of Jerusalem's inviolability (Pss. 46:5; 48:8). If Jerusalem remains faithful, it can rely on the protection of the Divine Warrior. In this impregnable position, the city cannot be truly threatened by Syria and Israel, labeled here as "two smoldering stumps of firebrands" (Isa. 7:1–9). Another important component of Isaiah's message is the premonarchic tradition that considers Judah to have only one valid treaty, its covenant with Yahweh. This pact with Yahweh originally recognized the deity alone as king of Judah. And as Judah's Divine Warrior and king, it is Yahweh, not his representative Ahaz, who must provide for and protect the nation. In a final attempt to convince

Ahaz to remain neutral, Isaiah announces the verdict of the **divine assembly** against Israel and Syria. The divine assembly has indicted these nations for attempting to liberate themselves rather than accept Yahweh's plan for them (7:8–9). Yahweh alone is the liberator of the Israelites, and only Yahweh can set them free. God is willing to provide Ahaz with a sign to demonstrate this divine promise (7:11), for even if Assyria is a mighty power it is certainly no mightier than Egypt, from whom Yahweh previously had delivered Israel.

When Ahaz refuses to ask for the sign that Yahweh will carry out this verdict against Judah's opponents, Isaiah proclaims the sign anyway. He predicts the birth of a child whose name will be Immanuel. On the face of it, this is just another **annunciation**, a birth announcement by a divine representative (Gen. 16:11–12; Judg. 13:3–5). The child's mother, simply referred to in the Hebrew text as a "young woman" (Hebrew *almah*), is most likely one of Ahaz's wives who has accompanied the king on his inspection tour. She may have even been obviously pregnant at the time and thus have served as an easily observable object of the prophet's words. This pronouncement is also a "time-based" prophecy—an unusual and risky thing to do, since a prophet's reputation was based on his veracity (Deut. 18:21–22). Isaiah predicts that by the time the child is old enough to know the difference between right and wrong (somewhere between five and thirteen years old), Israel and Syria will be destroyed and Judah will be impoverished (Isa. 7:13–25). The child's name, Immanuel, which means "God is with us," is a sign that the power behind Assyria's success at this point is actually Yahweh (10:5). Judah should therefore fear the coming of the Lord, not petty kingdoms such as Syria and Israel. Isaiah matches this prediction with a second annunciation, this time predicting the birth and naming of his own son, who will see the destruction of Samaria and Syria before he can say the words "my father" and "my mother" (8:1–4).

The likely backstory to these events is that Ahaz had already requested aid from Assyria and could not renege on that agreement. The Assyrians then use the opportunity presented by Ahaz's request for assistance to intervene before the rebellious states had sufficient time to organize their resistance. Judah's hopes for freedom from Assyrian rule are dashed, and it is placed under even more restrictive treaty obligations. Judah also has to pay for Assyria's "help." Its local autonomy is weakened even further, and it has to pay an even heavier annual tribute. In the end and within the time frame of a decade, Isaiah's prediction of destruction and impoverishment for the nation had come true.

End of the Northern Kingdom

The Syro-Ephraimitic war in the 730s was symptomatic of the discontent within the entire Assyrian Empire. Additional revolts continued to take place, and eventually Assyrian emperor Shalmaneser V, and his successor, Sargon II, decided to make an example of some of the rebels. Israel, once again a leader among the small states, was targeted in 722, and the Assyrian Annals describe its invasion. A year later the capital city of Samaria was captured, and the nation of Israel ceased to exist as an identifiable political entity. Though it is likely that many refugees escaped to Judah, the Assyrians deported the majority of the survivors, and the tradition of the "ten lost tribes of Israel" was born (2 Kings 18:9–12). Although these people survived the destruction of their nation, they lost their national identity as a distinct people. Furthermore, Assyrian efforts to rebuild Samaria signal the eradication of Israelite culture in that region, since Sargon II repopulates it with peoples from other parts of his empire, including rebellious Arab tribes (17:24).

The effect of this traumatic event on Judah is manifest in the prophets who point to Israel's demise and warn Judah and Jerusalem that they may well suffer the same fate (Isa. 9:8–21; Jer. 7:15; Mic. 1:2–7). Some, including the Deuteronomistic editors of Joshua–Kings, take this as vindication of the Davidic monarchy and its covenant with Yahweh. Israel, which had broken away and perpetuated the **sins of Jeroboam**, had finally and justifiably been punished (2 Kings 17:2–18, 21–23). With the Assyrians still a very real threat to their own existence, however, the more likely reactions among the people of Judah are shock, fear, and apprehension for the future. The psychological effects of the disaster may have been fueled by the lurid tales of Assyrian atrocities carried south by the refugees from Israel's cities.

In this charged atmosphere, Hezekiah succeeds his father, Ahaz, as ruler of Judah around 726. While his assessment of the political situation is probably quite similar to that of his father, he is portrayed as a king more open to the message of Isaiah. The much more sympathetic account of Hezekiah's reign in the book of Kings indicates that, unlike his father and most of the other kings of Judah, "he did what was right in the sight of the LORD" (18:3). Among his accomplishments is his attempt to purify the Jerusalem temple (18:4–6) by removing images of other gods (including the Nehushtan, the bronze serpent from Moses's day). He also invaded Philistine territory "as far as Gaza" and presumably extended his hegemony over them (18:8). These actions are in fact a series of political moves defying the Assyrians, who had imposed set boundaries within their provinces and expected vassal states throughout Syria-Palestine to demonstrate their deference to Assyrian religion and culture.

Hezekiah's rebellious actions were made possible by the Assyrians being distracted by other, more dangerous rebellions in significantly more strategic areas of the empire (Babylon). The result is that they did not initially punish Hezekiah for his defiance. Still, Hezekiah did exercise some caution. For instance, in 711 when Philistine king Azuri and his **city-state** of Ashdod organized a revolt at the instigation of the Egyptians, Hezekiah does not immediately join the new alliance. Instead, like his father before him, he remains neutral. Isaiah may have influenced this decision by performing a rather unusual **enacted**

Symbolic Use of Clothing

Clothing not only served a utilitarian purpose but also symbolized social status, wealth, power, and gender. Clearly the cut, style, decoration, color, and quantity of clothing served as social markers to immediately identify a person. Isaiah's symbolic use of clothing is one of many examples in the biblical text:

- Judah's daughter-in-law Tamar is typecast while wearing a set of "widow's garments," but she is able to transform herself and her social status by changing into another style of clothing, including a veil, which identifies her as a prostitute (Gen. 38:14–15).
- David's daughter Tamar is known as one of "the virgin daughters of the king" by her robe with long sleeves (2 Sam. 13:19; cf. 13:31). When she is raped and shamed by her brother Amnon, however, she tears her robe as both a sign of mourning (3:31) and a signal of her change of status.
- When Elijah designates his successor, he casts his robe over the shoulders of Elisha to signify that he will eventually take up the prophet's tasks (1 Kings 19:19). That same garment is used as an instrument of power to open the waters of the Jordan River (2 Kings 2:8–14).
- Amos condemns rich landowners who do not return the day laborers' garments according to the law (Exod. 22:26–27; Amos 2:8). Without his robe, the laborer sinks to the social level of a slave, just as Isaiah's "naked circuit" portrays the fate of a disobedient people who will fall into slavery as prisoners of war (Isa. 20:2).
- Jeremiah removes his "linen belt" and buries it in the bank of the Euphrates. His action is designed to signal the direction from which danger will come and to indicate that the exiled people will also be "buried/planted" in Mesopotamia for a period of time (Jer. 13:1–11).

prophecy. He strips off his priestly robes and parades naked around the city for three years to demonstrate the fate of those who rebel against the Assyrians (Isa. 20:3; compare Mic. 1:8). Given the devastation eventually visited on Ashdod and Gath by Sargon II, Hezekiah's decision is a wise one. In his annals, Sargon II boasts of stripping Ashdod of its inhabitants, treasury, and gods and of deporting a segment of the people. Isaiah's nakedness could not have more graphically portrayed the condition of war prisoners to his audience.

It is inevitable, however, that Hezekiah's attempts to gain a greater measure of political autonomy for his small kingdom will bring them to the attention of the Assyrians. During the third year of his reign as the Assyrian emperor (701), Sennacherib invades Judah and ravages the countryside as part of his general campaign to suppress rebellious nations in Syria-Palestine. Sennacherib's chronicle is filled with the self-serving, boastful language typical of

Assyrian political propaganda. Its grandiose style is reflected in the account of Sennacherib's invasion in 2 Kings and in the Assyrian Annals:

> In the fourteenth year of King Hezekiah, King Sennacherib of Assyria came up against all the fortified cities of Judah and captured them. King Hezekiah of Judah sent to the king of Assyria at Lachish, saying, "I have done wrong; withdraw from me; whatever you impose on me I will bear." The king of Assyria demanded of King Hezekiah of Judah three hundred talents of silver and thirty talents of gold. Hezekiah gave him all the silver that was found in the house of the LORD and in the treasuries of the king's house. (2 Kings 18:13–15)

> Because Hezekiah of Judah did not submit to my yoke, I laid siege to forty-six of his fortified cities and walled forts and to the countless villages in their vicinity. I conquered them using earthen ramps and battering rams. . . . I took 200,150 prisoners of war. . . . I imprisoned Hezekiah in Jerusalem like a bird in a cage. . . . Hezekiah, who was overwhelmed by my terror-inspiring splendor, . . . was forced to send me 420 pounds of gold, 11,200 pounds of silver, precious stones . . . and all kinds of valuable treasures. . . . He sent his personal messenger to deliver this tribute and bow down to me. ("Annals of Sennacherib," *OTPar* 191–92)

The savage destruction of many of Judah's cities, including the important border fortress of Lachish (2 Kings 18:14), forces Hezekiah into a situation in which his only means of saving the kingdom is to pay a huge ransom. While stripping the capital of its wealth saves Jerusalem from destruction, it provides little solace to villagers outside its walls whose houses and fields have been destroyed. One unfortunate side effect of the ransoming of the city is a strengthening of the belief in the inviolability of Jerusalem. Despite the shame attached to Hezekiah's capitulation and the emptying of the city and temple treasury, Jerusalem had not fallen to the Assyrians. Therefore, the conclusion is drawn by many of its inhabitants, especially the priestly community, that God will not allow the "place where his name dwells" to be destroyed. This **myth** of inviolability remains in place despite the contemporary prophet Micah's prediction that "Jerusalem shall become a heap of ruins" (Mic. 3:12) and even surfaces in the hope expressed a century later in Jeremiah's time that God will continue to spare the city (Jer. 26:17–19).

Additional details of the Assyrian siege of Jerusalem are provided in Isa. 36–37 (mirrored in 2 Kings 18). These chapters recount the taunting speech of the Assyrian military official and diplomat bearing the title Rabshakeh, or "Chief Cupbearer." During a truce he stands outside the walls of Jerusalem, at "the conduit of the upper pool on the highway to the Fuller's Field" (Isa. 36:2), and negotiates with Hezekiah's officials. Just like Isaiah, who had previously used this strategic spot to confront King Ahaz (7:3), the Assyrian official uses a significant place to address the obvious threat to the life of the city. The people who have retreated inside the walls for safety must have strained to hear the negotiations despite the protests of Hezekiah's advisers. To further discomfort the king's men and add to the tension created by his statements, the shrewd Rabshakeh speaks in the Hebrew language so all the people can understand his words (36:11–12).

Careful analysis of his formal discourse shows that he is a skillful orator. He alternates between negative and cajoling statements. For instance, he sarcastically chides Judah for making an alliance with Egypt and calls it a worthless exercise. He describes that nation as a "broken reed" that will cut the hand of anyone who deals with it (36:6). He then employs a sanctimonious tone, pointing to King Hezekiah's decree to have all altars torn down in the shrines and villages outside Jerusalem, and says that this action has actually angered God. Next, in a comic and ingratiating manner, he ridicules Judah's lack of soldiers, saying that even if the Assyrian king supplied them with the horses, Hezekiah could not provide the riders. Then, returning to the results of Hezekiah's efforts to centralize worship in Jerusalem, he tells them that the Assyrian army is besieging Jerusalem at the behest of Yahweh: "Is it without the LORD that I have come up against this land to destroy it? The LORD said to me, Go up against this land, and destroy it" (36:10).

This use of a **theodicy** by a foreign diplomat is a powerful but not unusual tactic. Isaiah himself describes Assyria as Yahweh's tool to punish the nation (10:5–11). And Isa. 40–55, dated to the end of the exilic period (ca. 539), argues that Yahweh has anointed King Cyrus of Persia as the liberator of the exiled people of Judah. The Persian version of this event, recorded on the "Cyrus Cylinder," is yet another theodicy that claims the god of the Babylonians has allowed Cyrus to conquer Babylon: "Marduk, the ruler of the divine assembly, heard the people of Babylon when they cried out and became angry. Therefore, he and the other members of the divine assembly left the sanctuaries which had been built for them in Babylon. Marduk . . . searched all the lands for a righteous ruler to lead the *akitu* New Year procession. He chose Cyrus . . . and made him ruler of all the earth. . . . Because Marduk . . . was pleased with Cyrus's good deeds and upright heart, he ordered him to march against Babylon" ("Decree of Cyrus," *OTPar* 208). In yet another example of this particular usage of theodicy, found in Jer. 21:4–10, the prophet Jeremiah condemns Jerusalem's leadership for adherence to the myth of the city's inviolability and asserts that God actually "will fight against you [Jerusalem] with outstretched hand and mighty arm."

A second siege event is described in Isa. 37, but it is somewhat difficult to separate from the events of the first in 701, although 2 Kings 18:13–16 seems to contain additional information that attempts to differentiate the two events. The episode in Isa. 37 appears to be a part of the siege narrative of Isa. 36; however, it more directly involves Yahweh's assurance that Jerusalem shall be saved: "For I will defend this city to save it, for my own sake and for the sake of my servant David" (37:35). The narrative is an example of an **apology,** a literary device used to defend an individual, in this case Hezekiah. When Hezekiah prays for Yahweh's assistance, an angel brings a plague that kills 185,000 Assyrians overnight (37:36). Hezekiah's trust in Yahweh thus results in a miraculous deliverance of Jerusalem, as Sennacherib strikes camp and goes home. The narrative ends with a reference to Sennacherib's assassination by his sons (2 Kings 19:36–37; Isa. 37:37–38).

Historians remain intrigued by this account of Jerusalem's deliverance. It is possible that the death of the Assyrian soldiers was the result of a plague; certainly plague in overcrowded army camps was well known in the ancient world. Apart from a story reported by Greek historian Herodotus, however, there is no evidence to confirm that such a plague struck Sennacherib's army while it was in Palestine. And while the Assyrian chronicles report that Sennacherib's sons assassinated him, there is no reason to connect that event, which took place in 680, with Isaiah's prophecy.

Since the historicity of Isa. 37 cannot be confirmed, it is better to interpret it as a pious tale based on the tradition of Jerusalem's inviolability. The story thus underscores the belief that Yahweh will protect Jerusalem, especially when its Davidic kings put their trust in God. But perpetuating the idea that Jerusalem cannot be destroyed will have disastrous consequences for its citizens. One hundred years later, a mob nearly kills Jeremiah because he prophesies the destruction of Jerusalem and the temple (Jer. 26:7–9) and thereby challenges the veracity of this cherished tradition. But when Neo-Babylonian king Nebuchadnezzar destroys Jerusalem along with the temple in 587, it becomes clear that the tradition of Jerusalem's inviolability merely generated false hopes and a sense of overconfidence that prevented true repentance.

The Remnant

Isaiah is particularly harsh in his oracles against the northern kingdom of Israel (Isa. 17:4–6; 28:1–4). This may be the result of the Syro-Ephraimitic war or other tensions between the two kingdoms. It may also reflect the prejudices that the southern priesthood held against the maverick kings and priests of the northern kingdom. Reversing God's covenant promise to Abraham that his descendants would be "as numerous as the stars of heaven and as the sand that is on the seashore" (Gen. 22:17), the prophet declares that only a remnant will return: "For though your people Israel were like the sand of the sea, only a remnant of them will return" (Isa. 10:22).

This reversal of the terms of the covenant is reminiscent of the symbolic name of Hosea's child Lo-ammi ("Not My People") in Hosea 1:9; and Isaiah's declaration, if it had a wide circulation, must have been frightening to both Israel and Judah. The fertility of the land and the people had always been a concern, but now the decimation of the population by the rampaging

Assyrian armies underscored the impending reality of the death of Israel. The poignant nature of their plight is seen in Isaiah's statement that "my people go into exile without knowledge; their nobles are dying of hunger, and their multitude is parched with thirst" (Isa. 5:13). Like Hosea (4:1–6), who also points to a lack of knowledge among the people, Isaiah squarely places the blame for the people's demise on their leaders.

To soften this specter of destruction and to make the case once again for God's faithfulness to those who obey the covenant, Isaiah matches nearly every prediction of destruction with a promise of the restoration of a faithful remnant and the punishment of Judah's enemies. Thus "on that day" when God restores the fortunes of the nation he will extend a hand to bring back "the remnant that is left of his people" (Isa. 11:11), and they will once again "lean on the LORD" to give them strength (10:20). When God returns the full blessings of the covenant to the land, "the surviving remnant of the house of Judah shall again take root downward, and bear fruit upward; for from Jerusalem a remnant shall go out, and from Mount Zion a band of survivors. The zeal of the LORD of hosts will do this" (37:31–32).

Coupled with this is the prophet's assurance that on that day of restoration God will raise up a representative of the ruling house of David to lead the remnant in wisdom and righteousness. Centuries later Isaiah's assurance that

---

Knowledge and the Fear of the Lord

A common biblical theme is the idea that the fear of the Lord leads to the kind of knowledge essential for life (Ps. 111:10; Prov. 1:7). The association of fear and knowledge is also reflected in Job's admission that he did not truly know God until he saw God with his own eyes (Job 42:5–6). The fear of God is often described as a quality of righteousness:

Gen. 20:11   Abraham justifies his own unethical actions in Gerar because "there is no fear of God at all in this place."

Exod. 18:21   Jethro encourages Moses to select elders to assist him: "Men who fear God are trustworthy."

1 Sam. 12:24   Samuel describes a just king as one who rules in the fear of God.

Proverbs   Several proverbs state that the fear of the Lord "is hatred of evil" (8:13) and brings honor and life (22:4; 10:27).

Jer. 5:24   Jeremiah claims that Israel's punishment is due to the unwillingness to "say in their hearts, 'Let us fear the LORD our God.'"

Mal. 2:6–7   Malachi reminds the Levitical priesthood that it is their responsibility to "guard knowledge" so that when the people come seeking instruction from their lips it can be trusted.

"a child has been born for us" (9:6–7) will find its way into the interpretation of the Gospel writers and their efforts to authenticate Jesus's tie to the house of David and the role of **Messiah** (Luke 2:11; Matt. 1:16). In this way and in another time they connect with Isaiah's original promise of hope to a nation under siege and in danger of total destruction.

Isaiah returns to this theme of restoration in 11:1–2, where he describes how from the ruin of the nation will spring "a shoot . . . from the stump of Jesse" (David's father). From what appears to be a lifeless stump, green shoots will emerge to demonstrate conclusively that the people of the covenant will be restored. Furthermore, their ruler will be imbued with Yahweh's wise counsel and will serve as the model for a people who must have the knowledge and fear of Yahweh in order to survive (11:3). This idealized Davidic king will, unlike Ahaz, lead the people with courage and strength while faithfully adhering to the terms of the covenant.

The remaining portions of the book of Isaiah will be examined below when postexilic prophecy is discussed. Isaiah of Jerusalem apparently completed his activities with the end of Hezekiah's reign (Isa. 38–39) in 697. It is apparent from examination of the similarities of language and themes that appear in Isa. 40–66, that Isaiah's message was passed on to a school of his disciples (the group mentioned in 8:16 receive his testimony and teachings). They kept his message, vocabulary, and style alive and revived it after the exile to speak to the needs of the community that returned to Jerusalem to rebuild their lives and the temple after 535.

10

The Book of Micah

An exact contemporary of Isaiah of Jerusalem, the prophet Micah has a distinctively different perspective on the events that occur during the last three decades of the eighth century and the beginning of the seventh century (Mic. 1:1). He lived in a satellite village of the former Philistine city of Gath (1:14). Moresheth-gath was located about six miles northeast of Lachish in the **Shephelah** and twenty miles southwest of Jerusalem. Along with Lachish, Adullam, and Mareshah, Moresheth served as a fortified settlement on the western border of Judah (2 Chron. 11:8). Micah's view of the conditions of that period are therefore based on his proximity to the area first invaded by the Assyrians in 711 during the Ashdod Revolt (Isa. 20:1), the first to feel the full wrath of an army known for its cruelty and ruthlessness. Furthermore, the prophet, unlike the Jerusalem-based Isaiah, represents the feelings and concerns of the rural farmers and villagers who had to bear the brunt of the Assyrian army's rape and pillaging.

When Shalmaneser III invaded Israel and the northern kingdom in 724, the ravenous army stripped the land of its food during the siege. Finally, once Samaria fell two years later, the surviving population was resettled in a far region of the Assyrian Empire (2 Kings 17:5–6, 22–23). In the next generation, when the people of Jerusalem were bottled up under siege by Sennacherib's army (701), the rest of Judah's population was subjected to rape, execution, and enslavement as the Assyrian troops once again foraged the countryside for food and supplies.

Weary and sick over the magnitude of these waves of relentless destruction, Micah identifies the true enemies of the people, in a sharply critical oracle, pointing to the Israelite capital of Samaria and Judah's capital at Jerusalem. He declares that the kings and priests are cannibals (Mic. 3:2–3) who have stripped the flesh from the people through excessive taxation and misled them by their deceitful and corrupt leadership (3:11). His message can be divided into three main facets: social criticism in the face of high-level injustice (1:2–2:11; 3:1–12; 6:9–16; 7:17), a **covenant** lawsuit against the nation for its violations (6:1–8), and a depiction of a future idyllic and peaceful restoration (4:1–5), including a royal **Messiah** figure (5:2–5) and a shepherd image for God (2:12–13; 7:8–20). Throughout his message, Micah emphasizes the simple terms of the Mosaic covenant and condemns the monarchy and the priesthood for seizing authority that had not been given to them by God.

Social Criticism Theme

In the turmoil caused by a succession of political crises and weak leaders during the late eighth century, large landowners and wealthy individuals took the opportunity to prey upon small farmers, seizing their land for debt, squeezing them off their holdings, and depriving them of their covenantal inheritance (2:1–2, 8–9). Isaiah also refers to these members of the rapacious elite as those "who join house to house, who add field to field" (Isa. 5:8). Micah taunts the landed gentry and defies them to close their eyes and ears without trembling when confronted with the reality of God's call to the Assyrians to turn the tables on them. Like their own victims, they will be dispossessed and deprived of the ability to pass their lands on to their heirs (Mic. 2:4–6).

Like other prophets before and after him, Micah charges these leaders with the crime of indifference to reality. Instead they reject the words of the prophets, saying "one should not preach of such things" and assuring themselves that "no harm shall come upon us" (2:6; 3:11). As Amos and Jeremiah assert, the people of Israel listen only to prophets who proclaim "peace, peace, when there is no peace" (Amos 2:12; Jer. 6:14; 8:11). Only "empty falsehoods" are acceptable to a blinded people (Mic. 2:11). Regardless of this official attitude, these celebrated and rewarded false seers and diviners ultimately will be put to shame, forced to cover their lips like lepers (Lev. 13:45) in order to hide their disgrace and to mourn their fate (Mic. 3:5–7; compare Ezek. 24:17).

Judging his society to be utterly corrupt, Micah charges that the political leaders, judges, priests, and prophets of Israel are unjust and greedy. They daily demonstrate that they "hate the good and love the evil" by selling their influence, their teachings, and even their prophecies for a price, while saying to themselves that "surely the LORD is with us!" (Mic. 3:2, 9–11; 6:10–12; 7:3). This charge, which depicts a world turned upside down, occurs frequently in the **wisdom literature** of the ancient Near East. For example, the "Eloquent Peasant" of ancient Egypt charges that lawmakers "tolerate injustice" while so-called respectable members of society are willing to "condone what is crooked" (*OTPar* 235). In another piece of Egyptian wisdom literature, a man considering suicide justifies his choice by saying that "everyone chooses evil, everyone rejects good" (*OTPar* 227). Similarly, the "Babylonian Job" laments what he sees of human misery caused by people who "listen to the wicked" and by the wealthy, who are so corrupt that they are even willing to "steal a beggar's bowl" (*OTPar* 243).

Just as Amos had decried the innumerable false business practices that had deprived the people of what little resources they still possessed (Amos 8:5–6), Micah also takes up this refrain, calling for social justice in the face of "wicked scales and a bag of dishonest weights" (Mic. 6:11). Because of their greed and their acceptance of violence against the weak in society, these wealthy landowners and businessmen are condemned to see all they have accumulated through criminal activity siphoned away as tribute payments to the Assyrian kings and as loot taken by foreign armies (6:15).

Compounding their current unjust actions, the leaders and people of Israel are condemned for having "kept the statutes of Omri and all the works of the house of Ahab" (6:16). Like the **Deuteronomistic Historian**'s catchphrase, **sins of Jeroboam** (2 Kings 13:2; 17:21–23), Micah uses the phrase "statutes of Omri" as another label applied to the rulers of Israel. They both signify in a collective way the ultimate reason for Israel's downfall: multigenerational adherence to idolatry and the rejection of **Yahweh**'s statutes under the covenant. In this way Micah points to the sins of the Omride dynasty and its successors, who contributed to Israel's destruction by walking "in all the way of Jeroboam" (1 Kings 16:26) and "did evil in the sight of the LORD more than all who were before him" (16:30).

From a political standpoint, Micah's angry message is also directed at the kings of both nations, who have glorified themselves in their capital cities of Samaria and Jerusalem (Mic. 1:5–7). Through their actions they had brought the wrath of Assyria upon the countryside when they listened to Egypt and opposed Assyrian **hegemony** or refused to pay their tribute (2 Kings 17:4). Evidence of these foreign entanglements is found in the Annals of Shalmaneser III (*OTPar* 179) and that Assyrian monarch's "Black Obelisk" inscription (*OTPar* 180). The latter inscription includes a depiction of Ahab's successor, Jehu, paying tribute and bowing to the Assyrian kings as a sworn vassal. Although this action is not recorded in the biblical account, it is very similar to what King Ahaz does when he submits to Tiglath-pileser III (2 Kings 16:7–18). In confronting the nation over these political choices, Micah's oracle also echoes the judgment of the Deuteronomistic Historian, who denounces those kings who willingly chose to perpetuate the sin of Jeroboam (1 Kings 15:26, 34; 22:52–53).

Micah also targets Jerusalem for destruction because of its widespread corruption and self-deception. In Mic. 3:12 he repeats his statement about Samaria (1:6) that the city will "become a heap of ruins" and adds that Zion, the Temple Mount, "shall be plowed as a field." This extremely harsh message demonstrates just how complete the destruction is to be and is also targeted at the complacent inhabitants of the cities who had witnessed the destruction of the villages and towns outside their walls. A field cannot be plowed or planted until it has been completely cleared of vegetation, stones, and other debris. The clean sweep will not only clear away the homes but also their inhabitants. With that accomplished, the Assyrians will then be able to draw upon the benefits of the land that had been promised to the people under the covenant but that they have now forfeited. Apparently, this horrendous statement stuck in the popular mind, since it is quoted nearly a century later by the elders during Jeremiah's trial (Jer. 26:18). It also provides evidence of the continuing belief in the **myth** of the inviolability of Jerusalem. It still serves for them as a precedent showing that God had apparently relented in Hezekiah's day and had chosen not to destroy the city and temple after all. Thus, when Micah's statement is quoted by the village elders at Jeremiah's trial, they do so in the hope that "the LORD [would] change his mind [once again] about the disaster that he had pronounced against them" (26:19).

In his own day, however, Micah very likely witnessed the burning of villages throughout the countryside of Judah and at least heard from eyewitnesses of the utter destruction of the nation of Israel. Therefore he is justified in his **lament** to say that "the faithful have disappeared from the land" (Mic. 7:2). At the same time he uses that sorrow to charge that some still "lie in wait for blood" while their "hands are skilled to do evil" (7:2–3). This unjust world represents a complete reversal of the ideals of the covenant community. Under these conditions, trust between friends is impossible; children treat their parents with contempt; and entire families are at war with each other (7:5–6). There can be no withholding of God's displeasure in the face of such corruption. Drawing on familiar agricultural images from his village background, Micah illustrates the fate of a land without law:

> You shall eat, but not be satisfied, . . .
> you shall put away, but not save. . . .
> You shall sow, but not reap;
>> you shall tread olives, but not anoint yourselves with oil;
>> you shall tread grapes, but not drink wine. (Mic. 6:14–15)

Judicial Oracles

Micah frames his charges against Jerusalem and Samaria and their corrupt leadership in the form of a divine lawsuit (6:1–2; compare Hosea 12:2). During this same time period, Isaiah uses a **juridical parable**, the Song of the Vineyard, to create a courtroom atmosphere for God's judgment of the nation (Isa. 5:1–7). However, Micah, like Amos, is a member of the village culture, and it is therefore not surprising that he chooses to direct his venom at the urban centers that he felt were the cause of the peoples' deprivations and calamities. The worship of foreign gods that continued to be fostered in their shrines and temples and the forging of foreign alliances had incurred both God's wrath and the heavy hand of the Assyrian conqueror on Israel and Judah (Mic. 1:15). While invaders first trampled the fields throughout the countryside, now they will turn their attention to capturing and depopulating the capital cities. These centers of power will become "a heap in the open country, a place for planting vineyards" (1:6). When Samaria at last falls to the Assyrians after a two-year siege in 721, Micah contends that the city's once mighty walls will "pour down . . . into the valley" leaving only the remnants of its foundations to mark the place (1:6).

The itinerary depicting the path of destruction created by the Assyrians may be reflected in the list of cities in 1:10–15, from Gath to Maroth to "the gate of Jerusalem." During the Assyrian scorched-earth campaign in Israel, helpless peasant farmers who attempt to defend their homes are slaughtered or rounded up and deported. In the wake of such general destruction, the prophet calls on the people to repent and mourn their fate. Like the **enacted prophecy** employed by Isaiah during the Ashdod Revolt of 711 (Isa. 20:2), the mourners are told to strip themselves naked and walk barefoot into exile to the sound of scavenging jackals (Mic. 1:8). Their shaved heads signify that they are no longer "pampered children" but are reduced to the status of prisoners of war (1:16; compare Ezek. 5:1–4).

Widening his condemnation of those in authority, the prophet also takes aim at the hollow rituals orchestrated by the priesthood and then performed by the people. He makes it clear that they cannot expect that by simply presenting their sacrifices on the altar they have obligated God to protect or reward them. Micah's lawsuit (Hebrew *rib*, "contention") over their hollow worship begins with Yahweh calling upon all of creation to witness the testimony in this case (Mic. 6:1–2). This is an unusual feature since most lawsuit oracles are addressed to "people of Judah" (Isa. 5:3–4) or the "people of Israel" (Hosea 4:1). Then, in a series of questions and answers in Mic. 6:3–8, the prophet makes his case by presenting the traditional litany of saving events that had previously character-ized God's care for the people of the covenant (6:3–5; see Ps. 78). He reminds them that they had been "brought up" from Egypt; redeemed from slavery; guided by Moses, Aaron, and Miriam; blessed by foreign prophets like Balaam (Num. 22:5–6); and repeatedly forced to recognize divine anger and retribution when they fell into idolatry and disobedience as they did at Shittim (25:1).

Some scholars suggest that the next set of questions (Mic. 6:6–7) is an ex-ample of the whining refrain of the people, who believe that God is actually burdening them; and they illustrate this by listing extravagant demands that would have drained them of their resources. It is more likely, however, that the mounting tone of indignation over the query "with what shall I come before the LORD?" is actually an example of Micah's anger. He is mocking the people when he voices these impossibly large offerings of "ten thousands of rivers of oil" and the sacrifice of a "firstborn" child (6:7). In fact, Micah's harsh criticism is directed at Israel's empty cultic practices (compare a similar sarcastic tone in Amos 4:4–5). Just as Amos contended (5:21–24) that Yahweh rejects their "solemn assemblies" and "burnt offerings" and the raucous noise of their songs, Micah attempts to drive a stake into a belief system based on quantity rather than on the quality of faith.

The prophet then provides a much simpler model of devotion to Yahweh's covenant. Micah points out, as Samuel had (1 Sam. 15:22), that obedience to God's covenant is more important than ritual sacrifice. They are admonished to "do justice, . . . love kindness, and . . . walk humbly with your God" (Mic. 6:8). This simple statement echoes that found in Hosea 12:6, where the people are called on to "hold fast to love and justice, and wait continually for your God." It is also voiced in a later generation by Jeremiah (7:21–23), who states that God's desire is not for burnt offerings, but for the people to "walk only in the way that I command you, so that all may be well with you" (compare Exod. 15:26). In each of these cases, the result is a sense of true peace that comes with the knowledge of God (Hosea 6:6). The catalyst for this welcome condition is found in strict adherence to and a true understanding of *hesed*, "everlasting love" (Mic. 7:18–20).

Restoration

Some scholars suggest that later Judean editors inserted the passage that describes the restoration of the Davidic monarchy (Mic. 5:2–5). It would not be completely out of character, however, for an eighth-century prophet to employ this theme. One of Micah's most important restoration statements concerns the rise of a new Davidic ruler from Bethlehem (5:2; see the quotation of this verse in Matt. 2:5–6). A prophecy such as this one serves two purposes. First, it takes the monarchy back to its primal roots, since Bethlehem is David's birthplace. It also removes the taint of "career politician" or "political insider" from the monarchy. David did not inherit the throne; instead he is chosen by God, anointed by the prophet Samuel, and recognized by the civil authorities after the death of Saul's son Ishbaal (2 Sam. 5:1–5). Like the idealized figure of David, this new king will be an obedient shepherd (Mic. 7:14), willing to respond to Yahweh's voice by "feeding the flock" and providing the people with security and peace (5:4–5; compare Ezek. 34:23–24).

Micah's vision of restoration also includes cleansing the nation of every vestige of foreign worship, including the various forms of magic employed by diviners and incantation priests. There is also to be a general removal of all of the sacred stones (*massebot*) that had been installed in shrines and worshiped for centuries, like those in the originally Canaanite cities of Gezer, Shechem, Hazor, and Arad. And finally, the worship of **Asherah**, the mother goddess of Canaanite and Ugaritic religion, is to be eliminated. Her sacred poles and groves are to be cut down and all manifestations of her cult outlawed (Mic. 5:12–14; this false worship practice is also condemned in Isa. 17:8 and Jer. 17:2).

When Yahweh has removed the evildoers from the land and justice is restored at last, then the shame that had been incurred by the nation will be removed. Witnessing this transformation, the nations of Assyria and Egypt will become desolate and "stand in fear" of Yahweh (Mic. 7:8–20). They will be humbled, forced to lick the dust like the cursed serpent in the garden of Eden (Gen. 3:14; see Isa. 14:29; Jer. 8:17). And, in their awe of what Yahweh has accomplished "in days to come," they will "go up to the mountain of the LORD . . . that he may teach us his ways" (Mic. 4:1–2; see Isa. 2:3). Like many of the prophets, Micah's initial task is to serve as a voice of condemnation in the present and as a beacon of hope for a better future. His simple theology calls for the people to set aside their extravagant sacrifices and useless, empty rituals and "walk humbly" with God while they strive "to do justice and to love kindness" (Mic. 6:8)—all attributes of their covenant obligations. In addition, he assures the people that their God "does not retain his anger forever" for those who form the **remnant** of the faithful and will form the nucleus of the restored nation (7:18–20).

11

Prophetic Voices
of the Late Seventh Century

While it may seem strange that no prophetic voices are associated with the mid-seventh century, careful reading of the very brief chronicle of events during this period (2 Kings 21:2–9) provides clear evidence that the people and culture of Judah were completely subordinated to Assyrian influences during the long reign of Manasseh (687–642). In fact, Assyrian records demonstrate that Mesopotamian imperial power was at its height, with a series of strong rulers and little chance for the vassal states to revolt as they had in the past. Frustration over their political situation and the growing influence of Assyrian culture among the people of Judah may be found in the litany of crimes and apostasies attributed to Manasseh by the **Deuteronomistic Historian**. Manasseh

- rebuilt the **high places**, erected altars to Baal, and set up an **Asherah pole**;
- built altars for all the "host of heaven" and set up an image (*pesel*) of Asherah in the Jerusalem temple; and
- made his son "pass through fire" and practiced soothsaying and augury (Nah. 3:4).

A less condemning appraisal of the king is found in the fifth century. The **Chronicler**'s account portrays both Manasseh's religious crimes (2 Chron. 33:2–9) and his transformation into a repentant sovereign and reformer (33:10–17). While the Deuteronomistic Historian used Manasseh's overt **apostasy** as a major contributing factor in Jerusalem's destruction by the Neo-Babylonians in 587, the Chronicler is looking back at these events and has chosen to make a theological point about the reshaping of the king's role and character. This may be a response to the length of his reign (fifty-five years), since, for the Chronicler, it would be unconscionable for an unrepentant ruler to remain on his throne so long without experiencing God's wrath. It is unlikely, however, that the story of the penitent Manasseh, who is held captive in Babylon by the Assyrians and in his despair calls on **Yahweh** for deliverance (33:12–13), reflects historical reality. His only real captivity was to the political realities of his time when it was necessary to accept Assyrian **hegemony** or be deposed and his people conquered.

In any case, in the decades following the prophetic pronouncements of Isaiah and Micah, no new prophetic voice is raised, or at least none is recorded. It is possible that they had all gone into hiding, as they did during Ahab's reign (1 Kings 18:4). Since Yahweh worship is not totally extinguished during that half century it is likely that the harsh words of Isaiah and Micah served to keep a flame of belief alive among the **remnant** even during this period. To be sure, this was a time when Judah lay completely submerged, a backwater region in the Assyrian Empire. It was nominally ruled by a puppet king, who obtained a measure of support from the people by allowing the old Baal culture to creep back into their worship practices. He also was forced to include Assyrian religious rituals as part of his vassalage, while Yahweh worship is subordinated to the realities of the politics of the day. Certainly, there had been other occasions when Israelite culture and religion were threatened with extinction; however, the writer of 1–2 Kings treats this period as a dark age during which the people are led astray by King Manasseh and the nobility (2 Kings 21:9). As Assyrian power begins to wane, prophetic activity in Judah resumes in the latter half of the seventh century during the reign of the good king Josiah (640–609). The decline of the Assyrian Empire and a brief period of political resurgence for Judah create a brief opportunity to celebrate their old enemy's demise, but very shortly a new power will emerge in Mesopotamia to take its place, and the Hebrew prophets will turn once again to strident warnings.

The four short prophetic books contained in this time frame—Nahum, Zephaniah, Habakkuk, and Obadiah—serve as a bridge to the turbulent times of Jeremiah and Ezekiel and the more momentous events of the sixth century. Each will continue the pattern of prophetic pronouncement set by previous divine spokesmen while speaking to specific aspects of their own time and demonstrating a piece of their own personalities.

The Book of Nahum

Other than the **superscription** to this book, no surviving sources describe the author of Nahum. In fact he is not even referred to as a prophet here, although his message is identified as an oracle (1:1). Furthermore, the clan name or place name Elkosh is unknown, although some traditions locate it in either the region of Galilee or the rural region of southwestern Judah. The book cannot be dated with any precision; however, its extreme optimism suggests a date prior to the end of Josiah's reign (609). The oracle predicting the fall of the Assyrian capital of Nineveh most likely dates between 663, when Ashurbanipal captured the Egyptian city of Thebes (3:8), and 612, when Nineveh was destroyed by a coalition army led by Neo-Babylonian King Nabopolassar and his Median allies. If its composition and/or editing are actually postexilic, then that reflects an effort to demonstrate that Yahweh is the divine force behind the destruction of Nineveh and the elimination of this hated enemy nation.

Unlike most of the prophetic works, the book of Nahum does not address itself to Israel or Judah and does not warn or condemn them for their violations of the **covenant**. Instead it is focused entirely on the defeat of Assyria and the destruction of that mortal enemy's capital city by Yahweh the **Divine Warrior**. Its inclusion in the **canon** of prophetic literature may be based on the theme of the Divine Warrior at work, but its content would also be a welcome hymn of triumph for the people of Israel and Judah, who had experienced firsthand the many atrocities committed by the Assyrian armies as they ravaged the land. The prophet's celebratory and vengeful tone reflects the theme of Yahweh's righteous jealousy (compare Ezek. 8:5). Because Assyria had attempted to subordinate Yahweh to its own gods, Yahweh's vengeance had been aroused. In retribution, all of Nineveh's graven images and idols are to be cast out of its temple (Nah. 1:14). The removal of these sacred images from their temple symbolizes the complete overthrow of Assyria's power, as it was manifested in its gods. Furthermore, the destruction of Nineveh, the deposing of its king, and the complete defeat of the Assyrians illustrate the theme that God would avenge the crimes of nations who exploit other peoples (3:4–7; compare Joel 3:19–21).

Yahweh's majesty takes the form of controlling all of the dynamic elements of nature. The first appearance of Yahweh as commander of the winds (Nah. 1:3) is reminiscent of the **theophanic** appearances found in Habakkuk (esp. 3:10), Zechariah (9:14), and Job (38:1). Of particular importance in this regard is these powers being representative of those associated with the high gods of Israel's neighbors. For instance, the whirlwind or the "Cloud Rider" is a common symbol for divine majesty in Ugaritic epic as well as in the Mesopotamian creation story *Enuma Elish* (also in Pss. 68:4; 104:3):

Kothar-wa-hasis said: "Listen to me, Mighty Ba'al, hear me out, Rider of the Clouds. Now is the time for you to strike. Slay your enemies and eliminate your rivals." ("Stories of Ba'al and Anat," *OTPar* 269)

> He [Marduk] brought forth Imhullu "the Evil Wind," the Whirlwind,
>   the Hurricane,
> the Fourfold Wind, the Sevenfold Wind, the Cyclone, the Matchless
>   Wind. ("The Creation Epic," *ANET* 66)

Yahweh also displays divine authority over the waters, including rivers, seas, and life-giving rains (Nah. 1:4). God's rebuking the flood (as in Isa. 50:2; Ps. 104:7) puts him on an epic par with the god Baal in Ugaritic **myth**. But whereas Baal can only temporarily subdue Yamm, the sea god, Yahweh's sovereignty is complete and everlasting. The effect of his "voice" in Nah. 1:5 resembles the depiction in Ps. 29, which concludes that Yahweh's incomparable power cannot be matched by any other god:

> The voice of the LORD is powerful. . . .
> The voice of the LORD breaks the cedars;
>   the LORD breaks the cedars of Lebanon.
> He makes Lebanon skip like a calf. . . .
> The voice of the LORD flashes forth flames of fire.
> The voice of the LORD shakes the wilderness. . . .
> The voice of the LORD causes the oaks to whirl,
>   and strips the forest bare. (Ps. 29:4–9)

Nahum's description of Nineveh's destruction in Nah. 2 employs images similar to those found in the Assyrian Annals. The clash of arms and the turmoil of battle are evoked through vivid descriptions of heavily armed and massed armies, armored chariots, disconsolate prisoners being taken into exile, and the battering down of gates and palace walls (2:3–7). All of these images speak of the total devastation of a formerly great people. With Yahweh personally fighting against them, they can no longer hope to recover their former glories (2:13). It is no wonder that their "hearts faint and knees tremble" while their "loins quake" and "faces grow pale" (2:10).

Particularly apt in this passage is the use of the lion metaphor in 2:11–12. The chief deities of Nineveh are Ishtar and the sun god Shamash. Artistic representations of Ishtar often depict her with a lion, and Shamash is portrayed as a winged lion. In addition, King Esarhaddon of Assyria (680–669) refers to himself in his Annals (Prism B, *ANET* 289) as a rampant lion, a favorite of the gods, who came to power at their command and was able to vanquish all opposition to his rule. Now, according to Nahum, the lion will have no more cause to roar. Its den will be empty, and the sword will devour the "young lions."

Finally, Nahum employs a series of taunts that begin by asking the Assyrians, "Are you better than Thebes?" (3:8). This Egyptian city, also dedicated to a god (Amon), had been captured and destroyed by Emperor Ashurbanipal of Assyria in 663. Lots had been cast (3:10) to distribute its nobility as slaves to the conquerors (a practice also found in Homer's *Iliad* and Joel 3:3), and its rich palaces had been plundered and destroyed. Now it is Nineveh's turn. Although the city is admonished to go ahead and prepare for a siege (Nah. 3:14), the people of Nineveh are told that their efforts will not save them because their "troops . . . are women in your midst" and "the gates of your land are wide open to your foes" (3:13). Then, using a phrase common in the Assyrian Annals identifying the kings as the shepherds of the people, Nahum derisively tells them that their "shepherds are asleep" (3:18) and their enemies now are able to "clap their hands" in anticipation of their demise (3:19). Clapping hands and stamping feet are common gestures of both celebration (Ezek. 25:6) and derision. The latter instance is found in Lam. 2:15, where Jerusalem is the destroyed city, having become an object of scorn in which clapping is accompanied by hissing and the wagging of heads (compare Ezek. 6:11).

> Esarhaddon: "King of Assyria, regent of Babylon, king of Sumer and Akkad, king of the four rims (of the earth), the true shepherd, favorite of the great gods." (Prism B, *ANET* 289)

> Ashurbanipal: "Those peoples which Ashur, Ishtar and the (other) great gods had given to me to be their shepherd and had entrusted into my hands." (Rassam Cylinder, *ANET* 298)

Since no nation or tyrant can remain in power forever, the author of Nahum may be allowed to gloat over Nineveh's destruction. From the perspective of the oppressed, the hated Assyrians, who had employed psychological warfare, torture, and heavy-handed administrative practices, had at last received the justice they deserved. The use of a **theodicy** in which Yahweh is the force behind Nabopolassar's Babylonian army is typical of Israelite prophecy (compare Isa. 45:1–4, as King Cyrus of Persia captures Babylon). The theodicy demonstrates a God who is both "jealous and avenging" (Nah. 1:2) as well as "slow to anger" (1:3). This is especially satisfying to the Israelites, who believe that a just God never leaves the guilty unpunished. The graphic descriptions of shields dripping blood and war chariots careening through the streets (2:3–4) must have been pleasing to the people of Judah, who had suffered greatly at the hands of the rampaging Assyrian armies.

The nation of Judah, however, would be able to revel in Nineveh's destruction in 612 for only a few years. They were quickly swept up in the imperial ambitions of Egypt and Babylonia's new king, Nebuchadnezzar, as these revived superpowers filled the vacuum created by Assyria's demise. After a brief period of hopeful rebuilding under King Josiah and the regeneration of national ambitions (2 Kings 23:1–27), Judah fell once again under the control of rulers no less demanding than the Assyrians, and the beleaguered nation spiraled into a crisis that would eventually consume it and its people.

The Book of Zephaniah

As the Assyrian Empire began to come apart after the death of its last great emperor, Ashurbanipal, Judah too embarks on a new path. The days of the puppet rule of Manasseh are left behind, and new prophetic voices begin to be heard. Of course, their message contains the familiar condemnations of kings and priests who failed to eliminate Baal worship and encouragement of the people and leaders of Judah to restore Yahweh as their supreme deity. That these prophetic figures can voice an anti-Assyrian message is an indication of how far the empire's power had faded.

Among these late seventh-century prophets is Zephaniah, whose name may be an assertion that "Yahweh is Zaphon." Like Elijah's name, which proclaimed "Yahweh is my God" during a time when Ahab and Jezebel were working to eliminate Yahweh worship, Zephaniah's name made the claim that Yahweh is the sole source of power even over the Baal stronghold/sacred mountain of Baal. According to the superscription in 1:1, the prophecies of Zephaniah date to the reign of Josiah (640–609). However, even though it is likely that Zephaniah prophesied during the reign of Josiah, it is difficult to reconcile his oracles with the actual events of Josiah's reign. In addition, his fierce condemnation of Judah's **syncretized** religious practices suggest that Zephaniah may have been active before Josiah began his religious reforms in 621 (2 Kings 23:1–25). But it could also be argued that Zephaniah's prophecies were part of the effort to institute this reform movement (22:1–23:30; 2 Chron. 34:1–8).

The book contains oracles against idolatry and foreign religious practices and confirms God's judgment of Judah's sins and those of its neighbors. One image he repeatedly employs, like several other prophets, is the image of the "day of the LORD [Yahweh]" (Zeph. 1:8–18; 2:2; compare Amos 5:18–20). This image is associated with God's judgment of Judah and all of the nations (Zeph. 1:14–15). For instance, in Isa. 13:9–11 and 17:7–9, the "day of the LORD" will coincide with the nations being confronted by the reality of Yahweh's true power when God will put an end to their pride, arrogance, and useless sacrificial altars. The same theme in Zephaniah warns the people to show proper respect to the Lord of creation. All of the officials and "princes" of the land, who have adopted foreign attire and introduced fraudulent religious practices (i.e., "leap over the threshold"; compare 1 Sam. 5:5), will find themselves prepared as the sacrifice on their tainted altars (Zeph. 1:7–9). Those who have become wealthy by promoting foreign influences while discounting Yahweh's ability to do good or harm will find the evidence of their wealth "laid waste" and others enjoying the fruits of their labor (1:12–13). God will rain down bloody ruin and destruction in a display of such wrath that it can easily be compared to the blaring of battle trumpets and the crashing of arms in battle, while the survivors walk about in a befuddled daze (1:14–18).

The Day of the Lord

The familiar theme of the day of the Lord initially must have contained expressions of hope for the nation and, with God's help, the renewal of the land and the elimination of their enemies. However, the prophetic literature often replaces these hopes for divine intervention with the triumph of Yahweh over foreign gods and the devastation of an unfaithful people, who have put their trust in these false deities:

> On that day the LORD will punish
>> the host of heaven in the heaven,
>> and on earth the kings of the earth. (Isa. 24:21)

> Alas for the day!
> For the day of the LORD is near,
>> and as destruction from the Almighty it comes. (Joel 1:15)

> Alas for you who desire the day of the LORD!
>> Why do you want the day of the LORD?
> It is darkness, not light. (Amos 5:18)

> For the day of the LORD is near against all the nations.
> As you have done, it shall be done to you;
>> your deeds shall return on your own head. (Obad. 15)

> The great day of the LORD is near,
>> near and hastening fast. . . .
> That day will be a day of wrath,
>> a day of distress and anguish,
> a day of ruin and devastation. (Zeph. 1:14–15)

See, the day is coming, burning like an oven, when all the arrogant and all evildoers will be stubble; the day that comes shall burn them up. (Mal. 4:1)

In a reversal of Yahweh's creative act in Gen. 1–2, the prophet's horrific vision is one of the total annihilation of all creation, in much the same way that God sweeps away humankind in the flood narrative (Gen. 7:11–24):

> I will utterly sweep away everything
>> from the face of the earth, says the LORD.
> I will sweep away humans and animals;
>> I will sweep away the birds of the air
>> and the fish of the sea.
> I will make the wicked stumble.
>> I will cut off humanity
>> from the face of the earth, says the LORD. (Zeph. 1:2–3)

Such massive destruction is reminiscent of the vision of devastation described in Isaiah's call story: "Until cities lie waste without inhabitant, and houses without people, and the land is utterly desolate" (Isa. 6:11). Clearly, the prophets were required to deliver an unwelcome message, but at the same time they could not allow God's warning to be set aside.

One particularly frightening image in Zephaniah portrays Yahweh searching Jerusalem with a lamp for "those who say in their hearts, 'The LORD will not do good, nor will he do harm'" (Zeph. 1:12). These blindly complacent people foolishly convinced themselves that God will take no direct role in the affairs of history, for either good or evil. Because of that stubborn attitude, it becomes the prophet's task to shake them out of their drunken stupor. He therefore predicts that the houses and vineyards that are the evidence of their wealth and pride will be plundered (1:13).

In the next generation, Jeremiah will also use this quest image in his search for the "one person who acts justly and seeks truth" (5:1–3). But this later prophet is actively looking for the righteous, not those who are to be punished. Zephaniah's image is reversed by Ezekiel, who envisioned a group of divine examiners who search Jerusalem and mark the foreheads of the innocents "who sigh and groan over all the abominations" so that they may be spared the coming destruction (Ezek. 9:4). Zephaniah offers little hope for mercy. Like Amos 5:4–6, he leaves only a simple path for those who hope to survive the destruction: "Seek the LORD, . . . seek righteousness, seek humility" (Zeph. 2:3). Zephaniah hints that those who do so *may* be among those who lie "hidden" during the day of God's wrath, although this cannot be guaranteed (compare Amos 5:14–15). Only when God has completed the coming judgment on the nation is there a hope for restoration. At that point, once the "proudly exultant ones" have been purged from them, a "people humble and lowly" will reemerge to "seek refuge in the name of the LORD" (Zeph. 3:11–12). Of course, in Zephaniah's time, with the demise of the Assyrian Empire, there is some hope that the nation will be spared further destruction. While God has punished the people for their unfaithfulness and continues to warn them, it is now time to condemn Israel's enemies in a set of **oracles against the nations** (Zeph. 2).

Zephaniah balances the destructive past with the assurance that Judah's foes will also suffer God's judgment in the coming time. Like other prophets, Zephaniah utters oracles against the nations. These oracles graphically describe Yahweh's anger against the enemies of Judah and Israel. Given his own experience of the Assyrians and their control of Judah during the majority of the eighth century, it is not surprising to find that nation among his targeted foes. Assyria's proud boast, "I am, and there is no one else" (2:15) cannot be left unchallenged (the counterpoint to this is God's assertion that "I, the LORD, am your God and there is no other" in Joel 2:27 and Isa. 45:5–6). While there is no denying that nation's former power, its pride will be turned to desolation, and its former

Oracles against the Nations

Major collections of the "oracles against nations" appear in Isa. 13–23; Jer. 46–51; Ezek. 25–32; and Amos 1–2. Their purpose is to warn other nations that they cannot act without impunity when dealing with Israel and Judah and to demonstrate that Yahweh uses them as an instrument of punishment. In their pride and extreme arrogance, they in turn will fall victim to the power of the Divine Warrior so that Yahweh can be glorified and the people of the covenant restored:

> The LORD of hosts has sworn:
> As I have designed,
>   so shall it be; . . .
> I will break the Assyrian in my land,
>   and on my mountains trample him under foot;
> his yoke shall be removed from them,
>   and his burden from their shoulders. (Isa. 14:24–25)

> Woe to you, O Moab!
>   The people of Chemosh have perished,
> for your sons have been taken captive,
>   and your daughters into captivity.
> Yet I will restore the fortunes of Moab
>   in the latter days, says the LORD. (Jer. 48:46–47)

I will lay open the flank of Moab from the towns on its frontier, the glory of the country. . . . I will give it along with Ammon to the people of the East as a possession. (Ezek. 25:9–10)

> Thus says the LORD:
> For three transgressions of Tyre,
>   and for four, I will not revoke the punishment;
> because they delivered entire communities over to Edom,
>   and did not remember the covenant of kinship.
> So I will send a fire on the wall of Tyre,
>   fire that shall devour its strongholds. (Amos 1:9–10)

victims will gladly use gestures of loathing designed to express their disdain: "Everyone who passes by it [Nineveh] hisses and shakes the fist" (Zeph. 2:15).

After his systematic condemnation of the foreign nations, Zephaniah once again turns his attention to Judah's shortcomings. He does this in the form of a **woe oracle** pronounced against Jerusalem and its corrupt judges, prophets, and priests (Zeph. 3:1–5). Like other prophets who cannot believe that God's actions against the nations have gone unnoticed by the people of Judah, Zephaniah can only sigh at their willingness "to make all their deeds corrupt" (3:7; compare Jer. 7:16–20; Hosea 9:7–9). In this instance, he may be addressing the past sins of Manasseh's collaborationist administration, or perhaps he is decrying the failure of the people to continue the Deuteronomic reform after Josiah's death in 609.

Even though this oracle envisions the destruction of Jerusalem, it is accompanied later in the chapter by a statement of grace for the righteous remnant. Following the inevitable destruction, God, who is described earlier as the source of true justice and as predictable as the coming of dawn (Zeph. 3:5), will transform the people's speech to "pure speech" (3:9; compare Isa. 6:5–7). In this new era the nation will consist of the humble and lowly, who "will pasture and lie down" as Yahweh's flock (Zeph. 3:12–13; compare Mic. 6:4–6).

The final segment of the book (Zeph. 3:14–20) contains a song of joy proclaiming salvation for the people and of the restoration of Jerusalem. This section is out of character with most of the message in the rest of the book. A comparison with Isa. 40:1–2 suggests that it contains postexilic themes (also Zech. 12:1–9) and is probably a late addition to the text designed to balance the prophet's harsh message:

> Sing aloud, O daughter Zion;
>   shout, O Israel!
> Rejoice and exult with all your heart,
>   O daughter Jerusalem!
> The LORD has taken away the judgments against you,
>   he has turned away your enemies. (Zeph. 3:14–15)

> Comfort, O comfort my people,
>   says your God.
> Speak tenderly to Jerusalem,
>   and cry to her
> that she has served her term,
>   that her penalty is paid,
> that she has received from the LORD's hand
>   double for all her sins. (Isa. 40:1–2)

The Book of Habakkuk

The book of Habakkuk consists of three distinct parts: a dialogue (1:2–2:5), a woe oracle (2:6–20), and a prayer (3:1–19). This well-defined structure suggests that these materials were edited and put in final form by the prophet in the decade or so after Josiah's death in 609. The dialogue and oracles in Hab. 1 can probably be dated to the reign of Jehoiakim (609–598) and, more specifically, to before 605, when the Chaldean armies of Nebuchadnezzar defeated the Egyptian-Assyrian coalition at the Battle of Carchemish. Habakkuk 2 reflects the prophet's familiarity with the Chaldean presence in Judah in the period after 605 and possibly as late as 598. Some concerns have been raised over the date and provenance of the psalm in Hab. 3 since it is not found in the Qumran scroll of Habakkuk. However, there is no reason to believe that it was not at least added to the text of Habakkuk even if it had previously been used as part of temple hymnody.

The first segment of this short book (1:2–2:5) is a complaint similar to that found in Jer. 12:1–4 and Pss. 13:1–2; 89:46–51. It begins with a plaintive cry of "how long?" and proceeds with a litany of the world's ills and the seeming victory of evil over good during the corrupt reign of Jehoiakim: "The wicked surround the righteous—therefore judgment comes forth perverted" (Hab. 1:4). The injustice of the situation is also the theme of the various complaints made by the Egyptian "Eloquent Peasant," who defines a world without justice as one in which "judges take sides in a dispute" and "magistrates are corrupt," while merchants are free to give "short measure" when distributing grain (*OTPar* 234). Instead of reassurance, however, God's response to the prophet's cry is that he is sending the Chaldeans and their war machine to ravage the land once again (1:6–11). At that point Habakkuk raises the poignant question whether the acts of the oppressor, personified here as a fisherman hooking and netting his victims, will be allowed to continue "without mercy" (1:15–17).

The Value and Wisdom of Patience

The plans of the diligent lead surely to abundance,
   but everyone who is hasty comes only to want. (Prov. 21:5)

The patience of the godly will not be frustrated. (Sir.16:13)

   My children, endure with patience the wrath that has come upon you
      from God.
   Your enemy has overtaken you,
      but you will soon see their destruction
      and will tread upon their necks. (Bar. 4:25)

   Thorns and snares are in the way of the perverse;
      the cautious will keep far from them. (Prov. 22:5)

Control your temper. . . . Do not let your tongue steer your life. ("Teachings of Amen-em-ope," *OTPar* 300)

Blessed is the man who thinks before he speaks. ("Teachings of Ankh-sheshonqy," *OTPar* 312)

   I wait quietly for the day of calamity
      to come upon the people who attack us. (Hab. 3:16)

God responds to Habakkuk's concerns with a command to write down the vision of things to come in letters large enough "that a runner may read it" (2:2). Since patience is still required for these things to come to pass, the prophet is instructed to "wait for it" and is reminded that the proud do not have a right spirit within them while "the righteous live by their faith" (2:4). In fact, the wealthy will be consumed by their own greed, with their open mouths a metaphor for the rapacity of death that will ultimately take them away (2:5).

The book places a high value on the person who can put hope in the eventual triumph of Yahweh and the people of Judah over their enemies: "If it seems to tarry, wait for it; it will surely come, it will not delay" (2:3). Because valuing patience over rash action is a theme found in many **wisdom** pieces from the ancient Near East, it is possible that Habakkuk was influenced by this wisdom tradition.

Habakkuk follows up God's call for patience with a series of five statements of reassurance and announcements of judgment against people and nations that temporarily prosper through illegal and violent means (2:6–20). These judgments are voiced in the form of a woe oracle. This distinctive **genre** of prophetic speech is intended to express deep emotional feelings of anger or grief. Other examples of the form are found in Isaiah's "woe to those who . . ." statements (Isa. 3:9; 5:8) and in Jeremiah's beseeching "woe to you, O Jerusalem!" (Jer. 13:27). Each of these cries of woe is followed by the threat of punishment to come. As a result, when Habakkuk points to the damage to be inflicted by the invading Babylonians, he intones, "Alas for you who heap up what is not your own! How long will you load yourselves with goods taken in pledge?" (Hab. 2:6). He also warns them of an eventual reversal when their oppressed creditors will "suddenly rise" and "you will be booty for them" (2:7). Similarly, Isaiah assures the wealthy landowners who have driven the small farmers off their land by joining "house to house" that they shall see these beautiful houses lying desolate "without inhabitant" (Isa. 5:8–9; compare Hab. 2:9–10).

Habakkuk completes his list of woe pronouncements with a condemnation of idolatry and the useless practices of priests who call on wood and stone images to "wake up!" and "rouse yourself!" (2:19). The background for this statement may be the Babylonian "opening the mouth" ritual, which was designed to transform a manufactured object into the physical embodiment of the god. But Habakkuk's words are similar to those of many other prophets who ridicule the very idea that an idol can be considered or treated like a god or in any way could be relied upon for help (Isa. 40:18–19; Hosea 4:12; 13:2).

The final section of the book, Hab. 3, is a hymn structured much like those found in the book of Psalms. It contains a superscription that includes the term *Shigionoth* (compare Ps. 7), which may indicate that this hymn is to be classified as a type of **lament**. This portion of Habakkuk is also the only place outside Psalms in which the rubric *Selah* is found (e.g., Pss. 46, 66, 140). The meaning of this technical term is unknown, but it may be an instruction associated with the poem's orchestration or performance by a choir. In addition, the poem's imagery suggests that it may have been used as a cadence in a priestly procession or dramatic ritual, since it depicts the marching forth of a **transcendent** creator to save the people: "In fury you trod the earth, in anger you trampled nations. . . . You trampled the sea with your horses, churning the mighty waters" (Hab. 3:12, 15).

Throughout, the poem employs natural phenomena to emphasize Yahweh's transcendent power as the Divine Warrior and the deity for whom all "glory covered the heavens" (3:3). Since the language of hymns and praise songs has a rich history in the ancient Near East, it is not surprising that Habakkuk seems to be drawing on figurative images commonly found in Ugaritic epic poetry. For example, Habakkuk describes God's divine rage manifested against the sea (3:8, 15; compare Baal's epic battle against the sea god Yamm in *OTPar* 270) and in the slaughter of enemy soldiers (3:13–14; compare the goddess Anat's "wading knee-deep in warriors' blood" in *OTPar* 265). As the Lord of creation, Yahweh is capable of stopping the moon in its course (3:11; compare Josh. 10:12–13), while the earth splits open as God treads upon the mountaintops (Hab. 3:6, 9) just as Anat's stamping foot causes "the earth to tremble" (*OTPar* 266). The idea of the mountains serving as a set of stepping-stones and trembling at the approach or tread of God is common in the Psalms and the prophetic literature:

> Then the earth reeled and rocked;
>   the foundations also of the mountains trembled
>   and quaked, because he was angry. (Ps. 18:7)

> For lo, the one who forms the mountains, creates the wind,
>   reveals his thoughts to mortals,
> makes the morning darkness,
>   and treads on the heights of the earth—
>   the LORD, the God of hosts, is his name! (Amos 4:13)

> For lo, the LORD is coming out of his place,
>   and will come down and tread upon the high places of the earth.
> Then the mountains will melt under him
>   and the valleys will burst open. (Mic. 1:3–4)

Despite the threat of violence contained in these manifestations of God's power, the prophet concludes his psalm with an exultant expression of trust in God's eventual gifts to a faithful people. Even though the basis of their economy (fig trees, vines, olive trees, fields of grain, and pasturing herds) are barren or stripped from their land, God remains the strength of the nation and a source for rejoicing (Hab. 3:17–18; compare Ps. 46:1–5). Evil may exist and hardship is the fate of the nation, but Habakkuk promises that faith in God's power does have its rewards. He confidently assures his audience that the Lord of creation, who is the one who treads upon the mountaintops in his majesty (Hab. 3:6), will lend his strength to the faithful so that they too can "tread upon the heights" (3:19).

The Book of Obadiah

Bearing another significant name, "Servant of the LORD," the author of the book of Obadiah, in just twenty-one verses, provides a glimpse of the rivalries that existed between the small states of Syria-Palestine and in particular between Judah and Edom. The book most likely dates to the period just after a repeated series of Babylonian invasions have ravaged Judah's countryside and destroyed Jerusalem in 587. Nothing specific is known about the author, but his rage against Edom at least suggests that he witnessed the perceived betrayal of Judah by a nation that had political and perhaps kinship ties going back to the origin of both nations (the story of the twins Jacob and Esau is found in Gen. 25–28, 32–33, 36). The book consists primarily of an oracle condemning Edom for having exploited Judah's weakness in the face of Babylonian incursions by raiding and pillaging its defenseless cities and towns (Obad. 10–14). During the political chaos of the times, Edom apparently had taken advantage of the opportunity to occupy a portion of southern Judah following the dismemberment of the Assyrian Empire in 605. Then with the Babylonian armies of Nebuchadnezzar besieging Jerusalem and cutting off all support from its allies, the Edomites either lent a hand to the Babylonians or refused to offer aid to Judah, "their brother" (Obad. 10–11).

Although there are occasional references to Edom as an ally of Israel (e.g., 2 Kings 3:9), generally the accounts of their relationship, from the reign of Jehoram (853–841) until Jerusalem's fall in 587, are filled with acts of violence and harsh dealings. For instance, the enmity between these two nations is demonstrated in Amos's geographically based oracle against the nations surrounding Israel. In the section on Edom (Amos 1:11–12), the prophet refers to blandishing swords, perpetual anger, and a lack of pity that has led God to rain down fire on Edom's major cities, Teman and Bozrah (compare Obad. 9).

In the middle of this harangue against Edom, we see the duplication of Jer. 49:7–22 and Obad. 1–7, particularly the sentiments found in Jer. 49:9 and Obad. 5: "If grape-gatherers came to you, would they not leave gleanings?" It is unclear whether one prophet or the editor of their work is quoting the other, or whether both are working from a common prophetic source. The repetition of phrases serves to indicate just how deeply these sentiments were felt—both the anger over Edom's pillaging of Judah and the relish with which the people of Judah witness Edom's subsequent and thorough looting by its former allies.

These traditions of national rivalry may be based on incidents throughout the monarchy (1 Sam. 14:47; 2 Sam. 8:12–14; 1 Kings 11:15–16) as well as events in Amos's own time when King Uzziah took and rebuilt the Edomite port of Elath on the Gulf of Aqaba (2 Kings 14:22; 2 Chron. 26:2). Perhaps a natural rivalry between these two neighboring countries contributed to long-standing tensions and animosities. Whatever its origins, the theme of Edom's betrayal of Judah is consistent with other anti-Edomite literature from this period (Isa. 63:1–6; Ezek. 25:12–14; Joel 3:19; Mal. 1:2–3). The theme also may be related to the legendary struggle between Jacob and Esau in Gen. 27:41–45 (Obad. 6 also interchanges Esau and Edom).

Possibly the most rabid of the exilic-period, anti-Edomite statements is the lament found in Ps. 137:7, which calls God to remember the crimes of the Edomites: "Remember, O LORD, against the Edomites the day of Jerusalem's fall, how they said, 'Tear it down! Tear it down! Down to its foundations!'" This exilic psalmist builds up to his devastating conclusion by first expressing a complaint over the dislocation of the people of Jerusalem, who have been taken into captivity by the Babylonians and who have mocked them, saying that their God had forgotten them. Instead of giving into depression, the faithful psalmist assures God that the people will never allow the vision of Jerusalem to dim, nor will they give up their desire to return to the land of the covenant. With this statement of faith in place, the poet then calls on God to take revenge on their enemies. A similar pattern of complaint-assurance-petition is found in the oracle against Edom in Obadiah. However, this lament is structured in a slightly different order: petition-assurance-complaint-assurance:

> petition: "A messenger has been sent among the nations: 'Rise up! Let us rise against it for battle.'" (Obad. 1)
>
> assurance: "On that day, says the LORD, I will destroy the wise out of Edom, and understanding out of Mount Esau." (Obad. 8)
>
> complaint: "On the day you stood aside. . . . You should not have gloated over your brother. . . . You should not have boasted on the day of distress." (Obad. 10–12)
>
> assurance: "As you have done, it shall be done to you; your deeds shall return on your own head." (Obad. 15)

Rhetoric such as this is designed to express the range of human emotions that are to be expected over betrayal and destruction. They form a litany of responses similar to those in the Psalms that acknowledge what has happened, but conclude that God will provide aid and restitution (Pss. 2:1–6; 65:1–8). Instead the faithful should look forward with hope for a "day" when Yahweh brings judgment on their enemies. The voicing of the lament form serves as a means of purging the sufferer of any bitterness while providing the assurance that evil cannot prevail when God takes a hand.

The Golden Rule

Do to others as you would have them do to you. (Luke 6:31; Matt. 7:12)

Follow this teaching: "Do unto others, as you would have others do unto you." ("A Farmer and the Courts in Egypt," *OTPar* 235)

Do not do evil to someone and thus encourage another to do evil to you. ("Teachings of Ankhsheshonqy," *OTPar* 313)

Evidence of this anti-Edomite tone persists into the Second Temple period. A relatively late account of Zerubbabel's effort to rebuild the temple accuses the Edomites of having destroyed it when the Babylonians captured the city (1 Esd. 4:45). This story contradicts 2 Kings 25:8–12, which blames only the Babylonians for the temple's destruction. Similarly, Judith 7:8–18 depicts Edomites and Moabites joining forces with the "Assyrian" army of Holofernes to attack Bethulia in Judah. It is likely that the distrust of Edom coincides with the growing hatred of the Herods in the century before the Common Era, who were ethnically Idumeans/Edomites (Josephus, *Jewish Antiquities* 14.403).

Obadiah bases his call for revenge against Edom and the total destruction of Judah's enemies on the law of reciprocity. All nations are called to participate (Obad. 1), not just Judah. They must observe the internationally sanctioned maxim that a people not at war should not do violence to their neighbors or gloat over their misery (Obad. 12). This is especially the case for those already in distress because of a catastrophe due to natural or human causes. Thus he confidently states, "As you have done, it shall be done to you" (Obad. 15). The law of reciprocity is a corollary to the Golden Rule found in the New Testament and in the Egyptian wisdom tale "A Farmer and the Courts in Egypt."

In retaliation for drinking a cup of celebration on God's "holy hill," Edom will in turn be forced to drink Yahweh's "cup of wrath" (Obad. 16; see Ps. 75:8; Isa. 51:17). With the Divine Warrior's assistance (using other nations as his tools; 10:5), there will be a general restoration of Judah's land, from Zarephath of Phoenicia in the north to the "towns of the Negeb" in the south (Obad. 20). The oracle of restoration contains the familiar image of Yahweh triumphant on Mount Zion while Mount Esau is humbled (Isa. 30:19–26; 31:4–9; Zeph. 3:14–20). In this case the day of the Lord is indeed a day of hope (compare the negative allusions in Amos 5:18 and Zeph. 1:14–15). It will bring forth justice on the plunderers and the occupation of Edomite, Phoenician, and Philistine territories by the people of Judah (Obad. 19–20). This reversal of political fortunes is matched by the restoration of Yahweh's name as the Lord of all nations: "Those who have been saved shall go up to Mount Zion to rule Mount Esau; and the kingdom shall be the LORD's" (Obad. 21; compare Ps. 22:28).

12

The Book of Jeremiah

The content of the book of Jeremiah spans the tumultuous period from about 622 until shortly after 587. Jeremiah's emergence as a major prophetic figure and his message coincide with the years following Josiah's reforms (ca. 622–609), the rather chaotic period immediately following his death in 609, and the subjugation of Judah by first Egypt (609–605, 601–598) and then Babylon (604–601, 597–538). The book thus reflects the wildly shifting fortunes of the nation, from its brief nationalistic exuberance under Josiah to a desperate search for security and leadership amid Egypt's and Babylon's international contest for control of Syria-Palestine.

Since Jeremiah doesn't emerge as a prophetic figure until after Josiah's death, he may have initially been a supporter of the king's reform efforts. If Jeremiah had been available and had established a firm reputation, it seems that it would have been more appropriate to consult him rather than Huldah when Josiah asked for authentication of the "book of the law" (2 Kings 22:14–20). However, it is possible that he was not considered because of his extreme youth at the time and his association with Anathoth, the site of a community of exiled priests from the line of Abiathar (1 Kings 2:26–27). In addition, since Huldah's husband was a ranking member of the temple priesthood in Jerusalem, she may have been consulted in the context of her role as an established court prophet and one they had had dealings with in the past. Whatever the reason, the death of Josiah at the Battle of Megiddo in 609 spelled the end of his expansionist plans to reunite the territory of Israel and Judah. It also reduced the energies necessary to continue to implement most of his reforms.

Judah's hopes for political autonomy were dashed, and a new era of superpower clashes drew Judah even more tightly into submission. When the Assyrians were defeated at the Battle of Carchemish in 605, Egypt claimed Palestine as part of its political domain. That shift in fortunes meant that Pharaoh Necho II had become Judah's new master, and he quickly placed a puppet king on the throne in Jerusalem. Josiah's oldest son and immediate successor, Jehoahaz, was taken hostage back to Egypt, and his pro-Egyptian brother Eliakim was put on the throne. His status as a servant of the Egyptians was made quite obvious when his name was changed to Jehoiakim by the pharaoh (2 Kings 23:34).

Having consolidated his control of the former territories of the Assyrian Empire in Mesopotamia and Syria, in 604 King Nebuchadnezzar of Babylonia wrested control of Palestine from the Egyptians. Suddenly, Jehoiakim found himself a Babylonian vassal (2 Kings 24:1). That did not mean, however, that he was truly loyal to his new master, and based on Egyptian promises of aid, Jehoiakim revolted three years later. Temporarily he enjoyed Egyptian protection, but this ended in 598 when Nebuchadnezzar once again invaded Judah and captured Jerusalem. That defeat marked the first time Jerusalem had fallen to a siege since David's time. It must have been a severe blow to those who had believed in the **myth** of the inviolability of the city (Isa. 31:4–5).

During this period, the prophet Jeremiah, from the village of Anathoth, condemned Jehoiakim's policies (Jer. 11:1–13; 22:11–19), derided the people's continued idolatry (10:1–5; 18:12–17), and denounced the reliance of the people of Jerusalem on the temple of **Yahweh** to save them from any threat (7:12–15). In examining the connection between Jeremiah's message and his social setting, one place to start may be his hometown. His fierce attacks on the monarchy and the temple may be fueled by the likelihood that he is a descendant of the Levitical group that had been exiled there in Solomon's time as punishment for Abiathar's support of Adonijah, Solomon's brother and rival for the throne (1 Kings 2:26–27). With the appointment of Zadok as high priest, Abiathar's group was forever frozen out of that prestigious office.

It is thus possible that Jeremiah's words condemning the prophets and priests, who "deal falsely" with the people (Jer. 6:13–15; 8:10–12) and ply their trade with "no knowledge" of what they should be doing (14:18; compare Hosea 4:6), may be an attempt to gain a measure of revenge while pointing out legitimate concerns about their leadership. Jeremiah's condemnation of the lavish offerings of expensive incense on the altar demonstrates a link to the words of earlier prophets who also denounced elaborate, but basically empty cultic ceremonies (Jer. 6:20; compare Amos 5:21–24). The prophet seems to be shaking his head at leaders who ignore or reject God's warnings to reform their worship practices (Jer. 6:16–17; compare Isa. 5:24; Zech. 1:4).

After Nebuchadnezzar's successful siege of Jerusalem in 598, Jehoiachin son of Jehoiakim, who had reigned as king for only a few months, was deported to

Babylon. There he joined a group of hostages that included many of Judah's high-ranking leaders and priests (2 Kings 24:10–17). The Babylonian king then installed the last of Josiah's sons, Mattaniah, as his puppet king and changed his name to Zedekiah to signify his new status (24:17).

The many shifts in literary style and perspective throughout the book of Jeremiah suggest that prior to its final redaction by the biblical editors its composition may have been the combined effort of the prophet Jeremiah and his friend and scribe Baruch. The first-person portions probably contain much of the prophet's own words; these powerful sections of the book demonstrate the prophet's deep emotions of anger, frustration, and great personal loss (8:18–22; 12:1–4; 20:7–12). In some respects, we can understand Jeremiah's personal traumas as a mirror of Judah's disintegration as a nation. The third-person accounts are less passionate and allow the reader to step away from the emotional intensity of the other parts of the book (21:1–10; 26:1–24; 28:1–17). These sections reflect on the reasons for Judah's destruction and offer a **theodicy**—that Judah is being punished for its many transgressions of the **covenant** by a righteous God, using the Babylonians as his instrument. Once the nation's period of purification is complete, the righteous **remnant** may then expect an eventual restoration to their land and fortunes (Jer. 31–32).

The way in which the book is structured makes it difficult to follow because the materials do not follow a set chronological order. For instance, Jeremiah's temple sermon is found in both Jer. 7 and Jer. 26, while the episode that immediately succeeds it, Baruch's mission to the temple, does not appear until Jer. 36. The seemingly random placement of events throughout the book may simply reflect the decisions made by the editors to highlight themes instead of a linear sequence in Jeremiah's narrative. Whatever the reason for the book's current structure, it does require the reader to step back and forth through the text in order to maintain a clear sense of the time line.

Jeremiah's Call

Scholars are still debating the actual date of Jeremiah's call as a prophet. His statement that he is "only a boy" (1:7) suggests that at the time he is a young adult, perhaps sixteen to eighteen years old. It is likely that he received his call sometime during the reign of Josiah (640–609) and that he therefore experienced and was influenced by that king's Deuteronomic reform (622–609). The question of his youth and lack of recognition as a prophet may also help explain why Josiah consulted the female prophet Huldah instead of Jeremiah when the book of the law (generally considered to be Deut. 12–26) was "found" during the renovation of the temple (2 Kings 22:14–20).

The account in Jer. 1 contains all the characteristic elements of **call narratives**, especially those of Moses (Exod. 3:2–4:23) and Gideon (Judg. 6:11–24).

Although there are slight differences between the accounts of Jeremiah's commissioning and those of these two earlier figures, they can be explained by the unique social setting of each individual. What seem most striking are the obvious parallels between Jeremiah's call and those of political leaders. Given the power vacuum that existed in his time period, these statements serve to enhance the prophet's authority and legitimize his role. Jeremiah's call story includes

a **theophanic** appearance,

a statement by the deity of intention and relationship,

an objection by the candidate and a negative label applied by the candidate to himself,

a transforming action,

an injunction and legal empowerment, and

a sign given by the deity to reassure and strengthen the chosen one.

Like several other prophets, Jeremiah is empowered to speak when God touches his lips (compare Moses in Deut. 18:18 and Isaiah in Isa. 6:6–7). Also interesting is God's commission that designates Jeremiah as a prophet "to the nations" (Jer. 1:5). The language used here resembles legal formulas found in royal coronation formulas (Pss. 2:7–9; 89:19–37). Since the term "prophet" carries with it the power-by-extension of the god for whom he speaks and acts, Jeremiah is able to wield power usually reserved only for kings or gods (Jer. 18:7; 31:28). For example, the powers with which Jeremiah is invested include "to pluck up and to pull down, to destroy and to overthrow, to build and to plant" (1:10). These elements of authority are quite similar to those granted to the Babylonian god Marduk in the *Enuma Elish* creation story. As part of their oath to accept Marduk's leadership, the other gods declare that "your word shall build up and tear down" (*OTPar* 15). Such a close parallel indicates either a familiarity with the Babylonian story by the biblical writer or a standardization of enthronement language among the cultures of the ancient Near East.

Jeremiah's transformation is completed when he receives a sign that confirms and reassures him in his mission. In Jeremiah's case, this involves a pair of visions of an almond branch and a boiling pot (1:11–13) and their interpretations (1:14–16) reassuring him of divine protection. Finally, Yahweh symbolically labels Jeremiah with the titles "a fortified city, an iron pillar, and a bronze wall" to denote his invincibility as God's spokesperson (1:18).

The Threat from the North

Jeremiah's ministry likely began around 622 and continued until the destruction of Jerusalem in 587. It is difficult, however, to identify with certainty the earliest oracles. Some argue that Jeremiah's vision of the boiling pot (1:13–15) alludes to the incursions of Scythian barbarians who overran this area but did not remain for long. Such a short-lived threat would have discredited Jeremiah, at least temporarily. Many other references suggest that the Babylonians and not the Scythians were perceived as this northern foe (4:6; 6:1, 22; 10:22; 50:3, 9, 41). While it is conceivable that some other group like the Scythians was originally meant in these passages, the references to an enemy from the north were reinterpreted and made to refer explicitly to Babylon and to the Chaldean leader Nebuchadnezzar after the Battle of Carchemish in 605.

Image of Judgment

The call to judgment for the people of Judah is found in an image of foreign kings placing their thrones at the gates of Jerusalem (1:15). This practice may refer to the manner in which commanders placed their thrones on high ground facing the city gates in order to direct an attack. The gate area, however, was also the traditional place of justice, decision making, and the granting of favors by kings and elders (38:7–10; Zech. 8:16). Thus David sat in the gate following the defeat of his son Absalom, reviewing his troops and thanking them for their service (2 Sam. 19:8). The heads of Ahab's sons were placed in two heaps on either side of the gate of Samaria as a judgment on his dynasty (2 Kings 10:8). And when they wanted to pass judgment on the veracity of Micaiah's prophecies, Ahab and Jehoshaphat placed their thrones in the gateway of the city of Samaria (1 Kings 22:10).

In Jer. 1:15 these foreign kings have been called to sit in judgment on Judah's sins, just as previously the kings of Assyria had been sent by God to plunder and destroy Israel (Isa. 10:5–6). Yahweh serves as a prosecuting attorney or witness (compare Mic. 1:2), making a case against the people in much the same way that parents were required to come to the city gate to testify against prodigal children (Deut. 21:18–21). The indictment contains the traditional charges made against the people by the prophets and psalmists: **apostasy**, idolatry, and unfaithfulness to the covenant (Jer. 1:16; Ps. 89:32–37; Hosea 4:12–13; Zeph. 1:4–6).

The Temple Sermon

Despite having been called as a prophet over a decade earlier, the first major event in Jeremiah's career is his temple sermon staged near the beginning of the reign of Jehoiakim (Jer. 26:1). The sermon reflects Yahweh's concern over foreign influences brought on by Egyptian control of Judah (starting in 609). While the prophet is aware of the political realities of that time, Jeremiah focuses on the covenant and proper worship practices. Accounts of this event are found in both Jer. 7 and Jer. 26. Jeremiah 7, written in the first person, contains a fuller version of the prophet's sermon. Jeremiah 26, on the other hand, is written in the third person and concentrates on the public reaction to Jeremiah's words and his trial, while providing only an abbreviated version of the sermon.

The setting where a prophetic speech is delivered is always important. At Yahweh's command, Jeremiah stages his confrontation with the Jerusalem leaders at the temple's entrance, which is the physical conduit between secular and sacred space. Since he comes here on a major feast day, his audience will include not only the people of Jerusalem but also persons and officials from all over the kingdom. Standing at this particular place, Jeremiah draws on the authority attached to the temple as the center of Judah's worship. Of course his presence also blocks the free movement of worshipers into its holy precincts. While that assures him of an attentive crowd, it also provides a reason for heightened emotions. For comparison, see Jeremiah's defense of **sabbath** regulations while standing in the "People's Gate" (17:19–27).

In his sermon, Jeremiah insists on two critical points. First, he discounts the mistaken belief that the physical presence of God's temple ensures that Jerusalem can never be destroyed. His purpose is to explode the myth of inviolability that had been part of the nation's mentality since the time of Hezekiah when the Assyrians had failed to capture Jerusalem in 701. Its apparent pervasiveness had been strengthened by the reforms instituted by Josiah. His centralization of sacrificial and festival practices in Jerusalem as the place that God had chosen "as a dwelling for his name" had magnified the temple's importance (Deut. 14:23; 16:2; 26:2). Second, Jeremiah insists that only strict obedience to the covenant and to the stipulations of the Ten Commandments will prevent Yahweh's ultimate destruction of Judah and Jerusalem (compare Jer. 11:3–5; 17:24–27).

The theological **framework** for this message consists of alternating slogans: Jeremiah's warning to "amend your ways and your doings" (7:3, 5) and the popular chant "the temple of the LORD" (7:4). The latter was apparently both a ritual utterance and a slogan reassuring the people of Yahweh's protection. As a ritual formula, it may have been used when people entered the temple and passed from the secular to the sacred world. Now, as the people push forward toward the entrance, Jeremiah mocks their ritually intoned slogan and declares that no chant will cast a protective spell over them if they are not in compliance with the covenant. This can be "the temple of the LORD" only if they are the people of the covenant.

Jeremiah uses the now defunct shrine at Shiloh, about twenty miles north of Jerusalem, as his prime example. Although Shiloh had once served as the seat of Yahweh worship prior to the monarchy (1 Sam. 1–4), the site had been destroyed by the Philistines because of the unfaithfulness of Eli's sons (2:12–17). No amount of ritual or sacrificial offerings could save them or that place (3:11–14) because, without due respect for Yahweh's covenant, it constituted hollow worship. Like Micah (6:6–8) in the previous century, Jeremiah decries such rote ritual behavior. It is incapable of attracting God's attention because empty worship practices are not accompanied by the desire to obey Yahweh's covenant (Jer. 7:23). This declaration, that sacrifice is worthless without the love (*hesed*) of Yahweh and the covenant, is a familiar prophetic theme. It is also found in Samuel's confrontation with Saul (1 Sam. 15:22–23) and in Hosea (6:6): "For I desire steadfast love [*hesed*] and not sacrifice, the knowledge of God rather than burnt offerings."

As a result the people of Jerusalem cannot expect the physical presence of the temple to save them, no matter how many previous occasions God has chosen to spare the city (Isa. 37:5–38). They cannot freely violate every law and then blithely call on Yahweh's name, expecting divine forgiveness and protection. Jeremiah assures them Yahweh is not blind to their rebellious actions (Jer. 7:11), and therefore God will abandon them just as the people of the northern kingdom were left to their fate (7:15).

Such a blatant attack on the foundations of their beliefs and upon the monumental icon that they had come to consider their safety net could not go unchallenged. Baruch's version of this dramatic scene describes an immediate, angry outcry against Jeremiah. A public trial is organized on the spot, with the religious establishment (priests and prophets) serving as his accusers and prosecutors; the king's advisers, who are justifiably concerned about civil unrest in the city, serving as judges; while "all the people" (a collective phrase meaning the citizens present at the time) serving as an ad hoc jury (26:7–11).

Once charges of blasphemy and false prophecy have been leveled against Jeremiah, he stands up to speak in his own defense. Jeremiah freely admits that he has "prophes[ied] against this house [the temple] and this city" (26:12–13). He insists as a true prophet should, however, that these are Yahweh's words, not his alone. If, in their unthinking rage, they choose to kill him, they will be shedding "innocent blood," one of the worst crimes an Israelite can commit (Exod. 23:7; Deut. 19:10). He also invokes the principle of **prophetic immunity**, a tradition that applies to royal messengers who may not be blamed for the message that they bring from their master (Jer. 26:16).

Apparently persuaded by Jeremiah's argument, the officials and the people decide to release Jeremiah. Their decision is further bolstered when yet another group of local officials, the elders of the land, stand up to speak. They are regional officials and are probably in Jerusalem for the feast day. As you might expect, the example they use is words of the rural-based prophet Micah. From his perspective as a local farmer during the Assyrian invasions, he had also spoken out against Jerusalem during Hezekiah's time (715–687). Despite exclaiming that "Zion shall be plowed as a field; Jerusalem shall become a heap of ruins," he had not been punished for his message (Mic. 3:12). Unfortunately for Jeremiah's argument, the elders also express the hope that the Lord will "change his mind about the disaster" as he did in Hezekiah's time (Jer. 26:19). Clearly, no one in the crowd had actually listened to Jeremiah's warning or the conditions that he had set forth for God to be willing to relent. Although Jeremiah is vindicated to a certain extent by this verdict, he is quickly removed from the scene by one of the king's officials, Ahikam son of Shaphan, in order to prevent any further disturbance or a resumption of violence. However, the prophet will not be silenced for long.

Baruch's Mission to the Temple

Jeremiah's temple sermon created enough of an uproar that the prophet was forced at least temporarily into hiding. As a result, during the fourth year of Jehoiakim's reign (605), he uses Baruch to deliver once again a scathing denunciation of Jerusalem and its leaders (Jer. 36). In one of the few biblical examples in which a prophetic speech is instructed to be written down (e.g., Isa. 8:16; Hab. 2:2), Jeremiah dictates to Baruch a scroll containing Yahweh's message (Jer. 36:4), and the scribe then carries the scroll to the temple on a fast day. The story of Baruch's mission contains a spatial strategy designed to link together four separate and distinct locations as part of a chain of events and a series of staged dialogues. Each link—from the confines of Jeremiah's apartment, to the temple, to the private chamber of the king's officials, to a royal audience chamber, and back to Jeremiah's room—magnifies the importance of the scroll and God's warning.

The social frame for these events takes place in the period of political uncertainty during the early years of Jehoiakim's reign over Judah (609–604). Although the composition of this particular episode may have a complex history, based on the ideological agendas of the compilers of the book of Jeremiah, it functions within a set of well-known historical events and contains sufficient information on the temple and palace complex to evidence a basic familiarity with these precincts.

Jeremiah begins to forge the links of this spatial framework when he brings Baruch to his hidden rooms and dictates God's message containing "all the words that I have spoken to you against Israel and Judah and all the nations, from the day I spoke to you, from the days of Josiah until today" (36:2). From that point each link is connected as Baruch transports the scroll to various locations or it is taken by the king's advisers to significant places to be read.

The message of the prophet includes an indictment of Jehoiakim for playing a very dangerous diplomatic game. The king of Judah initially had been placed on his throne by a foreign monarch (Necho II of Egypt), but the political fortunes of the region had changed, and now he has been or is about to be forced to acknowledge the suzerainty of yet another king (Nebuchadnezzar of Babylon). Jeremiah declares that Jehoiakim's political vacillations (sometimes

Spatial Settings for Baruch's Mission

1. Baruch reads the scroll inside the temple, "in the chamber of Gemariah . . . , which was in the upper court, at the entry of the New Gate" (Jer. 36:10).
2. Baruch is ordered to come to a room in the "king's house" within "the secretary's chamber" to read the scroll before the king's advisers (36:12).
3. The scroll is read by a high-ranking adviser to the king and his officials "in his winter apartment" in an area of the palace restricted to a very select group (36:21–22).

supporting Egyptian efforts and sometimes declaring loyalty to Babylon) will result in Babylon's destruction of the land (36:29).

Micaiah, the grandson of Shaphan, is the first royal official to hear Baruch's recitation in the chamber of Gemariah, a place open only to officials and scribes such as Baruch (36:11). He discusses it with other royal officials, who become alarmed (36:16). They order Baruch to retell parts of the story for them before deciding to "report all these words to the king" (36:12–18). They also apprehensively ask him, "Tell us now, how did you write all these words? Was it at his dictation?" (36:17). These questions are part of their official inquiry into the matter, since these royal representatives would need to certify that (1) Baruch took the prophet's dictation and thus was not the author of the scroll and (2) that Jeremiah was the prophet who uttered this oracle. Clearly, Jeremiah's career and his prophetic standing may have been in question, considering Jehoiakim's brazen response. After due deliberation, they report the substance of his story to the king (36:20). Jehoiakim orders one of his advisers, Jehudi, to reread and perhaps reinterpret the message for him in a formal court setting (36:21).

The significance of this final scene is that it is set in a public audience hall that presumably contained the king's advisers and may well have included Neo-Babylonian messengers or diplomats, so Jehoiakim must show that he is still in authority. He haughtily denies Jeremiah's indictment and employs a grand gesture of denial. He uses a nearby charcoal brazier as a prop to replace the significance of the scroll and burns each segment as it is unrolled and read. By doing this he publicly rejects its contents and Jeremiah's authority to speak the word of the Lord (36:22–23).

Without speaking himself, Jehoiakim's political pantomime is as scandalous to the people of Judah who have remained loyal to their covenant with Yahweh as it may have been convincing to the Babylonian representatives present in Jehoiakim's throne room. But since the king does not want to provide the Babylonians with any evidence of his disloyalty to Nebuchadnezzar, no one in the court of Jehoiakim dares to show any emotions. They maintain a calm public face and do not appear to be "alarmed, nor did they tear their garments" as a sign of mourning (36:24). Given the precarious political situation, Jehoiakim must have felt it was essential that Judah remain officially faithful to its treaty obligations with Nebuchadnezzar, even if it meant that the nation must abrogate its covenant with Yahweh.

The drama and the linkage between these various settings are completed when Jeremiah dictates the message once again in his hiding place. Added this time, however, is a death sentence for Jehoiakim (36:32). Drawing on the account in 2 Kings 24:1–7 and further warnings in Jer. 25:1–14, it is clear that Jehoiakim continued to make private political overtures to Egypt. His actions may have been based on concerns over Jeremiah's indictment and the cautious advice given to him by his royal officials. In any case Jehoiakim made the decision to declare Judah's independence from Babylon in 600. Soon, however, the Neo-Babylonians bring their forces to the gates of Jerusalem, and Jehoiakim meets his end as the monarch during the siege.

Enacted Prophecies

Based on its common use by the prophets, clearly animated storytelling is a developed art in the biblical period. In delivering his message to the people of Jerusalem, Jeremiah makes effective use of physical acts, symbolic gestures, and street theater. Jeremiah 16–19 contains several **enacted prophecies** that allow the prophet to demonstrate his theatrical skills, while drawing on recognizable aspects of Judah's social customs and traditions. Each prophetic performance portrays an increasing sense of urgency on the part of the prophet as well as a graphic enactment of the events to come. From their emic or insider's understanding of the prophet's actions, physical props, and symbolic gestures, the original audience would have had a better grasp of Jeremiah's message than do modern readers. These enacted prophecies are designed to convey a message without the need for a long explanation and to capture the imagination of a people steeped in the material the prophet draws upon. Certainly, these prophecies were designed to shock the audience and to convince them of the urgency and the commonsense reaction to their dire situation.

One common feature of enacted prophecies is to have the prophet engage in actions that are uncharacteristic of his social station or age. That is the basis for the severe restrictions placed on Jeremiah's personal life and his normal emotional reactions in Jer. 16. He is forbidden to engage in the normal pursuits of life for a man of his age; he is not allowed to marry or raise a family (16:2–4). The symbolism of this enforced celibacy relates to the fast-approaching doom of the city and its people. Celebrations at this time would be inappropriate, and it would be cruel to bring children into a world in which they could experience only destruction and pain. Furthermore, Jeremiah's marital restrictions stand as a stark reversal of the covenant promise of fertility and God's injunction to Adam and Eve, Noah, and Abraham to "be fruitful and multiply" (Gen. 1:28; 9:1; 17:6).

Moving to another stage of his life, Jeremiah is denied the right and the normal obligation of a son to participate in any mourning rituals, even for his parents (Jer. 16:5–9; compare Ezek. 24:15–18). He may not gash himself or shave his head (Job 1:20; Jer. 41:5), nor may he attend funeral rites in which the dead are memorialized and the living comforted. Actions commemorating an individual death can only serve as a mockery of the approaching death of the whole nation. There will be so many dead that their bodies necessarily will lie unburied and unmourned by the few survivors of the siege (19:7–9; 33:5).

Jeremiah's horrific vision contains elements of a familiar **lament** form also found in the portrayal of a bereaved Zion with her hands outstretched in supplication and "no one to comfort her" (Lam. 1:17). The pain and suffering caused by siege warfare elicits the shattered cry of the victim who is so debilitated by weeping that her "eyes are spent" and they can no longer form tears (2:11). There are also direct parallels to the much older Sumerian lament form found in the twenty-first-century "Laments for Ur":

> Where crowds once celebrated festivals, bodies lay in every street,
> . . . corpses piled on every road.
> In the squares where people danced,
> heaps of corpses lay. ("Laments for Ur," OTPar 253)

Another type of enacted warning occurs in Jer. 18, where Jeremiah is instructed to go to the potters' district of Jerusalem and watch a potter attempt to shape a clay vessel on his wheel. However, what the prophet witnesses is the extreme frustration of the potter, who becomes dissatisfied with his creation and finally stops his work on it. He reforms the clay into a ball and with new determination begins once again to shape it (18:3–4). This scene would have been very familiar to the people of Jeremiah's day. Not only could they easily picture the potter at his wheel but they also could have easily made the connection that the clay symbolizes the nation of Judah and that Yahweh is the divine potter.

The idea that a god functioned as a creative craftsman is found in both stories and art from the ancient Near East. For instance, in the Atrahasis creation story from Mesopotamia, Nintu-Mami mixes blood and clay to form humans as servants for the gods (OTPar 35). Similarly, Egyptian tomb paintings depict Queen Hatshepsut being shaped on a potter's wheel by the ram-headed god Khnum (OTPar 61). Thus in Jeremiah's story, the pot taking shape on the wheel represents the creation of the nation by God the covenant maker (compare Isa. 29:16; 64:8). Because the people, like this poorly formed pot, have not conformed themselves to the desires of the divine potter, Yahweh has the prerogative to remold the clay and begin again. God chooses, however, to use the essence of the pot (the righteous remnant) to shape a new vessel/nation.

This enacted prophecy functions as an excellent example of the remnant theme. Although the prophet must warn the people of their inevitable punishment because of their failure to obey the stipulations of the covenant, total destruction will not occur. Just as the clay was reformed to create a new pot, so too will a remnant of the people be spared in order to restore the nation. Similarly, once Yahweh has punished the unfaithful "shepherds . . . who have scattered my flock," he will "gather the remnant" and "bring them back to their fold," and they will be provided with faithful shepherds who will truly shepherd them in obedience to God (Jer. 23:1–4).

The remnant theme also occurs in 6:9, where the prophet employs the image of a vineyard that has already been harvested, just as Judah has already been devastated by the Babylonian armies. Instead of a scene in which widows and the poor glean the remains of the fruit from the vines, it is an angry God who "gleans" the remnant of the people. What makes this image so effective is its express relationship to the law in Deut. 24:19–22 and its obvious reference to an everyday activity familiar to everyone in his audience.

As part of their covenant agreement with Yahweh, the Israelites were required to leave a portion of the harvest for "the alien, the orphan, and the widow." These protected classes representing the weakest members of their society serve as a metaphor for Israel itself. God provided for the nation, one of the weakest in the ancient Near East, and the nation in turn was expected to care for and provide justice to the poor and weak within its own community (Jer. 21:11–14; a similar social-justice theme occurs in Isa. 1:17 and Ezek. 22:6–12). Despite the socially transparent character of Jeremiah's message, its meaning apparently fell on deaf ears, and this then becomes the basis for God's wrath (Jer. 6:10). The act of gleaning becomes an expression of God's determination to gather all the people into the "basket" of the exile, just as a hungry widow reaches to break off a bunch of grapes. Those gathered in this final pass through the city become the remnant from which God may restore the nation (compare Ezekiel's image of the marking of the righteous remnant in Ezek. 9).

Jeremiah's use of enacted prophecies continues in Jer. 19 with a procession culminating in an **execration ritual**. His public denunciation of Jerusalem, similar to the curses found on Egyptian incantation bowls denouncing their enemies, provides an opportunity for the prophet to challenge the temple establishment and make the point that Yahweh has chosen to condemn the temple and the city. First, he makes a show of purchasing a pottery vessel and then marches in an informal procession to the Potsherd Gate, picking up witnesses and supporters along the way. At this strategic point, using the well-known symbolism attached to the gate area and its ties to justice and law (Deut. 22:15), he lists a bill of particulars of the people's sins: idolatry, the shedding of innocent blood, and sacrifice of children. Jeremiah then describes the imminent and utter devastation of the city and its population. The destruction will be so thorough that "everyone who passes by it will be horrified and will hiss because of all its disasters" (Jer. 19:8; compare Zeph. 2:15).

Then, in order to enact the curse, Jeremiah dramatically smashes the pot within the gate and declares that Yahweh will "break this people and this city, as one breaks a potter's vessel, so that it can never be mended" (Jer. 19:11). The pronouncement of the curse is horrifying enough, but to smash the pot before an astonished crowd within the gate area, a symbolically significant place that is culturally associated with legal judgments (Deut. 21:19; 22:15; Ruth 4:1), makes his gesture a living reality for all of the witnesses present. For them and for later audiences who hear these words, the stunning combination of physical gesture and significant place is decisively effective.

Such an overt challenge to the leaders of Jerusalem cannot be left unanswered by those in authority. Pashhur, one of the chief officials of the temple, has Jeremiah arrested and placed in public stocks (Jer. 20:2). What is at work here is the priest's desire to match Jeremiah's public act and to silence him by humiliating the prophet. The comic posture of someone helplessly displayed in the confines of the stocks is an easy way to ridicule that person before all passersby. It also can be a dangerous form of punishment since the prisoner is forced to submit to all sorts of abuse, including thrown debris. Pashhur's aim is to destroy Jeremiah's credibility. If that goal is accomplished, then Jeremiah's pride, along with his most recent and all future prophecies, will be damaged beyond repair.

Being put in such a humiliating position must have angered Jeremiah. Once he is released he demonstrates that anger by calling on Yahweh to take revenge on his enemies (20:12) in much the same manner as his cursing of his own neighbors from Anathoth when they plotted against him (11:18–12:6). Like so many others who feel they have been treated unjustly, he questions why the wicked are allowed to prosper and mislead the people (compare Hab. 1:2–4). Jeremiah also ponders the very purpose of his existence in much the same way as long-suffering Job (3:3; also Ps. 39:4–6) by cursing his own birth (Jer. 20:14). In the process, he calls into question the importance and relevance of the task that has brought him to this sorry fate. He acknowledges, however, that even if he wished to keep silent and thereby cause his persecutors to relent, he lacks that power. He describes his prophetic compulsion as an irresistible, inner force that cannot be denied (compare Elihu's compulsion to speak in Job 32:18–20):

> If I say, "I will not mention him,
>   or speak any more in his name,"
> then within me there is something like a burning fire
>   shut up in my bones;
> I am weary with holding it in,
>   and I cannot. (Jer. 20:9)

Cognitive Dissonance and Opposition to Jeremiah's Message

In the period between 597 and 587, Jeremiah and the people, both those who remained in Judah and those who were taken into exile in Babylonia, had to cope with conflicting emotions and prophetic voices that called for both hope and despair. While Jeremiah continued to warn of the ultimate destruction of Jerusalem, other prophets and officials were speaking out with a message of hope, saying that the end of exile is at hand (29:8–9, 21–23). They were promising the people of Jerusalem a speedy return of the exiled King Jehoiachin, the people, and the sacred objects taken from the temple. Furthermore, they played to the desires of the crowd by calling for divine retribution against the Neo-Babylonians (28:3–4). Clearly, optimistic words and a positive message, with a promised happy ending, would be more palatable to the people of Jerusalem than Jeremiah's words of a coming doom and destruction.

The most dangerous of Jeremiah's opponents is Hananiah, a recognized prophet from Gibeon. Confronting Jeremiah in the temple in the presence of the priests, Hananiah predicts that within two years the exiles will return and Babylon's power will be broken (28:1–4). With the assertion of such a diametrically opposite position to his, Jeremiah is forced to respond, but only after a period of reflection. He first expresses the hope that Hananiah's message will come true, but he then argues that peace has never been standard fare in prophetic speech: "The prophets who preceded you and me from ancient times prophesied war, famine, and pestilence against many countries and great kingdoms" (28:8; see Amos 4:6–13).

In this way, Jeremiah explains the role of the prophet (compare the list of prophetic characteristics in Deut. 18:18–22 and Jer. 14:13–16). Prophets were charged with the obligation to warn the people and their leaders in the name of Yahweh when they had strayed from the covenant. They were to remind them of the righteous anger of Yahweh and present the proper course that would bring the people back into compliance with their covenantal obligations to their God (Hosea 5:3–15; Zeph. 2:2–3). Peace without a real change in the people's actions and attitudes, however, was not part of the usual prophetic message because it implied two things: (1) a satisfying end to current troubles and (2) the people deserving to have Yahweh intervene to end these troubles because they are members of the covenant community. All Jeremiah can do therefore is fall back on the traditional adage that the true prophet is the one whose words come true (compare false prophets in Jer. 6:14; 8:11): "As for the prophet who prophesies peace, when the word of that prophet comes true, then it will be known that the LORD has truly sent the prophet" (28:9).

Faced with a clear case of **cognitive dissonance**, Hananiah performs an enacted prophecy of his own in order to physically break the impasse and gain the advantage. He removes the wooden yoke from Jeremiah's neck and breaks it (28:10). Jeremiah has been wearing around the yoke on his neck to signify that the people must submit to the yoke (political dominance) of Babylon and thus to Yahweh's will (27:2–8). By breaking this wooden yoke, Hananiah attempts to reinterpret Jeremiah's message and to proclaim that Yahweh's true intention is to "break the yoke of King Nebuchadnezzar" within just two years (28:11).

Temporarily defeated in this public debate, Jeremiah chooses to withdraw. After he receives a new revelation from Yahweh, he returns to confront Hananiah with a new and more remarkable symbol of submission—an iron yoke. The wooden yoke may have been broken, but Yahweh has forged a stronger restraint designed to hold his people in submission to Babylon while laying an even heavier burden on them for their willingness to be deceived by false prophets (28:12–14). Furthermore, Jeremiah knows that the lying message of Hananiah must be discredited and the cognitive dissonance ended. Therefore he goes on to predict the death of Hananiah, and the narrator subsequently notes that Hananiah died during that same year (28:16–17).

Not surprisingly, there are also voices of dissension among the exiles in Babylonia (29:8). Jeremiah deals with these voices of false hope by sending a very pointed letter to the exilic community (29:4–7). First, he disparages any hope that the exile will be over soon. He declares that Yahweh's plan is to hold them in captivity for a period of seventy years, during which the people must seek the Lord "with all their hearts" before they are returned to their land (29:10–14). Their redemption from exile cannot be obtained cheaply or through wishful thinking.

Jeremiah also sets aside the restrictions on where and how they may worship, which had been instituted by the reforms of Hezekiah and Josiah. These kings tried to centralize worship and their own political authority in Jerusalem. In this way they hoped to create a spirit of nationalism as they attempted to restore the fortunes of the Davidic monarchy and the Jerusalem temple community. Now, on the brink of the destruction of both the monarchy and the Jerusalem temple, Jeremiah tells the exiles that they no longer have to be in Judah or Jerusalem to worship or to have their prayers heard by God (29:7). Yahweh is not limited by space, nor is he a local god. He cannot be confined to the Jerusalem temple, and his fortunes are not tied to its existence. The people may worship Yahweh in exile or anywhere else, even without the temple priesthood to direct them. This revelation provides a new opportunity for the people to restore the covenantal relationship with Yahweh without the interference of groups that had in the past been more concerned with their own authority. Freed from the priestly agenda associated with the sacrificial cult, the community in exile will now set the stage for the development of **Diasporic Judaism** in the next two centuries.

The Final Days of Jerusalem

After nearly ten years of relative peace, Egypt once again lures Zedekiah into throwing off his allegiance to his Neo-Babylonian masters. Resolving to end

Egypt's clandestine meddling and to eliminate this troublesome kingdom on the fringes of the empire, Nebuchadnezzar besieges Jerusalem in 588. During these desperate days of the siege, Zedekiah sends messengers to Jeremiah to see if Yahweh will intervene to save the city (21:1–2). However, the prophet offers him no consolation whatsoever. Instead he warns the king that Yahweh, the **Divine Warrior,** has chosen to fight on the side of the Babylonians. As a result it is inevitable that the city will be destroyed, its defenders slaughtered, and the survivors taken away into exile (21:4–7).

The prophet offers only one chance for escape. They must open the gates of Jerusalem and surrender unconditionally to the Babylonians: "Those who stay in this city shall die . . . but those who go out and surrender to the Chaldeans . . . shall have their lives as a prize of war" (21:9). Such a dire response, repeated in the hearing of Zedekiah's advisers (38:1–3), must have shocked the king and his court, and it is no wonder that they imprison Jeremiah to prevent him from repeating his message in public and totally demoralizing the city's defenders. The prophet's temporary prison is a dry cistern carved out of limestone. It was apparently deep enough that Jeremiah had to be lowered by ropes into its depths. The empty cistern also provides ample testimony to the plight of a desperate city running out of water and other supplies (38:4–6, 9).

Eventually, Zedekiah is convinced to release Jeremiah by the pleas of one of his foreign advisers, Ebed-melech the Ethiopian. Interestingly, his decision is made during one of his sessions as chief magistrate. He is pictured sitting in the Benjamin Gate hearing any case brought before him as he might have during more peaceful times (38:7). Of course, these are far from normal times, and the facade of normalcy cannot hide the king's anxieties. After Jeremiah's release, Zedekiah requests a private interview with Jeremiah and questions him, yet again asking for some ray of hope. Knowing how weak Zedekiah is and how susceptible he is to the demands of his officials, Jeremiah hesitates until the king takes an oath in the name of the Lord that he will not be killed for speaking disturbing words. Jeremiah then repeats his message for a third time that surrender to the Babylonians is their only chance for survival (38:16–23). Although this must have frustrated and frightened Zedekiah, the king merely places Jeremiah under house arrest, and there he will remain until the fall of the city (38:28).

With the fall of the city only days away, Jeremiah performs one final symbolic act. While it is based on his legal obligation to redeem the property of one of his relatives that has died (Lev. 25:25; Ruth 4:4–6), his performance of a familiar legal transaction provides an excellent backdrop to his message of hope for a people about to go into exile. Jeremiah's actions demonstrate a public display of allegiance to the kinship rights of his extended household and his strict adherence to the duty to purchase the relative's fields so the land will remain within the family (Jer. 32:6–8). Of course, real estate of any kind at this point is totally worthless. The people of Judah are about to be taken into exile, and this property may well have been already occupied by Babylonian troops.

Despite that, Jeremiah buys the land without any hesitation. Weighing out the money and signing and sealing a deed before witnesses (32:9–10), Jeremiah performs an act that evokes the early days of Yahweh's covenant with Abraham and serves as a literary and covenantal **inclusio** of God's covenantal promise to the nation. Just as Abraham established his stake in the Promised Land by purchasing the cave of Machpelah and having his transaction duly recorded and witnessed (Gen. 23), now Jeremiah preserves a title to the Promised Land for future generations. He gives the copies of the documents to Baruch in front of witnesses and charges him to "put them in an earthenware jar, in order that they may last for a long time" (Jer. 32:11–14). This legal gesture assures the people that when the Lord's plan is fulfilled and they return from exile, Jeremiah's deed to a piece of the land will serve as their legal claim to the ownership of the Promised Land as redeemed members of the covenant community.

Since the prophet's role is not simply to condemn and cast judgment on the nation, Jeremiah also provides oracles of restoration, return, and recompense just prior to the fall of the city (16:14–15; 23:5–8). One particularly poignant example of the restoration theme is found in Jer. 24. Here the prophet describes a vision of a basket of figs, some good and some so bad they cannot be eaten (24:1–3). The good figs are identified as the people in exile for whom God has future plans to "bring them back to this land," to "build them up," to "plant them," so they will be given "a heart to know that I am the LORD" (24:5–7). In this way they will once again become "my people." The bad figs are equated with King Zedekiah and his officials, who have brought the Babylonians down on the people and who may have felt superior to those taken into exile. For them the future holds only "sword, famine, and pestilence" (24:8–10). While there is some debate over the authenticity of this vision and whether it reflects the hand of either a Deuteronomic or postexilic editor, its plea that the exiles taken away prior to 587 are still part of the covenant community fits well into Jeremiah's message.

Another reference to the future end to the exile and a reversal of the current destructive times for those "who survived the sword" and "found grace in the wilderness" is found in 31:1–2. The people are assured that God's love for them still endures (31:3) and that there will come a time when the cry will go out, "Come, let us go up to Zion" (31:6). Also contained in this character are the issue of individual responsibility and the casting of blame for the exile (31:29–30; compare Ezek. 18:2). The exilic community is told that they must recognize that in their punishment they are not paying for the sins of their ancestors, but for their own violations of the covenant. Once they have been purified as the people had been in the wilderness period after the exodus, then the exilic experience will have served its purpose. At that point a new covenant can be established, envisioned by both Jeremiah and Ezekiel as an internal one:

I will put my law within them, and I will write it on their hearts; and I will be their God, and they will be my people. No longer shall they teach one another, or say to each other, "Know the LORD," for they shall all know me, from the least of them to the greatest. (Jer. 31:33–34)

I will give them one heart, and put a new spirit within them; I will remove the heart of stone from their flesh and give them a heart of flesh. (Ezek. 11:19)

Furthermore, the exiles are reassured in a series of **oracles against the nations** (Jer. 46–51). The roster of nations includes Egypt, the Philistines, Moab, Ammon, Edom, Elam, and, of course, Babylonia. The prophet tells his people that it is certain that the Babylonians and all their allies will not benefit for long from their conquest and looting of other nations. They can be sure that God will demand an accounting for "all the wrong that they have done in Zion" (Jer. 51:24). When this occurs, the full power of God the Divine Warrior will turn against these enemy nations, transforming their lands into a desert and calling on foreign armies to campaign as God's "destroying sword" (50:11–16; 51:25–29).

When Jerusalem finally falls to the Neo-Babylonian army, Judah's royal court is dissolved permanently and will never be restored (52:1–30). Zedekiah is forced to watch his children being executed and then is blinded before being taken into exile (2 Kings 25:7; Jer. 39:6–7). The monarchy of Judah has now ended, although Jehoiachin will live on as a king in exile until his death (2 Kings 25:27–30; Jer. 52:31–34). Rather than chance their relations with another member of the Davidic royal house, the Babylonians appoint a non-Davidic official, Gedaliah, as governor, but he is assassinated after only a short time in office (2 Kings 25:22–26; Jer. 41:1–3). His assassins flee to Egypt, taking a reluctant Jeremiah with them (43:5–7). Thus ends the long career of a prophet whose work spanned the period from the exhilarating expectations of Josiah's nationalist movement to the depths of despair as Judah meets its fate at the hands of Nebuchadnezzar, and many of the people are scattered to Egypt and Mesopotamia.

13

The Book of Ezekiel

The physical location of the exiles, the events leading up to the destruction of Jerusalem, and the social context of a prophet who has also been a member of the priestly community are the keys to understanding the message of Ezekiel. He was taken into exile in 597 along with Jehoiachin, members of the royal family, and many of the chief priests. Ezekiel's message reflects his concerns for and continuing interest in Jerusalem and its temple priesthood. However, as one of the exiles in Babylonia, he must also deal with the effects of social dislocation and the exiles' mounting fears and concerns. Like many other prophets, Ezekiel's message is divided into two parts, statements of divine judgment and visions of restoration for the nation.

Prophetic compulsion forces Ezekiel to speak the harsh message given to him by God. But this is initially a selective message. Unlike other prophets, he is not allowed to "reprove" the people and thus give them a sense of hope in God's willingness to set aside their punishment yet again. He is able to speak only words of "lamentation and mourning and woe" (2:10) until the final fall of Jerusalem in 587. If he makes an attempt to speak any other message, God immediately silences him (3:26). Then, after the destruction of Judah's capital, Ezekiel is released from this selective compulsion and is finally able to speak words of reassurance to the exilic community. In reminding them of the just nature and merciful intentions of **Yahweh**, he tells them that once the people have been purged, they will be returned to their homeland, purified, and restored as God's **covenant** nation (36:24–25).

The principal theme in the book is the status of God's presence. Despite the people's assumption that God would never abandon them or the Jerusalem temple, Ezekiel, in a startling vision, describes the departure of God's "glory" from the temple (Ezek. 10). There can be no more telling or graphic means of signaling the doom of the nation. It is only after judgment has been executed and the nation purified that God's glory will be able to return to the temple (43:1–5). At that point the climax of Ezekiel's vision of restoration occurs with a detailed description of the restored temple (Ezek. 40–48).

The theme of Yahweh's presence is also implicit in the use of a recognition formula throughout the book. This formula appears sporadically elsewhere in the Old Testament/Hebrew Bible (1 Kings 20:13; Isa. 49:23; Joel 3:17), but in Ezekiel it is a recurring refrain. The prophet uses the phrase "and they shall know that I am the LORD" more than eighty times (e.g., Ezek. 6:10; 12:15; 20:26; 32:15; 39:6). In each instance, God declares that he is about to make manifest his divine power in order to demonstrate the magisterial ability of the deity to control chaos and exert total dominion over all creation. With that established, the conclusion can then be drawn that God is solely responsible for establishing the covenant with Israel and giving them the laws and decrees that govern the actions of Israel and, by extension, all other nations (compare Deut. 10:12–22).

Ezekiel's Call

Although the story of Ezekiel's call evokes images of those of Moses, Isaiah, and Jeremiah, it has its own very distinctive character. Perhaps most important is its sense of mystery. There is no hint of God manifesting overt **anthropomorphic** characteristics in this **theophany**. Whenever the prophet has to speak of God's appearance, he always uses a qualifying phrase, "in the likeness of" or "something like," so that he does not have to describe Yahweh in human terms. This practice creates a certain sense of majesty similar to the image created in Isaiah's description of the temple filled with smoke (Isa. 6:4). The sense of divine power is enhanced by Yahweh's addressing Ezekiel as a "son of man," a phrase that has the connotation here of being "mortal" (contrast the same title given to Jesus in Matt. 24:30 and Mark 2:10). In this way a clear distinction is drawn between the human and the divine being.

The sense of Yahweh's glory as a separate, roving aspect of the deity also appears in this scene. Instead of being a fixed being (like the enthroned figure in Isa. 6:1), Ezekiel's vision of God is one of ever-changing motion ("wherever the spirit would go"; Ezek. 1:12), which may imply the immediacy of action about to occur or a growing sense of omnipresence for God. Certainly, it would make it more difficult to determine the extent of Yahweh's glory or the degree of power behind all of this movement (especially 1:12–28). The universality of the image in motion may have also been intended to further separate Yahweh from the somewhat localized gods of Canaan and Mesopotamia.

Just as in other fully developed **call narratives**, Ezekiel is confronted in a theophany with a vision of God and is called to serve as a spokesperson for the deity. His task will not be an easy one, but unlike Isaiah and Jeremiah, he does not make the usual excuses. Instead Ezekiel's reaction demonstrates his fear and respect for divine power (1:28). That draws Ezekiel into the tradition often found when Israelite **wisdom literature** describes God (Ps. 2:11; Prov. 1:7; 14:2; Eccles. 8:12). Instead of making any excuses why he cannot serve, he obediently consumes the scroll presented to him (Ezek. 2:9–3:3). This gesture provides a parallel with the call narratives of the other major prophets, who also are empowered to speak by divine actions that involve their mouths (Isaiah's lips being purified and Jeremiah's mouth being touched). Afterward, the prophet can no longer demur, for he now possesses the divinely given ability to speak God's holy word. Once Ezekiel has eaten the scroll, however, he remains mute for seven days before taking up his task. For this amount of time, he sits "stunned" among his fellow exiles (3:15; compare Job 2:13). This period of reflection, in itself, suggests the magnitude of the message. It also links Ezekiel's message to other sacred acts such as the seven days of creation (another tie to God's power) and the seven days of the Passover festival (Exod. 12:14–16). It is also possible that his staged silence is an indication of the reluctance he may have felt in assuming the prophetic mantle.

Also contained in the call narrative is the idea of prophetic responsibility. Ezekiel is portrayed as a "guard" or "sentry" whose task is to cry out an alarm when an enemy army approaches (Ezek. 3:17–21; compare Isa. 21:11–12; Hosea 9:8). If Ezekiel fails to carry out this sacred task, he himself will be condemned for failing to warn the people of their doom. In this case, as previously (Isa. 10:5–6), the imminent danger faced by the people is the righteous anger of Yahweh and God's use of the Babylonians as the means of punishing Judah (Jer. 21:5–7; 28:14). Ezekiel experiences the weight of their approaching devastation and Yahweh's judgment on the nation when he is instructed to shut himself up in his house. Silenced by God, he can only await the inevitable (Ezek. 3:24–26). In this sense, Ezekiel differs from other prophets who announce judgment but retain some hope that God will relent (e.g., Jer. 26:19). The hope of being spared ultimate destruction does not appear in Ezekiel. That omission is consistent with a divine messenger who is already in exile and whose expectations for the future are based on the reality that he would soon be joined in exile by other members of his nation.

The idea that a god is in control of historical events is not limited to Israel. For example, the Mesha Inscription clearly attributes the misfortunes of the kingdom of Moab to the anger of its god, Chemosh (*OTPar* 168). This concept is known as a **theodicy**, and it provides another important indication of the purpose of Israelite prophecy. When national disasters occur, the prophets argue that such calamities are a result of the people's violation of their covenant with Yahweh. In addition, the prophets repeatedly had provided explicit warning of the disasters about to strike the nation. Therefore, it is possible to claim that God's willingness to provide a warning is essentially righteous and that harm to the nation does not occur without cause. This explanation of misfortune, which forms the heart of the theodicy, is based on the assurance that Yahweh is a just and righteous God. Such explanations would have been vital to the exilic community if it were to continue to worship Yahweh in the face of their own exile and the destruction of Jerusalem. Without this set of beliefs in place, there would be little reason for the Israelites to continue to worship a God who had failed to listen to their pleas or protect them.

Enacted Prophecies

During the period prior to the Babylonian siege and final fall of Jerusalem in 587, Ezekiel performs his message in a series of **enacted prophecies**, a form of street theater. These required him to engage in a series of symbolic and often outrageous acts designed to draw attention to him and make an indelible impression on his audience. In many of the enacted prophecies in Ezek. 4, the prophet employs a simple and easily understood strategy to portray Jerusalem's sad fate. God instructs him to take a clay brick, an item used in the construction of all buildings in Mesopotamia, and inscribe a simple outline of Jerusalem on it (4:1–3). Then, dispensing with his priestly dignity, Ezekiel plays in the dust like a child with toy soldiers, besieging his brick/city and showing how it will be destroyed. For a grown man, in particular a priest who would ordinarily scrupulously protect his pristine linen robes, to do this must have caused a great deal of muttering by his audience and perhaps accomplished the goal of raising apprehensions about the impending doom for Jerusalem.

Ezekiel's next piece of street theater involves lying on his side for an extended period—390 days on his right side and 40 days on his left side. If done in a public place, this act would have drawn a crowd as they counted out the days of Ezekiel's ordeal. His efforts in this case are designed to symbolize the number of years that the people of the northern and southern kingdoms, respectively, will remain in exile (4:4–6). The number forty is particularly significant in Israelite tradition since it is also the number of years the people were condemned to wander in the wilderness following the exodus (Num. 14:33). Thus this current exile can be interpreted as a new period of winnowing and transformation (Jer. 15:7). It may also serve as a reminder to the people that even though they are once again sentenced to a period of "wilderness" purification (Ezek. 20:33–38), that time of trial will come to an end (Isa. 40:1–2) and they will be restored to their land and to their proper relationship with Yahweh.

During the time that Ezekiel endures his painful ordeal, he is required to prepare very scanty meals for himself, demonstrating the starvation faced by the exiles and by those who are to be besieged in Jerusalem (Ezek. 4:9–13). At first God commands that these meals be cooked on an "unclean" fire using human dung, but at this point Ezekiel finally cannot restrain his protests. As a priest, he has dedicated his life to maintaining a "clean," ritually pure existence. If he is commanded to eat food contaminated by some form of impurity, it would likely make him gag and perhaps nullify, in his own mind, his ability to serve as God's prophet. At this reasonable protest, God relents, allowing him to use animal dung, a conventional fuel, to cook his meals and to continue the message that the people will face short rations during the siege (4:14–15).

In what could be described as yet another example of street theater, the prophet is told to shave his head and beard (5:1), acts often associated with mourning practices (Job 1:20). There are also instances in the biblical narrative when a shaved head and beard served as a sign of contamination or humiliation (Num. 6:9; 2 Sam. 10:4). At God's direction Ezekiel divides his hair into three piles. Then he chops up one pile with a sword, scatters another into the wind, and throws the third in the fire. With the bulk of the hair destroyed or scattered, he retrieves a few hairs and binds them up in the edges of his robes, signifying that only a few of the people, a **remnant**, will survive (Ezek. 5:3). Obviously, this performance is such a visually oriented set of actions that it would be most impressive in the open air, where the wind could play its part, and the fire and sword could be used effectively before the crowd. While the act provides no hope for Jerusalem's immediate future, it does signal the hope that a few of the righteous will survive the destruction.

As can be seen in these previous prophetic pantomimes, props can serve as an effective means of telling a story. Ezekiel employs this method once again by taking up "an exile's bag" in order to graphically predict the coming exile of the people (12:1–16). He carries it about with him day and night. To complete the image he digs a hole through the wall of his house, and toting the bag with him he mimics the defeated people forced to exit the breached walls of Jerusalem carrying only what they can quickly put together (12:5–7). Such a poignant picture is hauntingly similar to the pictures of refugees on the walls of Sennacherib's palace in Nineveh. Created as royal propaganda and designed to intimidate everyone who entered the Assyrian king's chambers, they depict the survivors of the siege of Lachish (701) as they trudge away from their destroyed city with nothing but a few possessions (OTPar 190).

One final and devastating aspect of this enacted prophecy occurs when Ezekiel is told about the fate of the "prince in Jerusalem." This oracle is possibly based on reports from witnesses of the fall of the city. It is remarkably the same as the account of Zedekiah's flight and capture by the Babylonians in 2 Kings 25:4–7. Just as the "prince" is instructed to cover his eyes as if he were blind (Ezek. 12:12), Zedekiah is blinded by the soldiers after they execute his sons (2 Kings 25:7). All of these events signal that the people of Jerusalem are no longer citizens of that place. The people will be taken into exile, "disperse[d] . . . among the nations" (Ezek. 12:15), and only a select few will survive sword, famine, and pestilence to tell the tale of "their abominations among the nations" (12:16; compare similar language in Jer. 21:9–10).

Explanations of Judgment

Like other prophets, Ezekiel's frightening message that condemns the nation and its leaders and his dire predictions of doom need to be justified. Otherwise, God would be perceived as unjust. The result is a series of visions that provide a more than adequate explanation for Yahweh's anger. The most devastating portrayal of the people's disobedience appears in the vision of the abominations in the temple (Ezek. 8). The substance of this vision is especially appropriate given Ezekiel's background as a temple priest. He would have been intimately familiar with the architecture of the temple and its ritual pattern. Naturally, he would also have been extremely concerned with the maintenance of proper worship of Yahweh in that place. In describing his out-of-body inspection tour, the prophet takes the reader from the outer court to the inner court, and everywhere he goes he sees the total defilement of the temple.

The vision opens with a scene in which Ezekiel is sitting with the elders taken with him into exile. These authority figures serve as his witnesses and, if necessary, can be asked to authenticate his experience. From the secular world, Ezekiel's spirit is carried away by a divine messenger, who grasps him by the hair and transports him through the air back to Jerusalem. As the journey ends, the prophet discovers that he has been returned to earth directly in front of the temple. However, he is unable to enter by the temple gate because that would take him directly into the path of an abominable "image of jealousy" (8:3) (probably an idol; see the "jealous God" language in Exod. 20:4–5). Rather than come into contact with this corrupting idol, he is told to go around to the side of the temple where a hole appears, and he is able to tunnel his way into the building.

As Ezekiel emerges into what should be a sacred chamber dedicated to Yahweh, he finds instead that its walls are covered with the drawings of other gods and their sacred symbols. The worst thing about this, however, is the presence of the **seventy elders**. Ordinarily these authoritative figures (comparable to the elders mentioned at the beginning of this vision) appear in more positive contexts as the representatives of the people's acceptance of the covenant (Exod. 24:9–10). In this instance, however, the seventy elders are busily engaged in burning incense and worshiping the gods portrayed on the walls (Ezek. 8:10–12). Their presence and inappropriate actions represent the entire nation's idolatry, and its magnitude is increased because it occurs within the sacred precincts of Yahweh's temple. The direct involvement of the seventy elders is a signal that Ezekiel will find the entire nation in violation of the covenant.

The panorama of disobedience continues to unfold as Ezekiel continues his virtual tour of the temple and finds one example after another of idolatrous behavior. First, he witnesses a scene in the outer court where a group of women are "weeping for Tammuz" (8:14). Tammuz is the Babylonian god of new growth and fertility, who dies each year during the dry season and enters the underworld (symbolic of the storage of the harvest in underground silos). Through the devout tears of his worshipers (symbolic of the returning rains) he is released from his imprisonment in the underworld so that he can bring back to the earth the new growth that spells the people's survival. Judean participation in this weeping ritual thus represents both a borrowing of Babylonian religious practices and a rejection of Yahweh as the land's true source of fertility and life.

Plan of Solomon's Temple

Ezekiel then moves on to the inner court, which lies between the porch and the altar. There he spies twenty-five men prostrating themselves toward the east as they worship the sun god. Significantly, this forces them to bow down with their backs to the altar of Yahweh and to the holy of holies (8:16), which would be a major indiscretion and a sign of absolute dismissal of Yahweh's presence. Significantly, at no point during his tour of Yahweh's temple does Ezekiel find any evidence of devotion to God or any person actually engaged in worshiping Yahweh.

Taking a more personal tack in his judgment oracles, Ezekiel uses a parenting image as a very powerful explanation for Yahweh's decision to abandon the temple and the nation (Ezek. 16). This oracle focuses on familiar aspects of nurturing a child and providing for its needs. In that sense it parallels the exodus event and the birth and nurturing of the new nation of Israel (compare Deut. 32:4–18; Hosea 11:1–7). In this metaphor, Jerusalem is portrayed as an unwanted female infant left to die in an open field. She has been abandoned very soon after birth and has not even been cleansed or wrapped in a garment (Ezek. 16:4–5). Since female infanticide was fairly common in times of famine or among impoverished families, Ezekiel's audience would not find this particularly strange. Modern audiences may be horrified, but it is a fact of life for cultures living on the margin of existence. Rather than pass by and leave the child to its fate, Yahweh takes pity on the abandoned child, adopts her, and provides for all of her needs (16:6–7).

Ezekiel then extends the metaphor as the girl grows up. When she reaches maturity God chooses to marry her and provides her with rich robes and jewelry (16:8–14). The new bride, however, is not satisfied with what God has provided, and she chooses to seek the favor of other lovers/gods (16:15). She squanders all that God has given her, including her children, whom she sacrifices to other gods (16:17–22). Of course, this abandoned child—now grown into an ungrateful wife and mother—symbolizes the nation and its infidelities. Israel and Judah had built **high places** and worshiped other gods (6:13; Hosea 4:12–13) and made alliances with Assyria and Egypt instead of trusting Yahweh (Ezek. 16:24–26; Isa. 30:1–7; Hosea 7:11; 8:9–10).

For their many crimes, the people of Jerusalem will be given into the hands of their enemies. Like the peculiar harlot in Ezekiel's metaphor, who pays her lovers instead of receiving payment from them, they will discover what it costs to reject Yahweh (Ezek. 16:33–34). Just as the northern kingdom (the "elder sister") and other disobedient sisters, such as Sodom, sinned (16:46–50) and were destroyed, now the "younger sister" (Judah), whose sins have made her older siblings "appear righteous," must face her judge. Despite condemning them for their failure to recognize who truly is God, Yahweh is still able to "remember my covenant with you in the days of your youth." Rather than abandon them, God will act once again to establish an "everlasting covenant" so that the nation will at last and truly "know that I am the Lord" (16:60–62). The divine generosity expressed here is designed to shame Judah so profoundly that she can "never open her mouth again" to betray the covenant (16:63). In that sense, silence is to be equated with submission to God's authority.

Ezekiel's vision of the abominations in the temple and the metaphor of Jerusalem's infidelity in the story of the foundling and the unfaithful wife provide a firm justification for Yahweh's decision to abandon the Jerusalem temple (Ezek. 10). At the core of this vision is establishing that the presence of Yahweh's glory is within the temple precincts (10:1–5). In fact, Yahweh's glory fills the temple one last time in the form of a cloud, while the wings of the cherubim provide a sense of a rushing wind (10:4; compare Isa. 6:2).

Then, as he does in his call narrative (Ezek. 1:4–28), Ezekiel takes particular care to describe a growing sense of movement facilitated by appearance of a conveyance supported by the cherubim (10:15–19). The amazing description of the chariot's wheels "full of eyes" and containing "four faces" adds to the potential for motion and is a signal that God has the ability to see all that has been occurring within the temple.

The drama begins when God commands a divine servant, referred to here as a "man clothed in linen," to gather burning coals from between the wheels of the chariot and cast them on the city (10:2). While some consider this an effort to purify the city in a way similar to Isaiah's purified lips (Isa. 6:6–7), it is more likely a reference to the approaching conflagration of the city when it falls to the Babylonians. With that accomplished, the glory of God is carried away amid clouds and fire in the chariot drawn by the cherubim (Ezek. 10:6–19). Just as Jeremiah had warned the people that their failure to "amend their way" would prevent God from being able to "dwell with you in this place" (Jer. 7:3–4), now Ezekiel graphically depicts the fruits of that failure—the actual abandonment of the temple by its God. Nothing could be worse!

Despite shattering the current hopes of the people of Jerusalem, Ezekiel does let them know that there will be an opportunity for a righteous remnant of the people of Judah to survive the destruction of the city. In what is clearly a parallel to both the Passover (Exod. 12) and the culling of the unfaithful who had bowed down to the golden calf in the wilderness (32:25–28), Ezekiel describes a vision in which seven men (six executioners and a scribe) instructed by God pass from one end of Jerusalem to the other (Ezek. 9). Wherever they find a person mourning the sins of the people, the scribe is told to mark that person's forehead with the Hebrew letter *taw* (an X shape). Then, during a second circuit of the doomed city, the executioners are ordered to slay everyone who does not bear this mark of innocence. In this way, the righteous are designated as worthy of survival (compare the effect of the blood on the doorpost in Exod. 12:7 and Rahab's "crimson cord" in Josh. 2:18). Even though Yahweh has chosen to physically abandon the temple and Jerusalem, these few survivors will constitute Yahweh's new people. The warning of the "sentinel" has been given (Ezek. 3:17–21; also 33:1–9), and the unity between word and action marks an end to one period and the beginning of a new one after the fall of the city.

Oracles against the Nations

In the structuring of the book, Ezekiel's enacted prophecies and statements of divine judgment are separated from his visions of restoration and hope (Ezek. 33–48) by the **oracles against the nations**, which comprise Ezek. 25–32. This may have been based on a decision by the editors to allow the oracles to serve as a transition or buffer between the two parts of Ezekiel's message. Their placement would also provide a further link to the historical events of the time as well as the inevitable destruction of Jerusalem. In his oracles against the nations, Egypt and several petty states that encircled Judah (Ammon, Moab, Edom, Philistia, and Tyre and Sidon in Phoenicia) are condemned. Of course, this **genre** is not unique to Ezekiel. It also appears in Amos 1:3–2:5; Isa. 13–23; and Jer. 46–51. In each case, it is unlikely that the foreign nations addressed in the oracles ever actually heard the judgments made against them. More likely, the Israelites are the audience for these prophetic messages, and it may be assumed that they would be pleased to hear that God intends to punish their enemies and make them pay for their oppression.

Although it is not possible to date the oracles with any certainty, they are all aware of the fall of Jerusalem in 587. Each oracle is arranged according to a geographical pattern (compare the similar scheme in Amos 1:3–2:5). Ezekiel looks to the east as he begins the cycle of condemnation, starting with Ammon. He then addresses the other nations, proceeding in a clockwise fashion from east to west, starting with Moab and then turning to Edom, Philistia, Tyre, and Sidon. The editors have treated the oracles against Egypt separately, perhaps because of the contrast between its political power and that of the petty states of Syria-Palestine. Tyre is also singled out for particular attention (Ezek. 26:1–28:19). That Phoenician port city is condemned for taunting Jerusalem at its destruction while relishing the prospect of increasing its trade empire with the elimination of a trading rival (26:2). Therefore God will use Nebuchadnezzar and the Babylonians as the instrument of punishment (26:7–14; 30:10–11). Furthermore, the king of Tyre is also condemned for presuming to possess the wisdom and power of a god (28:1–10). Because of his pride, he will be cast from his Eden-like kingdom, and everything he possesses will be turned to ashes (28:12–19).

The Israelites are to see a portion of their own future in the divine retribution against their neighbors: "The house of Israel shall no longer find a pricking brier or a piercing thorn among all their neighbors who have treated them with contempt. And they shall know that I am the Lord GOD" (28:24).

The elimination of all foreign threats marks the establishment of a restored Israel and the creation of an idyllic future (28:25–26). In addition, these examples of divine wrath echo the theme of the recognition formula and function as further proof to the Israelites and all the nations that Yahweh is indeed the Lord (28:24; 29:16, 21).

Visions of Restoration

Prior to Jerusalem's final fall in 587, Ezekiel lays the groundwork for the proposition, the theodicy, that Judah's sins have brought this evil upon itself.

He also emphasizes that the punishment will not continue if later generations prove faithful to Yahweh (11:14–21). To do this, Ezekiel makes two related statements in Ezek. 14 and Ezek. 18. In the first case, he gives a list of three righteous non-Israelite sages from antiquity: Noah, Daniel, and Job. All had survived trials because of their righteousness. In the primordial account prior to the introduction of Abraham, Noah and his family are the only survivors of the flood because Noah is judged by God to be righteous (Gen. 6:9). According to the "Tale of Aqhat," Daniel (not to be confused with the biblical Daniel) was a wise, but childless king in ancient Ugarit, who judged his people fairly and was rewarded with a son and heir (*OTPar* 71–83). And Job of Uz (possibly Edom) survived a legendary test in which he is afflicted with the loss of his property, children, and health. Still, he is able to rise from his misery and bless God's name (Job 1:13–21).

Earlier tradition held that the very presence of the righteous could justify God's sparing a city from destruction or could be the basis for the effectiveness of a righteous man's prayer on the city's behalf (Gen. 18:17–21; Jer. 5:1). Ezekiel now maintains that even if these three exemplary characters were all assembled, they could save only themselves. Jeremiah also applies this principle using Moses and Samuel as his example of righteous intercessors for the sinful nation (15:1). Like Ezekiel, Jeremiah voices God's message that even if these two men "stood before me, yet my heart would not turn toward this people." Therefore it is plain that the righteousness of any one individual lends merit to only that particular individual and cannot atone for the sin or set aside the punishment due to a land that consistently acted "faithlessly" (Ezek. 14:13–21).

Ezekiel expands on this concept when he quotes an old proverb, "The parents have eaten the sour grapes, but the children's teeth are set on edge" (18:2; compare Jer. 31:27–30). The proverb reflects the legal principle of **corporate identity**, by which children may also suffer for the sins of the father (Exod. 20:5). Thus, when Achan stole from the "devoted things" assigned to the *herem* when Jericho is captured (Josh. 7:15–26), his entire family is condemned along with him in order to purify the entire nation of sin. Until that happens the conquest of the land cannot proceed.

In this new world of the exile, however, Ezekiel tries to assure the people that they will not have to pay for the sins of their fathers—only "the person who sins . . . shall die" (Ezek. 18:4). This is not an argument for individual responsibility, nor is it the beginning of individualism, a Western concept that would have been incomprehensible to the communally oriented people of the ancient Near East. Rather, Ezekiel's argument follows the logic of Exod. 20:5–6, which warns of multigenerational punishment for those who reject God and promises benefits of God's "steadfast love [*hesed*] to the thousandth generation of those who love" God and keep the commandments. These principles apply to the entire exilic community and serve as an exhortation to them to remain faithful even though they may consider the pain of the exile to be "unfair"

(Ezek. 18:25–29). They must recognize that a purpose and opportunity are afforded by the exile as a period of purification and rededication. And in their displaced condition, God will judge "all of you according to your ways," for God wants them to "turn, then, and live" (18:30–32; compare Amos 5:4–6).

Once Jerusalem falls to Nebuchadnezzar's army in 587, Ezekiel is released from his compulsion to speak only words of judgment. From that point on, his new task is to explain what is ahead for the exiles in relation to their God. They must come to understand that Yahweh's decision to leave them unprotected has been the direct result of their own iniquity. The exile is therefore analogous to the time spent in bondage in Egypt, another era when they had lived "among the nations." During the exile they will be tested and purged, as in the wilderness period, and those who measure up to the stipulations of the covenant will once again be brought forth to reclaim their heritage in the land of Israel (Ezek. 20:33–38). When this period of instruction is complete, the name of God will be restored as the nations and exiles recognize Yahweh's power as they are returned to their land (39:25–29). Whatever dishonor has been attached to Yahweh's apparent failure to protect the people in 587 will thereby be vindicated and set aside as a false accusation (Ezek. 28–29; 39:1–16).

The prophet envisions a new world after the exile in which old injustices, poor leadership by kings and priests, and the very idea of wanting to violate the law and covenant will no longer exist. In his use of the "good shepherd" image in Ezek. 34, Ezekiel plays on a familiar theme of contrasted leadership found in Jer. 23:1–3. Both prophets condemn the "shepherds . . . who have

---

Davidic King Restored

Several prophets include a promise that after judgment has been fulfilled and the people have been punished there will be a restoration of the nation that will include a righteous king of the line of David. This ideal ruler will be raised up by God to ensure both social justice and obedience to the covenant.

> A shoot shall come out from the stump of Jesse,
>   and a branch shall grow out of his roots. . . .
> His delight shall be in the fear of the LORD. (Isa. 11:1–3)

The days are surely coming, says the LORD, when I will raise up for David a righteous Branch, and he shall reign as king and deal wisely, and shall execute justice and righteousness in the land. (Jer. 23:5)

For the Israelites shall remain many days without king or prince. . . . Afterward the Israelites shall return and seek the LORD their God, and David their king; they shall come in awe to the LORD and to his goodness in the latter days. (Hosea 3:4–5)

scattered my flock," and they indicate that their right to rule the people has ended because of their corrupt and selfish nature. Ezekiel (34:11–24) picks up on this judgment oracle and describes how Yahweh, the owner of the flock, will remove all authority from the false shepherds (kings and priests), who serve only themselves and neglect the sheep.

In contrast, Yahweh is the perfect shepherd who finds good pasture for the flock during the day and safe haven at night. Unlike their uncaring former masters, the divine shepherd administers to the sick and seeks out those who have strayed (compare Isa. 40:11). Once order has been reestablished with the flock and they are judged by their merit (Ezek. 34:17–22), Yahweh will appoint a new shepherd from the line of David who will follow Yahweh's example and properly care for the sheep (34:23–24).

For both Ezekiel and Jeremiah, the exilic experience serves as the divine mechanism that will make restoration possible because it is only by means of the exilic experience that the people realize the true nature of Yahweh's power and wisdom. As the prophets say, when Yahweh installs a "new heart" and a "new spirit" of obedience within them, they will come to understand the purpose of the exile and will recognize and be ashamed of their iniquities and "abominable deeds" (Jer. 31:31–34; Ezek. 36:26–32). Furthermore, both the destruction of the nation and its period of exile must be understood as a part of God's plan. God promises that the barren and depopulated land of Israel will blossom because the people will "soon come home" and all its fields and pastures will be restored to fertility (36:8–12).

God alone will be responsible for the end of their suffering and will cleanse them of their iniquities (36:33). Only Yahweh can make it possible for their homes to be rebuilt and their wasted land to be restored to a state "like the garden of Eden" (36:34–35). All this will be done to demonstrate to all the nations the power of Yahweh (36:22–24; 39:27–28; compare Isa. 40:5–26).

For those among the exilic community who have lost hope and believe that the exile means the end of everything, Ezekiel relates the vision of the "valley of dry bones" (Ezek. 37:1–14). This oracle uses the language of the creation story in Gen. 1–2. The prophet describes an ancient battlefield with its grisly debris scattered about to symbolize the current and future state of Israel's covenant relationship with Yahweh. Taken there by the spirit of the Lord, he is quizzed on whether the dry bones of the long-dead warriors that lay in lonely piles about the valley could rise and live again. Realizing that this is a question that only Yahweh can answer, Ezekiel simply says, "O Lord GOD, you know" (37:3; compare Job's recognition of the difference between human and divine knowledge in Job 42:1–6).

Having made it clear that he accepts the limits of human knowledge, the prophet is commanded to speak the word of God to the dry bones. As in the first story of creation (Gen. 1:1–2:4a), it is the creative word and spirit of God that fosters the beginning of life on earth. When Ezekiel speaks God's

Spirit of the Lord in the Prophets

One of the most commonly used images in the biblical text and especially in the prophetic literature for God's authoritative power is the "spirit of the Lord." Examples sometimes refer to the spirit of God as the motivating power behind prophetic speech, sometimes as a means of travel or rescue, and occasionally as a term synonymous with the person of God.

> The spirit of the Lord shall rest on him,
>   the spirit of wisdom. (Isa. 11:2)

And when he spoke to me, a spirit entered into me and set me on my feet. (Ezek. 2:2)

He brought me out by the spirit of the Lord and set me down. (Ezek. 37:1)

> I will pour out my spirit on all flesh;
> your sons and your daughters shall prophesy,
>   your old men shall dream dreams,
>   and your young men shall see visions. (Joel 2:28)

> But as for me, I am filled with power,
>   with the spirit of the Lord,
>   and with justice and might. (Mic. 3:8)

Not by might, nor by power, but by my spirit, says the Lord. (Zech. 4:6)

word, the bodies rearticulate and once again take on flesh. Then, recognizing that the creative work is not yet finished, God calls on Ezekiel to "prophesy to the breath" or wind (Hebrew *ruah*) (Ezek. 37:9). Again, the reference to the divine breath is reminiscent of the stories of creation. In Gen. 1 the first sign of order and life within the chaotic void is the spirit of God passing over the waters. Then, in the second story of creation, Yahweh "breathed . . . the breath of life" into the body of the first human, animating Adam as a living being with the spark only God could provide (2:7).

One cautionary note needs to be added about this story in Ezekiel. This description of the reanimation of dead bodies is not the basis for a belief in the general resurrection of the dead in Judaism at this stage in their history. Instead its purpose is to describe in metaphorical terms the seemingly dead relationship between the people and God. The covenant has been endangered by the people's disobedience, and their unfaithful had virtually killed their ties to Yahweh. Now, with God once again taking the initiative, a new creation becomes possible. The divine word combined with God's breath makes it possible for a dead nation to be revived. Resurrection as a theological concept will not enter Jewish thought until the Hellenistic period (ca. 300–100), principally among the Pharisee sect (Josephus, *Jewish Antiquities* 18.14–15), and appears in the Old Testament/Hebrew Bible only in Dan. 12:1–2, which dates to the time of Greek and Persian influence on Judaism.

Ezekiel's final portrayal of the restoration of the nation's fortunes is contained in his elaborate description of the restoration of the Jerusalem temple (Ezek. 40–48). In minute detail, he records the magnificent architectural design of the rebuilt temple, whose grand scale is intended to match the power and majesty of Yahweh's restorative act. The climax of the vision is the reestablishment of the throne of Yahweh (43:7–12) and the return of God's presence to the temple (compare Isa. 4:2–6). In that way he comes full circle from God's summary departure (Ezek. 10) to a glorious return. Since divine blessings are equated with God's presence, the full restoration of the land and the people is not possible without this divine return. When it occurs, the covenant promises of land and children will once again be in full effect (47:1–12).

The reality, however, did not match this grand vision. As we will see in the books of Haggai and Zechariah, there is a long delay in beginning the work of rebuilding the Jerusalem temple. When, with the assistance of Emperor Darius of Persia, a new temple is finally built in 515, it is only a fraction of the size of Solomon's temple and certainly not as beautifully decorated. While it is uncertain to what extent Ezekiel's glorious vision and the actual character and dimensions of the Second Temple were a disappointment to the people, only in Herod's time (ca. 30) will the magnificence of the Jerusalem temple approach Ezekiel's blueprint. But even that grand edifice is intended to reflect Herod's political connections with Rome, not Ezekiel's vision.

A sign that problems continue for the postexilic community can be found in the reforms instituted by Ezra and Nehemiah in the late Persian period (ca. 450–400). These Persian-appointed leaders found it necessary to issue strict orders on the organization of the temple personnel and their responsibilities (Neh. 12:44–47), took measures to ensure respect for **sabbath** regulations (13:15–22), and denounced the practice of mixed marriage (Ezra 9:1–4; Neh. 13:23–31). As we will see in the discussion of postexilic prophecy, the exilic experience will forever influence the people, but they will also find themselves at a crossroads as a community. Do they return to Jerusalem and Judah to rebuild the nation there, or do they take the advice of Jeremiah (Jer. 29:4–7) and make their life and worship their God in the lands where they have been resettled?

14

Postexilic Prophecy

Isaiah of the Exile (Isa. 40–55)

In chapter 9, on Isaiah of Jerusalem, I noted that the book of Isaiah generally is divided into three separate sections that reflect at least three separate time periods. Isaiah 1–39 is usually attributed to Isaiah of Jerusalem (ca. 740–697), whose message was discussed in connection with the prophets of the eighth century. In this chapter on postexilic prophecy, I will discuss the other two sections: Isa. 40–55, which prepares the exiles for return to the land (ca. 539–535), and Isa. 56–66, which reflects the years after the temple is rebuilt in Jerusalem (515–500).

Isaiah 40–55 is often referred to as Second Isaiah. This section of the book probably represents the work of a school of Israelite priests or scholars dedicated to the ideas espoused by Isaiah of Jerusalem. It would have been their task to carry their knowledge of the great eighth-century prophet with them into the exile and to preserve them for the community as a whole. The message found in Isa. 40 provides the key indicator that the author(s) is speaking to an audience distant in time from that of Isaiah of Jerusalem. It begins with a call to speak words of "comfort" to God's people because they have now "served their term" (40:1–2; 51:3), a message that clearly was not in the repertoire of First Isaiah, who had to shock the people of his time with God's harsh judgment in the face of Assyrian aggression and Israelite unfaithfulness.

The social and historical context of Second Isaiah is based on a later time (ca. 539), probably shortly after Babylon is captured by King Cyrus of Persia.

With that change in political control the opportunity now arises for the exiles to be released from their captivity and, if they wish, to return to their own land. It is therefore the primary task of Second Isaiah to accomplish two things: (1) voice a **theodicy** of the exile by explaining that the exilic experience has been necessary as a crucible of purification and that it occurred because of the people's unfaithfulness and God's judgment, and (2) encourage the people to begin making preparations for their return to Judah and Jerusalem and the restoration of the community in the Promised Land.

The most spectacular aspect of this change in fortunes, according to Second Isaiah, is that God now intends to restore a people who are known to have been vanquished and exiled. Such a miraculous accomplishment can be engineered only by God, and it is a piece of news that deserves to be shouted from Mount Zion to all "the cities of Judah" (40:9). Previously, defeat and exile would have been taken as undisputable proof that the God of Israel is a failure, a deity no longer worthy of any people's worship. It would not be surprising to find that many among the exilic community had become disillusioned with **Yahweh** and chose to assimilate into Babylonian society and transfer their allegiance and worship to the gods of Mesopotamia. Now, however, by freeing the exiles from their Babylonian captivity just as the God of their ancestors had freed them from their captivity in Egypt, Yahweh has proved once again to the Israelites and to "all flesh" that there is no God but Yahweh. This "new thing," once again making "a way in the wilderness" for a defeated people, is something that has never been accomplished by any other god (43:19). This mighty act marks Yahweh as supreme and the only true God. It also will become the basis, at last, for the formation of a monotheistic belief by the Jews. They will then accept Yahweh's declaration that "I am the LORD, and there is no other" (45:5).

Cyrus the Anointed

Historically speaking, the physical instrument of liberation for the exiles is King Cyrus of Persia. He began his rule in 550 by consolidating his authority over Persia and Media, to the east of the Tigris River. Over the next ten years, he systematically conquered and pacified the northern and western portions of the Chaldean Empire. By 542 Cyrus is preparing to take on Babylon, the final bastion of Neo-Babylonian power. He is aided in this by the dissatisfaction of the Marduk priesthood in Babylon. Nabonidus, Nebuchadnezzar's successor, had deemphasized Marduk's worship in the capital city, refusing to participate in the New Year festival staged by the Marduk priests and elevating his own patron deity, the moon god Sin, to the position of supreme god of the empire. Nabonidus had also been absent from the capital city a great deal of the time in an effort to protect trade routes in the areas south of Babylon, especially around the Arabian city of Teima. This provided ample cause for complaint and unrest within the capital—a condition that was not controlled effectively by Nabonidus's son and coregent, Belshazzar.

To provide legitimacy for his conquest of Babylon, a document that is a blatant piece of propaganda is prepared by Cyrus's administration. Designed to justify the capture of the city and the removal of Nabonidus, like many other royal documents it is shaped around a set of statements identified as theodicy. Very much like the accusations made by the Assyrian ambassador Rabshakeh during the siege of Jerusalem in 701, the argument is made that current events have been precipitated by an angry god, who has sent an avenging army against his own city and people in order to restore the proper order of the universe:

> Marduk, the ruler of the **divine assembly**, heard the people of Babylon when they cried out and became angry. . . . Marduk searched all the lands for a righteous ruler to lead the *akitu* New Year procession. He chose Cyrus, the ruler of Anshan. Marduk called him by his name and made him ruler of all the earth. Because Marduk . . . was pleased with Cyrus's good deeds and upright heart, he ordered him to march against Babylon. ("Decree of Cyrus," *OTPar* 208)

> But if you say to me, "We rely on the LORD our God," is it not he whose **high places** and altars Hezekiah has removed, saying to Judah and to Jerusalem, "You shall worship before this altar"? . . . Moreover, is it without the LORD that I have come up against this land to destroy it? The LORD said to me, "Go up against this land and destroy it." (Isa. 36:7, 10)

Like Rabshakeh's speech, Cyrus's victory decree is a piece of political gamesmanship and thus must be read carefully. By referring to Nabonidus's crimes against the god Marduk and the god's eventual decision to seek out a champion to liberate his people, Cyrus is claiming that he is not acting on his own volition but at the command of the Babylonian god. Therefore Cyrus's army is given permission by the wrathful god to travel unmolested through the countryside. In fact, when Cyrus reaches Babylon, the priests of Marduk apparently open the city's gates so that he can take it with only a minimum of fighting.

It is not surprising, then, that as the Persian army approached Babylon, discredited leaders and captive peoples, such as the Israelites, were quick to welcome Cyrus as their savior. Second Isaiah does this by taking the extraordinary step of applying the title "anointed one" (Hebrew *mashiyah*, from whence the English word **messiah** comes) to this Persian king. Naturally, he is careful to replace the role played by the Babylonian god Marduk with Yahweh:

> Thus says the LORD to his anointed, to Cyrus,
>   whose right hand I have grasped
> to subdue nations before him
>   and strip kings of their robes,

> to open doors before him—
>   and the gates shall not be closed. . . .
> So that you may know that it is I, the LORD,
>   the God of Israel, who call you by your name.
> For the sake of my servant Jacob,
>   and Israel my chosen,
> I call you by your name,
>   I surname you, though you do not know me.
> I am the LORD, and there is no other;
>   besides me there is no god. (Isa. 45:1–5)

The two documents are close parallels. Both Marduk and Yahweh provide a justification for the decision to bring down the rulers of Babylon. In both cases they name Cyrus as their champion and identify him as a person they each consider worthy of their favor. Cyrus is given the title "shepherd" in each document (Isa. 44:28a). Each proclamation includes a statement that Cyrus has been given the victory by "opening doors"—a physical reality, since the priests of Marduk are said to have opened Babylon's gates (43:14). Finally, each document contains a promise that the destroyed temples of the captive peoples' gods will be restored and that these people will be allowed once again to worship their local deities (44:28b).

The statement in Second Isaiah may have been written after Cyrus had already taken the city and issued his victory decree. Such an action would have been typical of persons or groups attempting to gain favor with the new ruler and his administration. Certainly, Isaiah's familiarity with the details of the decree and its language suggests at least an adaptation of its text. Moreover, his use of the term "anointed" and his recital of Cyrus's easy victory would have been pleasing to the Persians. Still, the insistence that Yahweh had chosen Cyrus even though the king did not know Yahweh (45:4–5) stands in contrast with the statement that Marduk had sought out a ruler who would keep Marduk's religious festivals and honor him as the chief god of Babylon. It also raises some question about whether the Persian ruler ever heard or received a copy of this flattering document. It is more likely that the only real audience for Second Isaiah's rendition of events is the exilic community. Just as the Assyrian and Babylonian armies had once served as God's tool to punish Israel (42:24–25), now Cyrus and the Persians function as Yahweh's means of freeing the exiles.

Most important to Second Isaiah is the claim that Yahweh alone is responsible for Cyrus's victory. No other god helped Yahweh, the creator of the earth and humankind (45:12), for Yahweh alone is the only extant divine being: "There is no god besides him" (45:14). The idols that Cyrus so magnanimously liberated are simply objects venerated by other peoples, but it is the God of Israel who has taken steps to save the people in the name of the **covenant** (45:16–17). In this way, the anonymous author (or authors) of Isa.

40–55 is able to assure his own people that the god responsible for Cyrus's great victory and their liberation is Yahweh, not Marduk.

It does not matter to this prophetic voice that Cyrus is unaware of Yahweh's actions. All that really matters is that the exiles are made aware that God has once again chosen a tool to effect historical events (compare 10:5). What is distinctive about this narrative is the use of the title "anointed" for Cyrus. No other non-Israelite ruler is given this honor, and it stands as a testament to the importance placed on this event—a new release from bondage, a new exodus. While Cyrus will not become a new Moses figure, his political stature as ruler of what will become during the reigns of his successors the largest empire in the ancient Near East up to that time underscores the prophet's claim of Yahweh's universal authority. Quite simply, Cyrus's rise to power is God's means of letting all nations know, "from the rising of the sun and from the west, that there is no one besides me; I am the LORD, and there is no other" (45:6).

The Servant Songs

In Second Isaiah, four "servant songs" develop an extended theodicy of the exile (42:1–4; 49:1–6; 50:4–9; 52:13–53:12). The identification of the servant has been a problem for scholars. In some passages, such as 49:3, Israel is clearly identified as the servant. In other cases, such as 53:2–5, the suffering servant appears to be an individual, perhaps the prophet himself. My position is that the servant represents Israel, and in particular the exilic community. It is their experience during the exile that purifies them and makes them worthy to return to the land of the covenant.

Given the length of the exile (598–539), it is necessary for this voice of Isaiah to make an argument why the people should resume their allegiance to Yahweh and return to their homeland. Because a viable community still faithful to the covenant has been maintained in the exile, the issue now arises why they should listen to the call to return. In addition, some justification is necessary that speaks to the purpose for the dislocation and pain caused by the exile. Therefore it is not surprising that Second Isaiah repeatedly uses allusions to God's purpose and saving character that closely parallel events found in the exodus narrative:

- Red Sea crossing (Exod. 14:21–29):
    "When you pass through the waters, I will be with you." (Isa. 43:2)
    "Who makes a way in the sea, . . . who brings out chariot and horse, army and warrior." (Isa. 43:16–17)
    "By my rebuke I dry up the sea." (Isa. 50:2)
    "Was it not you who dried up the sea, . . . who made the depths of the sea a way for the redeemed to cross over?" (Isa. 51:10)

- wilderness resources (Exod. 17):

  "They did not thirst when he led them through the deserts; he made water flow from the rock." (Isa. 48:21)

  "They shall not hunger or thirst, . . . for he who has pity on them will lead them, and by springs of water will guide them." (Isa. 49:10)

The point is that just as the people were tested during their bondage in Egypt and then purified in the wilderness prior to the conquest of the land, the exiles have been purified in Mesopotamia and will be led by God back to the Promised Land. Now that Jerusalem's "penalty is paid" (40:2), the exiles are free to return to their beloved city (49:14–18; Ps. 137:5–6).

Still, some were taken into exile, and some remained behind. What sense could God or the prophet make of this division? Why did the people have to suffer in this way? The answer comes in a classic theodicy, explaining that the exile was made necessary by the sin of the people who violated the covenant with Yahweh (Isa. 43:22–24): "Was it not the Lord, against whom we have sinned?" and is it not therefore the Lord who "poured upon him [the nation] the heat of his anger" (42:24–25)? Thus the pain and suffering associated with their exile coincides with Yahweh's justice (43:25–28), and the suffering of God's servant Israel (48:10; 49:3–4) expiates that sin for the sake of God's "name" and "glory" (48:11). Now, however, that time of suffering is past, and God will transform a wilderness into a gloriously restored land that will be "like Eden . . . the garden of the Lord" (51:3).

With the end of the exile also comes a new purpose for the servant. God will use this opportunity and saving act to make it known that the "former things" no longer have any hold on Israel and that God intends to perform a "new thing" (42:9) so that the nation will "sing to the Lord a new song" of praise to the ends of the earth (42:10). The exiles are reassured that suffering for the sins of the nation (53:3–6) is now at an end, and the servant, despite his marred appearance, will triumph and astonish kings and nations by returning to the Promised Land (52:14–15). The prophet assures the people that, as Yahweh's servant, their faith will be vindicated, and they will not be put to shame for their belief in their God (50:7–11).

In rejoicing over the triumph of Yahweh, the servant is given a new, even more important mission. It is not enough that Yahweh's power is demonstrated by the return of the people from exile. They must now become "a light to the nations" (42:6) to serve as "witnesses" to the Lord's majesty (43:10) and to spread the news of Yahweh's power, requiring the obeisance of kings and rulers (49:6–7). While this may be a reference to **universalism** and a further strengthening of the emerging concept of monotheism, Judaism will not become an evangelistic religion. Conversion or proselytizing has never been one of its tenets, and it is unlikely that this is the message of the prophet here. Their task is to serve as the proof of God's power so that "all flesh shall know that

I am the LORD your Savior, and your Redeemer, the Mighty One of Jacob" (49:26). Their mission is to demonstrate Yahweh's power above that of all other gods, not the enlightenment and conversion of the world's peoples to Judaism.

Predictive Prophecy

One of the most difficult issues in dealing with Isaiah and other prophets is to determine whether their prophecies were intended to predict future events, including those in the New Testament. The problem is especially acute in our treatment of the servant songs, because New Testament writers and many Christian interpreters read 53:1–9 as a prediction of Jesus's suffering and his role as redemptive savior (e.g., Matt. 8:17; 26:63; John 12:38; Heb. 9:28; 1 Pet. 2:24). Isaiah 53 is, however, extremely ambiguous in its description of the servant's suffering. While parallels can be drawn between the suffering of Jesus on the cross and the suffering of the servant, the servant songs in Isaiah do not name names or specify when this redemptive suffering is to take place. Quite likely, the servant was understood to have suffered while living in exile. But the indeterminate nature of this person or group known as the servant allows for multiple interpretations of these passages, and so it is not inappropriate for Christian writers to reinterpret the passages in light of Jesus's suffering and redemptive act. This is not, however, the only possible interpretation of the servant songs.

Another proof given for the validity of predictive prophecy is found in Hosea 11:1: "Out of Egypt I called my son." Careful study of the context shows that the prophet was once again retelling the story of early Israel and its **apostasy**. The theme of God's saving act bringing the Israelites "up from the land of Egypt" is similarly developed in many of the prophets (e.g., Jer. 2:6–7; 32:21–23; Ezek. 20:9–10; Amos 2:10; 9:7; Mic. 6:4). Yet Matt. 2:13–15 cites Hosea 11:1 as a prophecy fulfilled by Jesus's birth and sojourn in Egypt when his family was forced to flee from Herod's murderous intentions. This use of Hosea, and of Jer. 31:15 in Matt. 2:17–18, lends authority to his account and draws attention to God's ability to preserve his "son" (Jesus in Matt. 2 and the nation in Hosea) and provide comfort in dangerous times.

Interpretative use of Old Testament/Hebrew Bible prophetic speech by the New Testament writers is legitimate, but it must be recognized as an emic argument made to insiders. It was designed to reinforce the faith of the early Jewish Christian community and followed the pattern of discourse, common to that time, of citing ancient sources as proof texts to demonstrate to their audience that current events are the fulfillment of the prophet's message. The people of ancient Israel believed in a cyclic universe in which similar events continually recurred. Thus it was plausible that Hosea could speak of Israel's origins in the exodus event while at the same time later interpreters could quite legitimately use the prophet's words to bolster their claims about Jesus.

These insider arguments are quite satisfactory proof for members of the insider group. It is too much, however, to expect that modern etic observers, who are by definition outsiders to these texts and this ancient community, would find them completely convincing. In fact, outsiders are very likely to read the passage in question in light of their own interests and come up with an entirely different interpretation. Such a tendency is illustrated by Cyrus's and Isaiah's divergent interpretations of the fall of Babylon. For Cyrus, the fall of Babylon was a sign of Marduk's favor, while for Isaiah it was a sign that Yahweh had appointed Cyrus to free the Jews from their captivity. Babylon's fall serves the purposes of both Cyrus and Isaiah, but then what matters to their respective communities is to give credit to their own deity.

In a similar manner, the New Testament writers used the body of prophetic materials from the Old Testament/Hebrew Bible to make the case for their newly established religion and to reinforce and authenticate ancient prophetic statements that they felt provided ties to events in Jesus's life and ministry (e.g., Matt. 21:5 quotes Zech. 9:9 as part of the story of Jesus's triumphant entry into Jerusalem). Both practices are valid, but they must be seen for what they are. For our purposes in studying these texts, outsiders must make an effort to understand the position and social setting of insiders—to develop an appreciation for the positions of others while continuing to value their own conclusions. Ultimately, this respect of each side for the other is the basis for peace and harmony in a pluralistic society.

Response to the Call to Return

Despite Second Isaiah's rallying cry for the exiles to return to Zion, the question that stuck in the minds of most of them was, why should we leave all that we have created here and go back to Judah? During the seventy years of the exile, they had followed Jeremiah's advice (Jer. 29:5–6) by starting businesses, purchasing land, and establishing their families in a new country. If they chose to return to their homeland now, they could expect to start over in a place where large sections of land had lain uncultivated for generations. It would have taken hardy persons with a strong vested interest or those of real religious conviction or adventure to make the decision to go back. As it was, the majority chose not to leave. But in a series of waves starting about 535 (Ezra 1) and over a period of nearly one hundred years, perhaps 15 percent of the exiled community returned to Judah.

Who would choose to return from exile? There were four main types: (1) political appointees of the Persian government whose job it was to rebuild this area into a taxpaying province (Zerubbabel, Nehemiah, and Ezra); (2) persons with a stake in a restored temple and the higher status associated with the cult community (priests and their families could expect to play a major role in the revitalized nation, especially since there would be no restoration of the monarchy, but note the difficulties Ezra had recruiting Levites in Ezra 8:15–20); (3) speculators and opportunists who saw this as a land rush in which they could claim large tracts of land and make a fortune (among this group would have been younger sons who could not inherit family property in Mesopotamia and who saw the return as their chance for economic independence); and (4) those who saw the return as their religious duty to Yahweh and the covenant (like Isaiah, they envisioned a glorious procession, proclaiming the glory of God from the heights of Zion; Isa. 40:3–4, 9–11).

What these people discovered when they arrived must have shocked them. Jerusalem was not only in ruins after Nebuchadnezzar's systematic destruction (2 Kings 25:8–10), it was also overgrown after fifty years of neglect. Recent **archaeological** surveys have demonstrated that the land of Judah was not totally depopulated after the Babylonian conquest in 587. It would not have been in the economic interests of either the Babylonians or the Persians to totally depopulate the land of Judah (25:12). This region had value as a reliable buffer zone on the border with Egyptian territory as long as its people were not in rebellion. Therefore it is more likely that the leaders were taken away, while a few of the merchant class and small landowners would remain behind to pay taxes, feed the people, and maintain a presence in the land so that it would not become an uncultivated wilderness.

Still, the remaining inhabitants would have been hard pressed to continue to work all the fields that had once been cultivated. As a result, large tracts of once profitable farmland must have been allowed to lie fallow. The lack of enough hands to function as an effective labor force would have meant that in some areas of the country the carefully constructed terraced hillsides would have simply crumbled or eroded away.

Another factor to contend with was Samaritans—descendants of peoples brought to the former northern kingdom of Israel by the Assyrians (2 Kings 17:24–28) and Israelites who were not dispersed in the Assyrian Empire after 721. The Babylonians had not deported them when Judah was conquered, and they continued as an identifiable people in the Persian period. It is likely that until the return of the exiles from Babylon the Samaritans claimed political control over the entire area of what had been Israel and Judah. They were not pleased to see these returnees with their claims to land and political independence from the Samaritan governor's rule (the conflicts are described in Neh. 4:1–9; 6:1–14). In addition, the planned efforts to rebuild the Jerusalem temple would have come into conflict with the Samaritans' claim that the true altar of Yahweh should be situated on Mount Gerizim near Shechem (see the Elephantine Papyri, in A. Crowley, *Aramaic Papyri of the Fifth Century B.C.* [Oxford: Oxford University Press, 1923], #30).

Faced with a complex political situation and the need to quickly establish themselves in the land, the returned exiles focused on the immediate needs of resettlement and devoted their energies to building housing for their families, restoring and planting fields and terraces, and managing water resources. This not only occupied their time but also exhausted the funds that the Persian government had provided to rebuild their temple. As a result, only the foundation was completed during the first twenty years after the return of the exiles (Ezra 3:8–11).

The Books of Haggai and Zechariah 1–8

Frustrated with what had become a twenty-year delay in completing more than a foundation for the new temple, the prophets Haggai and Zechariah (only Zech. 1–8) began to exhort the people to resume work. These prophets were active during a three-month period of the second year of the reign of King Darius of Persia (518). Both seem unconcerned with the political realities of the time or the financial difficulties the people face to complete the construction process. For them, all that matters is that the temple be restored, because until that happens the covenant with Yahweh and the elements of the sacrificial cult cannot be fully restored.

Haggai

Haggai challenges the people's assertion that "the time has not yet come to rebuild the LORD's house" (1:2). He rebukes them for instead making time to build their own "paneled houses" while the Lord lacks a house (1:4). He reasons with his audience by making a direct connection between the effects of a drought and the subsequent crop failures and Yahweh's displeasure at the failure of the people to complete this task (1:9–11). Haggai's harangue includes a sequenced structure in which the people are repeatedly asked to "consider how you have fared" (1:5, 7). By pounding them over the head with the physical reality of their situation, the prophet hopes that they will wake up and reassess their priorities.

His message follows a pattern set by previous biblical writers (Deut. 28:20–24) and prophets who proclaimed that famine, war, and natural disaster were signs of God's wrath (e.g., Hosea 2:8–9; Amos 4:6–11; Mic. 6:9–16). One particularly poignant example of this prophetic pattern is found in Jer. 14:1–12. The prophet first records a **lament** in which the people call on God for help during a drought and the suffering that it has caused them. However, they do not receive the answer that they desire. Instead, like in Haggai, they are told that because they have continually "wandered" into idolatry and disobedience, "I do not hear their cry" (Jer. 14:10–12). And, in fact, Jeremiah is commanded not to pray for these people, for God has determined to no longer hear their pleas or accept their sacrificial offerings.

Haggai's efforts are designed to get the leaders and people to recommit to building the Lord's temple and to recognize who they are and how they had been able to return to Jerusalem. In order to accomplish this goal, he uses a phrase based on the social identity created for the community of returned exiles in **Yehud** and Jerusalem. He refers to them as "the **remnant** of the people" (Hag. 1:14; 2:2). This designation echoes Second Isaiah's reference to the exiles in Mesopotamia as "the remnant of the house of Israel," whom God has "borne" throughout their lives and whom he "will carry and will save" as they approach the opportunity to return to Jerusalem (Isa. 46:3–4). Similar terminology is found in Ezra's prayer (Ezra 9:8–15), where he refers to his assembled audience as "a remnant."

Each of these references is designed to remind the exiles and the returnees that they are the remnant, who has experienced dislocation and the purification of the exile. By that experience they are forever separate from "the people of the land," who had not gone into the exile (2 Kings 25:12; Ezra 4:4), and from any of the other peoples who had settled in the land while they had been in exile. This social label singles them out as worthy to take part in the building of the temple. All others who have been "adversaries of Judah and Benjamin" are to be rebuffed, just as they are by Zerubbabel and Jeshua in Ezra 4:1–3. Haggai, in this way, plays on the pride of the returnees, but also stirs up ethnic hatreds between Jews and Samaritans that will linger for centuries (Luke 9:51–56; John 4:9).

In addition to his general address to the people of Jerusalem, Haggai also engages in a separate effort to convince the leadership that the restoration of the Jerusalem temple is essential. Haggai calls on Zerubbabel—the Persian-appointed governor of the province of Yehud—to resume the interrupted construction project (Ezra 5:1–2). If Zerubbabel was actually a descendant, even possibly a grandson of the last Davidic king, Jehoiachin (1 Chron. 3:19), then Haggai's gambit would have also included a call to take on the mantle of Davidic kingship and, with courage in Yahweh's support, make a decision to help all the people. An indication that the prophet is making this connection is found when he calls Zerubbabel Yahweh's "signet ring" (Hag. 2:23; compare Jer. 22:24). Because signet rings were used to stamp and certify official documents, this title when applied to Zerubbabel indicates his legitimacy and his right to exercise the power of the office once held by David.

Given the political situation at the time, Haggai's efforts in this instance were probably unrealistic. Since Zerubbabel is an appointed governor he is in a tenuous position even if he is a true heir to the house of David. Should he accept the prophet's challenge to "take courage" and trust in the "abiding spirit of God" (Hag. 2:4–5), he would quickly find himself acting without explicit instructions from the Persian government. In that case, it is likely that he would have found himself quickly out of a job, and the province would once again be invaded by a hostile army. Of course, Haggai's attempt to influence Zerubbabel follows a tradition of prophetic confrontation similar to that employed by Isaiah when he confronted King Ahaz (Isa. 7:3–25). The real prophetic message, in both cases, is for the ruler to trust that God will provide what the people need in times of crisis. In Haggai's case, the promise for those who "do not fear" and are willing to trust in God is that "the treasure of all nations" is enough to "fill this house with splendor" (Hag. 2:6–7).

Zechariah's Parallel Efforts

Perhaps because Haggai's words bore no fruit, his contemporary, the prophet Zechariah, shifts his efforts to try to influence the high priest, Joshua (Jeshua). Zechariah employs a series of eight night visions, each of which includes a vision, question, and response. These interrelated visions present the prophet's concept of the universe as Yahweh's personal domain within which all the nations are given the opportunity to rule the earth. A major feature of the visions is the appearance of an angelic guide, who interprets the various symbolic images shown to the prophet. This element is a characteristic found in later **apocalyptic** literature, which is designed to move the prophetic figure into the background and place God's power and message in a more complicated and mysterious light (Dan. 7–12; Zech. 9–14). In Zechariah's visions, Yahweh promises that prosperity will return and Zion/Jerusalem will be comforted when the temple is rebuilt (1:16–17; 8:1–3). Even more comforting is the promise that God will once again dwell among the chosen people in the "holy land" (2:12; compare Joel 3:17–18). This is the only reference in the Hebrew **canon** to Judah as the "holy land."

In his fourth vision, Zechariah describes the high priest Joshua "standing before the angel of the LORD, and Satan standing at his right hand to accuse him" (Zech. 3:1). The term "satan" (Hebrew for "adversary") refers to an angelic being in Yahweh's heavenly court (compare 1 Kings 22:19). Like the satan character who appears in the book of Job (1:6–12; 2:1–7), this angel's function is to bring human sins to God's attention. We may think of him therefore as God's prosecuting attorney rather than as an adversary with powers or volition of his own. On a literary level, the satan character is a foil charged with the task of revealing a clue or setting up a puzzle that the more dominant character (God in this case) in the scene will solve.

The sins brought to God's attention are graphically represented by Joshua's filthy priestly robes, which signify the sins of the people and the priesthood (compare pristine priestly vestments in Ezek. 44:17–19). These soiled linen garments raise questions about the worthiness of the Jerusalem priesthood (compare Jer. 13:1–11). Instead of punishing these sins, Yahweh orders that Joshua be given a new, clean set of clothes and a fresh turban (Zech. 3:3–5; compare Isa. 1:18–20). This command plays on the exilic theme in Second Isaiah (51:9–11) that it is Yahweh's decision to restore the exiles. Their release is based not on human actions, but only on divine mercy (compare Ezek. 36:22–32). Of course, the injunction is predicated on their obedience to the

The Branch

A shoot shall come out from the stump of Jesse,
and a branch shall grow out of his roots. (Isa. 11:1)

The days are surely coming, says the LORD, when I will raise up for David a righteous Branch, and he shall reign as king and deal wisely. (Jer. 23:5)

In those days and at that time I will cause a righteous Branch to spring up for David; and he shall execute justice and righteousness in the land. (Jer. 33:15)

covenant. If they wish to ensure God's continued blessings, they must remain clean, functioning according to God's statutes. Only in this way can they ensure both Joshua's place as high priest and the priestly community's role in administering the temple and the courts (Zech. 3:6–7).

At this point, Zechariah draws on the traditions associated with the house of David and the concept of a messianic figure (3:8). He states that God will "bring my servant the Branch" to restore the temple and the nation under Yahweh's guidance. Comparable use of the image in Isa. 4:2 and 11:1 refers to ideal Davidic rulers. In Zechariah, the Branch will usher in an era of restoration and justice that will also include the return of Yahweh to Zion (Zech. 8:2–3) and an ingathering of people from all nations "to seek the LORD of hosts" (8:21).

Zerubbabel appears not to have accepted either the title "signet ring" or "Branch." Possibly he feared political repercussions from the Persian government. This decision would explain the change of reference in Zechariah's second use of "Branch" in 6:9–15. This passage, once referring to Zerubbabel, has apparently been changed, and the title is now bestowed on Joshua (6:11).

Despite the concerted urging of these prophets, Zerubbabel does not act to rebuild the Jerusalem temple until he receives additional funds and a political confirmation from Darius's imperial court. Part of the delay in construction had been opposition from the "people of the land" (persons not taken in exile) and the Samaritan leaders. They had attempted to stall any further efforts by playing on the somewhat unsettled political situation that followed Darius's swift accession to the Persian throne in 520 (Ezra 4:1–6; 5:1–17). Once internal impediments to his full authority over the government and the army had been removed through bureaucratic and diplomatic means, Darius was more open to dealing with the problems of his local administrators. Persian clerks were instructed to institute a search of the royal archives. Their efforts produced a copy of Cyrus's original decree (6:1–5). This document gave the king the justification needed for issuing additional funding and ordering that construction be resumed despite the protests of Tattenai, a regional governor who had questioned the

Jews' right to rebuild their temple (5:3–10). Although the Second Temple was in no way as grand as the one envisioned in Ezek. 40–48, its completion in 515 (Ezra 6:13–15) allowed the resumption of priestly sacrificial offices and the creation of a religious focal point for the returned community in Yehud.

Isaiah of the Return (Isa. 56–66)

The third section of Isaiah, Isa. 56–66, reflects the social and religious controversies of the period after 515. While it is conceivable that the same person or group responsible for the creation of Isa. 40–55 composed these chapters as well, this is not certain. For the sake of convenience, this section of Isaiah will be called Third Isaiah, and the issues it raises will be examined in the light of its own social context in the period after the construction of the Second Temple.

Third Isaiah and the Prophetic Tradition

The anonymous prophetic voice of Isa. 56–66 links itself with earlier prophets by asserting that "the spirit of the Lord GOD is upon me, because the LORD has anointed me . . . to bring good news to the oppressed, . . . to proclaim liberty to the captives, . . . to proclaim the year of the LORD's favor, . . . to comfort all who mourn" (61:1–2). There are many connections between Third and Second Isaiah, including similar vocabulary and themes. Both of these Isaian prophetic voices set aside "former things" (43:18; 65:16–17) and look to the eventual fulfillment of "new things" that are to come with God's help (42:9; 65:17; 66:22). The return of the exiles prophesied so enthusiastically in 40:1–11 (compare 49:8–13) is envisioned in Third Isaiah in terms of a restored Zion (62:10–12), whose light shines so brightly that nations and kings shall be drawn to it (60:1–3). Furthermore, Second Isaiah's servant image (43:5–13) is transformed in Third Isaiah into the righteous remnant that has returned to the land (60:21–22).

Another familiar theme presented in Third Isaiah that ties this prophetic voice to its own social context and also links it to the stream of prophetic oracles in the past is the refrain of God's judgment on Edom. Once again that neighboring kingdom is condemned for its participation in Jerusalem's destruction (63:1–6; compare Obadiah). Inclusion of this oracle again provides assurance of God's role as judge of the earth and points to the resumption of problems and enmity between Yehud and its Transjordanian neighbor on border issues, trade routes, and occasional military incursions.

Yet another of First Isaiah's themes is reiterated in Third Isaiah's vision of a purified creation centered on Zion and Jerusalem (Isa. 65:17–25), including the transformation of the earth into a new Eden-like world in which the wolf, lamb, and lion may dwell in peace. This functions as the ultimate expression of proper covenant relationship:

> The wolf shall live with the lamb,
>   the leopard shall lie down with the kid,
> the calf and the lion and the fatling together,
>   and the little child shall lead them. (11:6)

> The wolf and the lamb shall feed together,
>   the lion shall eat straw like the ox. . . .
> They shall not hurt or destroy
>   on all my holy mountain,
>   says the LORD. (65:25)

However, the "new age" that Second Isaiah had portrayed in his vision has been delayed by the social and cultic abuses that emerged in the newly established province of Yehud. Third Isaiah speaks of these problems using terms like "blind" (i.e., slumbering) "sentinels," "silent dogs that cannot bark," greedy shepherds without understanding, and leaders filled with wine and with no concern for tomorrow (56:9–12; compare 29:9; Nah. 3:18). These complaints are combined with the familiar charges of false or hollow worship (Isa. 58:13; 66:1–4, 17) and social injustice (59:1–8) found in earlier prophetic messages (Amos 4:4–5; 5:21–24; Jer. 6:16–20; Isa. 1:12–15).

With a resumption of the problems previously tied to God's judgment of the preexilic community, Third Isaiah provides a guide for proper behavior centered on what God truly expects from his people (Isa. 58; compare 66:2; Mic. 6:6–8). He points to fasting as a source of contention rather than a sign of religious piety and contrition (Isa. 58:3–4). The practice can have no real value because it is performed to "serve your own interest" (58:3; compare Zech. 7:1–7). What God actually requires is for the people "to loose the bonds of injustice, . . . to let the oppressed go free, . . . to share your bread with the hungry, and bring the homeless poor into your house" (Isa. 58:6–7). This statement is another example of the often repeated demand (Mic. 6:6–8; Jas. 1:27) that God sanctions only those rituals that come from a humble and contrite spirit, not personal acclaim or thoughts of gain.

Third Isaiah and the Second Temple

The period after the return from exile was one of readjustment and a striving for normalcy. The fierce desire of prophets such as Haggai and Zechariah to see the temple restored was a way to refocus the people's attention on the former modes of living in Jerusalem and the covenant they had made with Yahweh. Simply building a new temple, however, did not eliminate the abuses of power and excesses of exclusivism that are a part of any institution and its leadership (Isa. 59:9–11). Thus Third Isaiah finds it necessary to call the people to remember the simplicity of their covenant agreement and to make their community more inclusive.

With the restoration of the temple in 515, the people of the province of Yehud once again had a national shrine that gave tangible proof of the majesty of the God who had released them from exile. The temple became a focal point of religious identity and sparked a renaissance of priestly activity and regulation. The reconstruction of the temple and the reestablishment of cultic worship, however, created some new social and religious conflicts. With the restoration of the priestly community to serve in the temple complex (Ezra 6:16–18) came restrictions on who would be allowed to enter the temple and who had the authority to make use of its facilities and tithes. Also in place during the First Temple period, these priestly prerogatives reflect the typical purpose and design of temples.

Every facet of a temple's architecture is designed to create increasingly more restricted zones of sacred activity. In this way the hierarchy of the priesthood justified their prerogatives as the sole protectors and officiants within the temple complex. By restricting access they controlled the number of worshipers (all of them male) who could enter its gates. Further restrictions were added to create strict boundaries within the temple and designate sections into which only the priests could enter. Finally, only a select few were allowed into its innermost chambers. In fact, just one person (the high priest) was allowed to enter the most sacred precinct of all within the temple, the holy of holies (Exod. 28:40–43; Lev. 16:2–5).

These rigid guidelines can be traced in the Second Temple period to competing challenges between the returning exiles and the "people of the land," descendants of the kingdoms of Judah and Israel who had never been deported (Ezra 4:1–5; 6:6–12). Eventually, a detailed set of criteria determined who was a Jew and what privileges one could enjoy, especially within the priesthood. These criteria were primarily based on kinship (2:59–63), but also included considerations of gender and physical infirmity (Deut. 23:1–2). These regulations seem to contain a more stringent policy than had existed in Solomon's Temple, when there would have been less concern about the dangers of cultural assimilation (23:3–8). However, the postexilic community was ruled by a foreign power (Persia), and thus the restored priesthood chose to exercise even stricter regulations over those sacred areas that it still effectively controlled.

One sign of the concern over these restrictions is found in Third Isaiah's discussion of the treatment of eunuchs and **proselytes** (converts). Restrictions had been placed on them, forbidding their entrance into the temple to offer sacrifices. In each case Third Isaiah asserts that the sole criterion for full membership in the covenant community, other than obedience to the law, is the celebration of the **sabbath** (Isa. 56:2–8). He reassures them that the "eunuchs who keep my sabbaths" shall have a place "in my house." Despite their physical inability to have children, God will grant them "a name better than sons and daughters." Foreigners "who keep the sabbath . . . and hold fast my covenant" will find joy on God's "holy mountain."

During the exile the sabbath had become a centerpiece of Jewish identity (see details in chapter 15 on Daniel). Its heightened importance to the exilic community is based on the sabbath rituals not requiring the presence of a temple or the ministrations of a priest. Although the restrictions on work associated with the sabbath were intended to honor God as the creator and to set the exiles aside from their neighbors, once the priestly community was reestablished in Jerusalem, this practice may not have been kept with the solemnity it required (Nehemiah's efforts to enforce sabbath keeping in Jerusalem are recorded in Neh. 10:31; 13:15–22). Thus Third Isaiah's emphasis on sabbath observance may be a call to return to proper respect for this commandment (Exod. 20:8–11). However, it is also tied to his call to the people to maintain justice and refrain "from doing any evil" within their community (Isa. 56:1–2). By proclaiming that no person, not even foreigners and eunuchs, should be excluded from entrance into the temple if they "keep [the] sabbaths . . . and hold fast my covenant" (56:3–6), the prophet is upholding the basic rights these powerless persons have to justice.

In addition, Third Isaiah's championing the rights of all sabbath-keepers reflects the prophet's concern over the growing separation created within the Jerusalem community. It had become common practice to label "those of Israelite descent" as superior to "all foreigners" and "the peoples of the lands" (Neh. 9:2; 10:28). Third Isaiah's more inclusive vision of those who will be gathered to God's holy mountain, to "my house of prayer" (Isa. 56:7), reminds us again that prophetic voices often represent minority viewpoints and that they do not always have a profound effect on those in control of events or institutions during their own time.

The Book of Zechariah 9–14

This last section of Zechariah appears to have been written by an unknown author and attached to Zechariah's name during the middle Persian period (ca. 500–425) by editors of the material. It consists of two oracles that contain many familiar prophetic elements:

- **oracles against the nations**, including Syria, Tyre, and the cities of Philistia (Zech. 9:1–8; compare Amos 1–2; Ezek. 25–32)
- the phrase "on that day" or the "day of the LORD" (compare Jer. 30:8; Hosea 1:5; Obad. 8; Zeph. 1:7–18): "On that day the LORD their God will save them for they are the flock of his people" (Zech. 9:16); "on that day the LORD shall shield the inhabitants of Jerusalem so that the feeblest among them on that day shall be like David, and the house of David shall be like God, like the angel of the LORD, at their head" (12:8)

- condemnation of false prophets (Zech. 13:3–6; compare Jer. 29:8–9; Ezek. 13:9): "And if any prophets appear again, their fathers and mothers who bore them will say to them, 'You shall not live, for you speak lies in the name of the LORD'" (Zech. 13:3)

Zechariah 9–14 also contains elements of apocalyptic style similar to that found in Dan. 7–12. Among these elements is the vision of the final victory of Yahweh over the earth: "And the LORD will become king over all the earth; on that day the LORD will be one and his name one" (Zech. 14:9).

Zechariah 9–11 is the first oracle in this section of the book. It is written primarily in poetic form and features a call to return to Jerusalem from exile (9:12; 10:6, 10–12; compare Isa. 40:2). It continues the theme of the establishment of a messianic era of peace, prosperity for Judah, return of the exiles, and establishment of a righteous ruler. This theme had first been developed in the visions of Zechariah where the high priest Joshua is proclaimed to be "the Branch" (Zech. 6:9–15), and that assures the remnant that nothing, even the restoration of Zion, is impossible for their God. In doing this mighty act, Yahweh ensures an ingathering of many people "to entreat the favor of the LORD" (8:21)—an ironic request that the Jews allow these foreigners to go with them because they "have heard that God is with [them]" (8:23). Now in 9:9–10 the prophetic voice reiterates the theme by calling out to Jerusalem to rejoice for "your king comes to you . . . and he shall command peace to the nations." And in 10:6–12 even the remnant of Israel (called **Ephraim**) will be returned to the land from all the places where they have been scattered.

This oracle in Zechariah may have been influenced by a similar oracle in Ezek. 11:14–21, which assures the exiles that they will return home and cleanse the land of all foreign influences and false worship practices:

> Return to the stronghold, O prisoners of hope;
>   today I declare that I will restore you double. (Zech. 9:12)

> Speak tenderly to Jerusalem,
>   and cry to her
> that she has served her term,
>   that her penalty is paid,
> that she has received from the LORD's hand
>   double for all her sins. (Isa. 40:2)

> I will gather you from the peoples, and assemble you out of the countries where you have been scattered, and I will give you the land of Israel. When they come there, they will remove from it all its detestable things and all its abominations. (Ezek. 11:17–18)

The vision also incorporates a militant image, as the people are transformed into Yahweh's bow and used against the Greeks (Zech. 9:13–14; contrast Hosea 1:5). This most likely alludes to the repeated Greek mercenary and allied presence in Syria-Palestine during the fifth century. Ezekiel's reference to the Greeks—using the geographical term "Javan" (Ezek. 27:13)—perhaps indicates that they had been involved in the politics of Syria-Palestine as early as the sixth century. In Zechariah's time, they were political allies of Egypt and trade rivals of the Persians. Zechariah would therefore see them as an enemy people to be condemned by Yahweh.

The militant tone continues in the vision of the prophet-shepherd, sheep merchants, and the breaking of the staffs that are given the names "Favor" and "Unity." The first key to this vision is found in Zech. 11:6–10, with its abdication of control over human actions. Initially world leaders are allowed the opportunity to exploit the people and engage in savage slaughter. These actions are sanctioned, symbolically, by the breaking of the first staff, annulling the covenant with the nations (compare Jer. 12:7). There is then an interlude involving the payment of thirty shekels of silver as wages to the prophet shepherd. This payment is a pittance so unacceptable that God calls on him to throw it back into the temple treasury (Zech. 11:12–13). This gesture and the breaking of the second staff are symbolic of the dissolution of any recognized political link between the kingdoms of Israel and Judah. It also sets the stage for God's command that a "worthless shepherd" be raised up, who will act in a manner completely foreign to that of the true shepherd (compare the "good shepherd" in Ezek. 34:11–16).

The false shepherd will not care for the flock or seek out the "wandering, or heal the maimed, or nourish the healthy" (Zech. 11:16; compare Ezek. 34:2–6). The task of this shepherd is to devour rather than guide, to literally strip the flesh from their bodies, "tearing off even their hoofs" (Zech. 11:16). At this point, the prophet cannot accept such an abomination, and he expresses his frustration in a **woe oracle**, cursing the "worthless shepherd" with the sword, a withered arm (compare 1 Kings 13:4), and blindness (Zech. 11:17). His cry in turn provides a transition to the second oracle, which is more **eschatological** in tone.

The second oracle (Zech. 12–14) is written in prose style and begins with a short prologue (12:1) that clearly sets this section off from the first oracle. By contrast with Zech. 9–11, which emphasized God's immediate act of aiding the returning exiles and the difficulties they had faced, this section contains oracles that begin with the phrase "on that day" and emphasize God's future action. It contains a mixture of military action, lamentation over the losses incurred during the fighting (12:7–11), and images of restoration in which God provides "living waters" to a wasted land (14:8).

Of particular interest is the restructuring of the cosmos after a long and devastating struggle in which Jerusalem as well as the foreign nations will experience great suffering. The oracle depicts a scenario similar to that of the Babylonian destruction of Jerusalem in 587. The magnitude of the crisis is especially apparent in Zechariah's declaration that Yahweh "will gather all the nations against Jerusalem" to ravage the city and its inhabitants (14:2; compare Jer. 21:4–6). At a point when it appears all is lost, God enters the fray along with the "holy ones" to participate in a cosmic battle against the enemy nations (compare Dan. 10). As a result of that divine intervention, peace and an idyllic world ruled by God will emerge (Zech. 14:6–9). The survivors of the great conflagration will at last gather in Jerusalem to worship Yahweh and to keep the Feast of Booths, celebrating Yahweh's rule and the restoration of the covenant (14:16–19). This apocalyptic vision reflects similar images in earlier prophetic messages that describe a time when all the nations will be brought to a full understanding of Yahweh's power:

> At that time Jerusalem shall be called the throne of the LORD, and all nations shall gather to it, to the presence of the LORD in Jerusalem, and they shall no longer stubbornly follow their own evil will. (Jer. 3:17)

> I will gather all the nations and bring them down to the valley of Jehoshaphat, and I will enter into judgment with them there, on account of my people and my heritage Israel, because they have scattered them among the nations. (Joel 3:2)

The Book of Malachi

Despite the book of Malachi being placed last in the prophetic corpus of both the Hebrew and Christian canon, it probably dates to the period between 500 and 450 and reflects the activities of the priestly community immediately after the reconstruction of the Jerusalem temple. Authorship is uncertain, since Malachi is not a personal name but simply means "my messenger," a reference perhaps to the promised messenger of God mentioned in 3:1.

The book consists of six oracles, each following a question-and-answer format or an instructional theme. This style of discourse is also found in Mic. 6:6–8 and, in more extended form, in the Egyptian "Dispute over Suicide" (*OTPar* 223–29) and the "Babylonian Theodicy" (*OTPar* 239–44).

> *Question:* You say, "How have we despised your name?"
> *Answer:* By offering polluted food on my altar. (Mal. 1:6–7)

> *Question:* Yet you say, "How have we wearied him [the LORD]?"
> *Answer:* By saying, "All who do evil are good in the sight of the LORD, and he delights in them." (Mal. 2:17)

Question: But you say, "How are we robbing you?"
Answer: In your tithes and offerings! (Mal. 3:8)

Five of the discourses are concerned with the failures of Judah and the priests to obey the stipulations of the covenant. The sixth, a condemnation of Edom (1:3–4), seems out of character, but may simply reflect the continued Jewish enmity against Edom during the Persian period of the late sixth and early fifth centuries (compare Ps. 137:7; Obad. 6–14, 18–21). In Mal. 1:6–2:9, the accusations against the priests are similar to those made by Hosea 4:4, 6 and Jer. 6:13–14. The writer begins with a proverb categorizing the duties of a son to his parent and a servant to his master (compare Exod. 20:12; Prov. 29:3). The proverb evokes poignant prophetic statements that decry the shame attached to unfaithful and forgetful children. Similar axioms on the relationship between parent and child are also found in ancient Near Eastern **wisdom literature:**

A son honors his father, and servants their master. If then I am a father, where is the honor due me? (Mal. 1:6)

When Israel was a child, I loved him,
    and out of Egypt I called my son.
The more I called them,
    the more they went from me. (Hosea 11:1–2)

The faithful have disappeared from the land. . . .
For the son treats the father with contempt,
    the daughter rises up against her mother. (Mic. 7:2, 6)

Those who do not honor their parents' name are cursed for their evil by Shamash, the divine judge. ("Teachings of Ahiqar," *OTPar* 307)

Honor your father and mother and you will prosper. ("Teachings of Ankhsheshonqy," *OTPar* 310)

The emphasis on parental concern and filial obedience continues in Mal. 2:10–12. Here the issue is tied to false worship practices. The prophet charges that the people continue to profane the temple by introducing aspects of foreign worship, including "marriage" with the "daughter of a foreign god," possibly **Asherah** (compare 1 Kings 15:9–13; 18:19). For this reason an indignant Yahweh curses them (compare Jer. 3:6–10). That the Canaanite goddess Asherah continued to be venerated into the Persian period speaks to the persistent nature of religious practice in that area and the people's unwillingness to change.

Yehud contained a mixed population, made up of both returned exiles and "people of the land." That reality practically ensured that Yahweh-alone adherents lived side by side with practitioners of the old Canaanite ways. Dissatisfied with this situation, Malachi denounces the worshipers of false deities, calling them unfaithful persons who must be "cut off from the tents of Jacob," a metaphor for the community of the faithful (Mal. 2:12; see Jer. 30:18; Zech. 12:7). Only in this way can the nation maintain the purity of its temple practice and ritual. This emphasis on purification and an abhorrence for any contamination of Yahweh worship ties Malachi to the themes of the preexilic prophets Elijah (1 Kings 18:20–40) and Hosea (2:13–17), who also called for Israel to abandon its mixed allegiances and worship only Yahweh.

The issue of unfaithfulness leads into a condemnation of divorce in the postexilic community. If this passage were taken as a reference to human marriages, it would stand in contrast to the demands made by Ezra and Nehemiah that mixed marriages between Jews and non-Jews must be dissolved or annulled (Ezra 9:1–10:5; Neh. 13:23–31). However, God's forceful statement that "I hate divorce . . . and covering one's garment with violence" (Mal. 2:16) is actually a metaphorical reference to the marriage between Israel and Yahweh under the covenant. In this case, Israel is the husband who by law (Deut. 24:1–4) may divorce his wife, and the "wife of [Israel's] youth" is Yahweh. But in a reversal of the marriage metaphor in Hosea 1–3, the idolatry of the husband/Israel is covered up by rejecting the wife's/God's charges of infidelity/idolatry.

Furthermore, the marriage garment ordinarily symbolizes the conjugal agreement between the parties (Ezek. 16:8), but here it disguises the husband's crimes instead of providing the legal protections due to the wife under the covenant (compare the web of lawsuits that form an iniquitous garment in Isa. 59:4–6). In this way, what should have been a festal covering, symbolizing the couple's union with its garlands and jewels (61:10), has been transformed into a physical indictment detailing broken pledges. The divorce is in fact a sham allowing Judah/the husband to claim the status of a victim while continuing to worship other gods. This duplicity cannot be allowed, and therefore the divorce between Israel and Yahweh is denied. Malachi's concluding admonition charges them all to act faithfully under the terms of the covenant.

These metaphors and charges draw attention to the responsibilities of those who should be most cognizant of their duties and of the law. As a result, the specific charges made against the Second Temple priests speak of a lack of knowledge that in turn has led to false teachings (Mal. 2:7–8). They are also charged with improper attention to their sacrificial duties: "You bring what has been taken by violence or is lame or sick, and this you bring as your offering!" (1:13; compare Isa. 43:23–24). The law explicitly states that sacrificial animals are to be healthy and without blemish (Lev. 22:17–25; Deut. 15:21), yet these priests think they can cheat God (compare a similar self-deception in Jer. 7:8–11).

The question-and-answer format then resumes, reiterating the theme of instruction in Malachi. In this case it allows the author to point out specific cultic abuses. When the question is asked, "Will anyone rob God?" (Mal. 3:9), God's answer is unequivocal: "Yet you are robbing me!" They are cursed for robbing God of the required tithes and offerings (3:8–9). This illegal practice is actually a twofold problem involving the grain and animal offerings of the people. By law a portion of these offerings belongs to the Levites (Num. 18:21), and a tenth of the Levites' portion is supposed to be given to God (18:26–27).

The complaint of a systemic failure to comply with prescribed sacrificial rituals may be compared with the more common prophetic complaint that sacrifices have become a form of insincere worship and have therefore become unacceptable to Yahweh (Hosea 8:11–14; Isa. 1:11–14; Jer. 6:20). Clearly, Malachi's emphasis is to see that the newly reestablished temple community and the people of Yehud are in full compliance with God's command for prescribed tithes and offerings. With that in place, they can be assured of continuing prosperity. That promise is made clear in the contrasting statement that those who bring their "full tithes" (Lev. 27:30–32) into the temple storehouse can be assured that Yahweh will reward their faithfulness by giving them abundant harvests and protecting their crops from locusts and other natural calamities (Mal. 3:10–12; contrast Hag. 1:7–11).

Weary of such unfaithful servants, Yahweh resolves to send a messenger to "prepare the way" for the coming of the Lord to the temple and the reestablishment of the covenant relationship (Mal. 3:1). The promised divine reformer will take up the task of purifying temple rituals and transforming the priesthood into the faithful company that would not even consider committing fraud or engaging in greedy actions (3:2–3). Once that occurs, the offerings of the nation "will be pleasing to the LORD as in the days of old," and God will bless the faithful (3:4). As part of this general purification of the people, all vestiges of sorcery and other false religious practices will be eradicated (Deut. 18:9–14). At that point the people will at last be in full compliance with the law (Mal. 3:5). Malachi's glimpse of a perfect society is a complete reversal of Ezekiel's vision of the "bloody city" in which the commands to protect the weak and uphold all facets of the law are ignored (Ezek. 22:1–12). Based on the parallels between these two passages, it is possible that Malachi is drawing on the Ezekiel materials to heighten the contrast with his vision of a purified nation.

To add even greater authority to the messenger figure, an appendix added to the book identifies the messenger as the prophet Elijah (Mal. 4:5–6). That mysterious ninth-century figure, who, according to tradition did not die like other mortals (2 Kings 2:11–12), is an appropriate harbinger of change. A Gospel writer, seeing the coming of a new age in his own time, applies this same label to John the Baptist, perceiving him to be the Elijah-like messenger whose mission is to herald the coming of the Messiah (Luke 1:17).

The book of Malachi concludes with the declaration of a day of judgment when "those who revered the LORD" will be recorded in a "book of remembrance" (compare Dan. 12:1). Those whose names are recorded represent the righteous remnant that will be spared when God separates the righteous from the wicked (Mal. 3:16–4:3; compare a similar image in Rev. 20:12). The reader of these words is solemnly commanded to obey the law as given to Moses and to await the coming of Elijah, whose appearance will serve as the harbinger of the "day of the LORD." These final verses serve as a **colophon** to the entire set of prophetic books and set a tone of finality (Hosea 14:9 is another example of a wisdom colophon).

The Book of Joel

Because the unknown author of the book of Joel is quite dependent on other prophetic literature, proffers an eschatological tone in his message, never mentions the kingdom of Israel by name, and seems to be familiar only with the cultic practices of the reconstructed Jerusalem temple, most commentators assign the work to the postexilic period, probably after 400. The reference in 3:6 to the slave trade further bolsters this position, since the **cosmopolitan** Persian rule encouraged increasing contacts with Greek merchants. There are sufficient affinities to Amos 1–4 and Isa. 13, however, to make a case for an earlier date.

The name attached to this work means "the LORD is God," an appropriate declaration of allegiance in the postexilic period. The message of Joel reflects the uncertain existence of the Jewish community in Yehud and emphasizes adherence to the Mosaic covenant. Joel shows clear affinity with the language of Deut. 32: its depiction of Yahweh as righteous judge (32:3–4), divine judgment in the form of invasion and famine (32:23–24), and ultimate recompense for injuries caused by Israel's enemies (32:43). Although Joel mentions none of the other prophets by name, he draws upon well-known covenantal traditions and prophetic themes. He also draws upon his own experience of his world, which is primarily agricultural, and on the growing apocalyptic movement. The apocalyptic themes are especially evident in Joel's dire portents of a darkened sky and the "moon [turned] to blood" (Joel 2:30–32; compare Isa. 13:10) and in the gathering of the nations "in the valley of decision" for a final confrontation (Joel 3:11–16; compare Isa. 13:4–6; Zech. 14:2).

This short prophetic book centers its attention on the day of the Lord, first symbolized in a series of locust plagues that strips the land like an invading army (Joel 1:4; 2:1–11; compare Amos 8:9–10). It is possible that this is a mention or a memory of Assyrian or Babylonian invasions of Judah, but it could just as easily represent any invading force, human or insect, that God would send to punish both covenant breakers and enemy nations (Amos 4:9; Nah. 3:15). In the middle of the devastation caused by enemy attacks (Joel 1:6–7) and drought (1:10–12), the prophet reminds the people again that it is better to repent than to perform empty mourning rituals (2:13; compare

1 Sam. 15:22; Hosea 6:6). If they fail to be true penitents, then God will refuse to hear their pleas (Isa. 59:2; Mal. 2:2).

Their return to God must be characterized by full submission, "with all your heart, with fasting, with weeping, and with mourning" (Joel 2:12). Thus they are told to "rend your hearts and not your clothing" and return to a God who is by nature "gracious and merciful" (2:13; compare Exod. 34:6; Jer. 3:12–14). The reference to rending garments is a common mourning practice or a sign of extreme stress (2 Sam. 3:31; Jer. 36:24). Here, however, it refers once again to the prophetic complaint that ritual has replaced true faith by the people. To "rend their hearts," they would have to set aside those things that distracted their attention from God and shift their efforts to obedience to the covenant (compare Pss. 15:2; 24:4; Hosea 6:4–6).

Joel also refers to the day of the Lord as the moment of Judah's restoration, when plenty will replace want, and the presence of God will be made manifest in the people's words and hearts (Joel 2:17–27). An embedded pattern of pleas for help followed by reassurance of hope and restoration is also found in Lam. 3:55–57. In Joel's case the plea to "spare your people, O Lord" (Joel 2:17) is immediately followed by a series of clauses outlining what God, who is "jealous for his land, and had pity on his people," will do to redeem them (2:18). Yahweh will send "grain, wine, and oil" (2:19), which are the usual elements associated with both a marriage bond and God's covenantal promise of fertility (compare Hosea 2:21–22). Furthermore, the "northern army" will be driven off, to trouble them no longer (Joel 2:20).

At that point the litany of God's saving acts are combined with a twofold "do not fear" injunction and a set of assurances of the divine promise for the

"Do Not Fear" Admonitions in the Prophets

A common practice in prophetic literature is for the prophet to express a reassurance and a challenge to the people and their leaders not to fear because God will protect and provide for them if only they trust in him.

- In his confrontation with King Ahaz, Isaiah cautions the king to "take heed, be quiet, do not fear" as he faces the prospect of invading armies from Israel and Syria (Isa. 7:4).
- Second Isaiah gives the exiles God's assurance: "Do not fear, for I am with you," for the exiles will be gathered from all of the nations (Isa. 43:5–6).
- Jeremiah extols God's promise of eventual return for the exiles, telling them to "have no fear" for the Lord is "going to save you" (Jer. 30:10).
- The prophet's song of joy of God's restoration of the nation includes the admonition to Zion: "Do not fear" for "the Lord, your God, is in your midst" (Zeph. 3:16–17).

Return to Eden-like Conditions in the Restored Nation

Joel's prediction of the revival of Judah's fortunes follows the pattern set by earlier prophets of the restoration of the land's fertility and the creation of an almost Eden-like perfection. In these revived circumstances the people will also be transformed and will be obedient to the requirements of the covenant. On that day, with God's help, all their needs will be met, and the land and people will reach their full potential.

- In the early eighth century, Amos prophesies a time when the land's fertility outproduces the efforts of the workers to cultivate it and "the mountains shall drip sweet wine, and all the hills shall flow with it" (Amos 9:13).
- In the late eighth century, Hosea envisions the "day of the LORD" as an idyllic time when the earth responds to the divine "answer," God's creative word, and brings forth an abundance of grain, wine, and oil for the people of the covenant (Hosea 2:21–22).
- Ezekiel describes how God "cleanses" the nation and in the process transforms a desolate land into one "like the garden of Eden" (Ezek. 36:34–35).
- Joel echoes Amos's message, describing how "the mountains shall drip sweet wine, the hills shall flow with milk, and all the stream beds of Judah shall flow with water" (Joel 3:18).

land, its creatures and vegetation, and its people (2:21–27). All that has been destroyed by the swarming locusts/army shall be restored so the people will "eat in plenty" and never more "be put to shame" (2:25–27).

Since the world of the postexilic community is so environmentally fragile (Hag. 1:6), a plague of locusts that strips the fields clean can lead to famine and starvation. The community can also be victimized by their neighbors and sold into slavery, either for debt or because they cannot defend their borders (Joel 3:4–6). Into this reality of want and misery, Joel injects a ray of hope in his vision of a newly revived creation in which God's people will fully enjoy the benefits of the covenant promise of land and children (2:23–24).

Joel's apocalyptic language and visions are quite powerful and fit well into the unsettled period following the return from exile. Among his assurances is a passage that promises salvation to "everyone who calls on the name of the LORD" (2:28–32). Acts 2:17–21 quotes this Joel passage as an example of the last days and final judgment and associates Joel's promise of salvation with Christian ideas of the resurrection of the dead. The first-century CE understanding of salvation and afterlife, however, has not yet emerged in the Judaism of Joel's time. For Joel, the promised salvation involves the transformation of this world and the judgment of Judah's enemies (3:1–8). The use of warfare as a means of righting injustice and gaining revenge, also found in Esther 9:1–15 and Nah. 2:1–12, sounds cruel, but it reflects the pain and suffering of an oppressed people that wishes to strike out against its enemies Edom, Phoenicia, and Philistia (Ps. 137:7–9). Their hopes and fears are expressed by Joel's message, and they set a tone for further dislocations that will occur in the Hellenistic period after the conquests of Alexander of Macedon (post-325).

The Book of Jonah

Although the book of Jonah is set in the period when the Assyrian Empire held an iron-fisted control over much of the ancient Near East (850–605), it more likely was composed during the postexilic period, after 500. This date is based partially on the inability to trace the events described in the book to any established historical sources or the reign of any particular Assyrian king. In addition, the book's development of the theme of universalism seems to address and argue against the postexilic tendency to enforce Jewish identity through claims of exclusivism and cultural isolation. The book of Jonah thus represents a minority voice within the biblical tradition of the Persian period, calling for a wider understanding of Yahweh's concerns for creation. The author uses humor, satire, and irony to claim that Yahweh is concerned about all the nations of the world, not just Israel. Jonah's stubborn refusal to serve as Yahweh's prophetic messenger to Nineveh becomes a lightning rod attracting God's attention and drawing other people into an awareness of Yahweh's power. The prophet, like many of his people, must also be convinced that there is no such thing as undeserved divine forgiveness.

Universalism in Jonah

The book of Jonah showcases the principle that Yahweh has the power to control the fate of all peoples, even the sworn enemies of Israel. When God calls Jonah to preach repentance to the people of Nineveh, Jonah refuses to go (Nah. 2–3 also expresses hatred toward Assyria). Instead, he boards a ship sailing to the port of Tarshish (probably in southern Spain), a destination that will take him in the opposite direction (Jon. 1:3). Jonah's reluctance is quite understandable. It could even be argued that Jonah may have been trying to protect his own people by refusing to save the Assyrians from their destruction at the hands of Yahweh (2 Kings 8:9–13 records Elijah's similarly reluctant message to Hazael in Syria). In any case, from the perspective of an Israelite there is no good reason why he should want to aid the people who destroyed the northern kingdom of Israel in 721, devastated the towns and villages of Judah during the siege of Jerusalem in 701, and repeatedly ravaged every other country in the Near East. It seems more likely that Jonah's attitude would be similar to that of the seventh-century prophet Nahum (Nah. 1:15), who declared a national holiday to celebrate the destruction of the Assyrians.

What we have discovered, however, about prophetic calls is that no matter how outrageous the mission, there is no easy way to derail God's plan. God's instruction to Jonah to go to Nineveh, the hated capital city of the Assyrians, and warn the "wicked" people of God's coming judgment is really more than the prophet can bear. And yet this warning follows the same pattern encountered in previous prophetic literature. It is based around the concept that a righteous God is obligated to warn people of their failings before issuing a final judgment and imposing a sanction upon them (compare Amos 5:14–15; Joel 2:12–14). The paradox in this case is that the prophet will not be speaking to his own people.

When God declares to Jonah that "their wickedness has come up before me," that phrase evokes a memory of the prelude to the flood story in Gen. 6:5–7 and God's concern over the evil being committed in the cities of Sodom and Gomorrah (18:20–33):

> The LORD saw that the wickedness of humankind was great in the earth, and that every inclination of the thoughts of their hearts was only evil continually. (Gen. 6:5)

> Then the LORD said, "How great is the outcry against Sodom and Gomorrah and how very grave their sin!" (Gen. 18:20)

> Go at once to Nineveh, that great city, and cry out against it; for their wickedness has come up before me. (Jon. 1:2)

God's instruction to Jonah thus resembles other examples of the theme of sparing a righteous remnant. As part of God's creation, even the Assyrians must be given the opportunity to repent, lest God be placed in a situation in which a righteous person is destroyed without a warning.

As the story begins, Jonah chooses to resist God's command to warn Nineveh. He flees his country, leaving from the port of Joppa. Apparently, he hopes to travel to the very edge of the known Mediterranean world by sailing to Tarshish in Spain. In this way, if Yahweh is merely a local deity, he thinks he can escape "the presence of the LORD" (1:3). When his ship is threatened by a storm, Jonah discovers that there is no place to hide from Yahweh, who commands the elements throughout the world (compare Job 34:21–22).

Humor now enters the text, with the audience entertained by the contrast between the reactions of the sailors, all of whom were polytheists, and Jonah, who knows that Yahweh is the one true God. While the sailors madly rush around and begin to throw cargo overboard, they also frantically pray to their own gods. Jonah does nothing. He lies asleep in the hold, seemingly unafraid and secure in the mistaken belief that he has escaped God's ability to touch him. Jonah comes on deck only when the sailors rouse him with their plea to add his prayers to their own. They hope that, by attracting yet another god's attention, they will be able to still the raging sea before it engulfs them (Jon. 1:5–6). When they take the further step of casting lots to determine the cause of their misfortune (compare Josh. 7:16–20), Jonah has to admit the fault is his. The sailors cannot believe anyone could be foolish enough to try to flee from a god, but when the storm prevents them from reaching land they finally take Jonah's advice and cast him into the sea. Of course, at that point the seas subside and the sailors acknowledge their "fear" (respect) for Jonah's god by praying to Yahweh, offering a sacrifice, and taking vows (Jon. 1:14–16). Taken together, this episode illustrates the theme of universalism since it is the non-Israelites who discern the power of the Israelite God even if Jonah stubbornly has tried to ignore it.

After being cast into the sea, Jonah's temporary sojourn in "the belly of the fish" for three days provides him a place of safety and the time to mull over his actions (1:17). Finally, convinced that his call to prophetic activity cannot be denied, he prays for his release (2:2–9). The fish and the storm function in the story as evidence of God's control over the natural world (1:17; 2:10; see Job 41:1; Ps. 104:26). Later the bush that provides Jonah with shade serves the same literary function, although Jonah will have to be reminded of this. Having accepted his mission, however reluctantly, he now enters the Assyrian capital city (the penitential prayer in Jon. 2 may have been added later by an editor who felt it necessary to make Jonah appear a bit more submissive to God's call).

The resolution of the initial drama comes when Jonah enters Nineveh and without much enthusiasm begins to proclaim the message: "Forty days more, and Nineveh shall be overthrown!" (3:4). Even as he carries out this task, he shows his stubborn and rebellious nature. He walks a full day into the city before saying anything, perhaps hoping to find some corner where no one will hear him (3:4). The curious thing about this is that the people of this "great city," which required three days to walk from one end to the other, immediately believe Yahweh's prophet: "They proclaimed a fast, and everyone, great and small, put on **sackcloth**" (3:5). Unlike Sodom, which demonstrated that all of its citizens were evil by ignoring the warnings of a righteous man (Gen. 19:4), Nineveh's entire population, including the king, demonstrates their devout contrition and quick willingness to repent. In fact, another comic element in the story emerges when their overzealousness leads to decking out the animals in sackcloth (Jon. 3:8).

The penitential actions by the people of Nineveh are based on the hope that Yahweh may relent and spare the city (compare Exod. 32:11–12; Jer. 18:5–11). There are close parallels between the statements in Jon. 3:9 and the subsequent explanation given at the end of Jeremiah's trial for his acquittal and release:

Who knows? God may relent and change his mind; he may turn from his fierce anger, so that we do not perish. (Jon. 3:9)

Did he [Hezekiah] not fear the LORD and entreat the favor of the LORD, and did not the LORD change his mind about the disaster that he had pronounced against them? (Jer. 26:19)

Clearly, these people recognized the possibility of "changing God's mind," and they were willing to go to extremes to obtain this goal.

Characteristically, Jonah's reaction to being the most successful evangelist in the history of ancient Israel is extreme displeasure and mindless anger (Jon. 4:1). In his disgust, he complains that God is too kindhearted and prone to forgiveness (4:2). After all, the Assyrians have been responsible for terrible acts of destruction against the peoples of the Near East. And now God has forgiven them! This is just too much for Jonah to stand, and he withdraws from the city in disgust (4:5).

The prophet is so beside himself over Nineveh's survival that he asks God to take his life (4:3). Suffering from despair and depression, Jonah's request is not surprising and in context not unheard of either. For instance, when Elijah flees into the wilderness to escape Jezebel's wrath, he asks God for the comfort of death: "It is enough; . . . O LORD, take away my life" (1 Kings 19:4). And, perhaps justifiably, after struggling with the horrible suffering inflicted on him, Job expresses a similar desire, saying that he would "choose strangling and death rather than this body" (Job 7:15–16). Neither of these examples, however, is based on the frustration brought on by too much success. Jonah is so "over the top" in his self-centered mutterings that he can be considered only a muttering curmudgeon.

What has angered Jonah is God's having expressed concern for the entirety of creation. The downside, as far as Jonah is concerned, is that this concern has also resulted in God caring about the fate of the most bloodthirsty people

---

Assyrian Campaign Rhetoric

They put their trust upon their own force while I trusted Ashur, my lord. I caught him [the king of Sidon] like a bird in his mountains and cut off his head. I hung the heads of Sanduarri [of Kundi] and of Abdimilkutte [of Sidon] around the neck of their nobles to demonstrate to the population the power of Ashur, my lord, and paraded through the wide main street of Nineveh with singers (playing on) harps. ("Annals of Esarhaddon," adapted from *ANET* 290–91)

I dyed the river red with blood of Rezin of Damascus's soldiers. . . . I captured his archers, his spearmen, and their supply train. . . . I impaled his generals alive on stakes and I laid siege to his city for forty-five days, confining him like a bird in a cage. ("Annals of Tiglath-pileser III," *OTPar* 84)

in the ancient world. Even the slim possibility that they might be spared is enough to drive Jonah mad. The key to Jonah's stubbornness is found in Jon. 4:2, which explains why he initially resisted God's call. He can proclaim Yahweh's loving and forgiving nature to his own people, but Jonah cannot forgive the Assyrians and does not want God to do so either.

The final expression of this theme comes when Jonah constructs a booth outside Nineveh. As in the case of the storm and the great fish, God demonstrates mastery over all creation, first by causing a bush to grow and providing Jonah with a leafy canopy (4:5–6). Then the Lord of creation supplies a catalyst for further conversation with Jonah by sending a worm to destroy the bush and a hot wind to parch his throat and make him faint with the heat (4:7–8). Again, just as he did when Nineveh was spared, Jonah fails to see beyond his own discomfort. He angrily responds that this is simply the last straw and reiterates the desire to depart this life: "It is better for me to die than to live."

God now gets the final word and teaches Jonah the lesson of concern for all of creation by condemning Jonah's self-centered philosophy. The prophet's anger has been based not on the death of the plant but on the end of its comfort-giving shade. God criticizes Jonah's attitude in a typical wisdom statement that emphasizes the deity's prerogative to exercise judgment and to deal with creation as he sees fit:

> You are concerned about the bush, for which you did not labor and which you did not grow; it came into being in a night and perished in a night. And should I not be concerned about Nineveh, that great city, in which there are more than a hundred and twenty thousand persons who do not know their right hand from their left, and also many animals? (Jon. 4:10–11)

> Justice is a divine gift. ("Teachings of Amen-em-ope," *OTPar* 300)

> Divine plans are one thing. Human desires are another. ("Teaching of Ankh-sheshonqy," *OTPar* 317)

God corrects the prophet's shortsighted attitude and in doing so makes a point that should be learned by the nation as well. Because Jonah had nothing to do with the creation of the bush or of the people of Nineveh, he has no right to deny the creator the opportunity to be concerned with them (Jon. 4:10–11). Like Job, who had demanded the right to make his case before God, to "learn what he would answer me" (Job 23:3–5), Jonah gets a response that is hard to take. In other words, God asserts his full sovereignty over all of creation (compare God's question to Job, "Where were you when I laid the foundation of the earth?" [38:4]). Any compassion God chooses to exercise with respect to that creation is a divine prerogative. In this way the book of Jonah provides a full expression of the universalism theme.

Connection with the Postexilic Period

The members of the exilic community who remained loyal to Yahweh during the exile and in the subsequent postexilic period generally identified their God with themselves and their own country. It was quite easy to identify God as dwelling in Zion and from that seat of power judging the enemies of Judah (Joel 3:17; Zech. 8:3). The postexilic prophetic writers surely enjoyed the task of describing how Yahweh has promised to crush their oppressors (Zech. 14:13–15; Mal. 1:4–5). Furthermore, the return of the exiles demonstrated abundant proof that the God of Israel is truly supreme over all other nations and their gods.

What is not so pleasing is a portrayal of Yahweh helping their enemies to repent and be delivered from justified destruction. A message such as this would have been difficult to accept during the period of Assyrian control of the Near East or for that matter in any subsequent period of Israelite history. For many years the people's hopes were kept alive by promises of the impending annihilation of Nineveh and its rulers (Isa. 10:12–19; Nah. 2–3; Zeph. 2:13). The book of Jonah, however, was composed in the postexilic period, a time when the former nations of Israel and Judah have been reduced to living either in a small area around Jerusalem or in various countries of the exile. Within that social context it is clear that some voices, perhaps only a minority, saw the logic that if Yahweh is truly the only God, then all peoples are part of Yahweh's creation, even the seemingly unredeemable Assyrians of hated memory. Therefore, they too deserved a chance to accept a message of repentance. In this way, in the postexilic period, as new enemies emerged to oppress the Jews in Jerusalem or in the **Diaspora**, it became possible to pray for the welfare of their enemies as Jeremiah had once suggested (Jer. 29:7). If the nations of the earth could be convinced that Yahweh was indeed an all-powerful and universal deity (Isa. 49:7; 60:8–14), then their desire to extinguish the light of Judaism might also be set aside (the drama of survival is portrayed in Esther 8–9).

15

The Hellenistic Period
and the Book of Daniel

Although the book of Daniel is not included in the prophetic corpus of the Hebrew Bible, it provides insight into issues that were crucial to the late postexilic period and contributes to our understanding of the **apocalyptic** literature found in the books of Ezekiel and Zechariah. Confusion over the classification of the book of Daniel is created by its inclusion in the Writings section of the Hebrew **canon**, its historical problems, and the mixed use of late Hebrew and Aramaic vocabulary. All these factors point to its composition during the second century. Moreover, there are many similarities between the tales of Daniel's trials and the literature of the Maccabean revolt, which began in the 160s.

Literary Analysis

The book of Daniel can be divided into two distinct sections. Daniel 1–6 contains the "Tales of the Young Men," stories about Daniel and his three friends, who are brought to Babylon with the first group of exiles in 597. These vivid narratives revolve around the heroic championing of their Jewish identity through strict adherence to the dietary laws and a staunch adherence to the monotheistic injunctions of the **covenant**—ideas and practices that develop most fully during the exile and postexilic period. In every possible way, Daniel and his companions resist being assimilated into Babylonian culture or

The Postexilic Jewish Identity Movement

In order to preserve their ethnic identity and avoid assimilation to the dominant culture, some exiles in Mesopotamia drew upon their covenant traditions and their history to create a Jewish identity movement. These standards of religious behavior worked to combat the very real possibility of cultural extinction during the exile and helped to establish Judaism as a monotheistic faith both in the **Diaspora** and later in the returned community in **Yehud**:

- editing materials from oral tradition and historical and religious annals to create a canon of literature;
- using Hebrew as a **liturgical** language;
- emphasizing **sabbath** worship in the absence of temple and sacrificial cult;
- emphasizing circumcision as a ritual of initiation and exclusivism;
- increasing emphasis on **ritual purity**, including ritual bathing and dietary laws;
- insisting on **endogamy** as a safeguard against the threat of cultural assimilation and as the basis for membership in the priesthood.

accepting any changes in their religious practices even under threat of death (compare the zeal expressed in 1 Macc. 2:15–38). Furthermore, Daniel's ability to interpret dreams reinforces the superiority of **Yahweh** over the gods of Mesopotamia and Persia (compare Joseph in Gen. 41:1–45). The familiar theme of a contest between gods, which had been developed previously in the contest between Moses and Pharaoh (Exod. 7–12) and Elijah's contest on Mount Carmel (1 Kings 18), acquires new relevance in these stories set in the exile.

The remaining chapters (Dan. 7–12) contain apocalyptic visions. Apocalyptic writings can be defined as a special type of literature that reveals secrets of the future, knowledge possessed only by God and revealed only to the elect. The visions are usually full of bizarre imagery and cryptic numbers that must be interpreted by angelic beings. The visions of Daniel deal with the eventual triumph of Yahweh over the kings, gods, and angel armies of the Babylonians and Persians. These visions are difficult for modern readers to interpret because they are based on ancient Israelite traditions and the political agenda of the writer at the time they were composed.

There is no direct connection between the earlier chapters and the apocalyptic visions. Even the sense of chronology is different in the two sections. In addition, linguistic differences make it difficult to determine the authorship of the book: Dan. 1:1–2:4a and Dan. 8–12 are written in Hebrew, while 2:4b–7:28 is composed in Aramaic. These differences may indicate that different authors were responsible for the Hebrew and Aramaic sections; if so, the two sections were joined during the editing process because both traditions were about

Daniel. The linguistic differences may also illustrate the use of Hebrew as a liturgical language (a facet of the Jewish identity movement) for the introductory and most of the apocalyptic portions of the book.

Because Daniel's visions are written in the style of apocalyptic literature, their characteristics differentiate them from other prophetic visions. Prophets wrote and spoke in their own names about events that were of importance to their contemporary audience, while apocalypticists used the authority attached to the name of an ancient hero or prophet as their pseudonym. In addition, the sense of time is different between these two groups. Prophets believed that God worked within history, while apocalypticists believed that this world had become corrupt and that God's deliverance would come outside history with a new creation. Thus it can be said that prophecy was a dynamic and creative movement, setting a standard for the delivery of oracles from God. Apocalyptic literature, on the other hand, made partial use of these prophetic oracles while placing greater emphasis on a coded form of Israelite tradition and history.

Tales of the Young Men

Following their capture and resettlement by King Nebuchadnezzar of Babylonia, Daniel and his friends are given Babylonian names: Belteshazzar, Shadrach, Meshach, and Abednego. This practice is only the first step in the policy of assimilating these young men into Babylonian culture. The aim is to seduce them into the affluent lifestyle of their captors, making them more loyal and sympathetic officials when they are sent back to Judah to serve as administrators. A similar policy was used by many empires in the ancient Near East (Neh. 2:1–9). The assumption was that conquered peoples would be less likely to revolt if their own people administered the policies set by the empire. And by bringing individuals at an early age to the capital of the empire and educating them alongside the sons of Babylonian nobles and officials, the Babylonians could ensure the loyalty of these local officials. The irony in these stories is that Daniel and his friends refuse to be "educated."

These tales have two different types of plots. First are the tests of courage. In these stories, Daniel and his friends stand as heroic role models for the oppressed exiles (Dan. 1, 3, 6). Since this material was most likely composed during the Hellenistic era, the danger of cultural extinction faced by the youths in these stories may exemplify the conditions faced by the Jews under the influence of Seleucid Greeks, who ruled Syria-Palestine during the first half of the second century. In that sense, the stories are a representation of a culture war in which one side (the Jews) fights for the survival of its cultural identity and the other (the Seleucid rulers) seeks to homogenize its kingdom and eliminate disparate and contentious elements.

The second plot type centers on Daniel's ability to interpret the visions and dreams of the Babylonian and Persian rulers (Dan. 2, 4, 5). Like Joseph in Gen. 41, Daniel is portrayed as an outsider who performs a remarkable service for the king. Both show greater wisdom and skill as diviners than anyone else in the court, and as a result they are elevated to positions of authority and influence. In both stories Joseph and Daniel are separated from common diviners or sorcerers by their firm attestation of their powers to God alone.

Stories of Heroic Fortitude and Wisdom

Dietary Laws Upheld. The Jewish trainees are given the desirable privilege of eating from the king's table. In other biblical stories, this privilege is a sign of membership in the ruler's official family (1 Sam. 20:29; 2 Sam. 9:7–13). But since these foods would not have been prepared according to Jewish dietary laws (Lev. 17:10–16; 20:25) and might also contain forbidden items (Lev. 11; Deut. 14:3–21), Daniel and his friends refuse to eat them. Instead they ask to be tested for ten days, during which time they will consume only water and vegetables while other trainees eat the king's rich food (Dan. 1:8–14). At the conclusion of the test, the healthier diet of Daniel and company is demonstrated, and they are rewarded by God with wisdom and insight (1:15–17; compare Solomon's gift of wisdom in 1 Kings 3:10–12). Here and in the other stories as well, Nebuchadnezzar rewards the men with positions of importance and makes an uncharacteristic statement acknowledging the power of the "God of gods and Lord of kings" (Dan. 1:18–20; 2:47–49; compare Gen. 41:37–45). The courage and intelligence shown by Daniel and his friends would have been a useful model of behavior for the people enduring the oppression of the Seleucid king Antiochus IV (1 Macc. 1:10–64), which led to the Maccabean revolt in 166–142.

Idolatry Refused. Shadrach, Meshach, and Abednego refuse to bow down and worship an idol as Nebuchadnezzar commanded (Dan. 3:1–12; compare 1 Macc. 2:15–28). Their punishment is to be thrown into a furnace, possibly a walk-in kiln intended to produce the thousands of clay bricks needed for construction projects in Babylon. Such an unusual form of execution by fire simply heightens the drama and provides a remarkable stage for these events (Dan. 3:13–23). Of course, the three faithful men miraculously survive the flames with the aid of an angelic being (3:25–26). The story allows for the further development of the theme of **universalism**, as Nebuchadnezzar declares his faith in the "God of Shadrach, Meshach, and Abednego" (3:28–30; compare 2:46–47; 2 Kings 5:15–19). Their refusal to worship an idol, of course, shows strict adherence to the prohibition of images (Exod. 20:4–6), but it is also remarkably similar to the story of the martyrdom of Eleazar, who also refused to go "over to an alien religion" during Antiochus Epiphanes's oppression (2 Macc. 6:18–31).

Daily Prayer Upheld. In an episode similar to the harrowing escape in Dan. 3, Daniel is placed in a den of hungry lions for disobeying the king's decree and praying to Yahweh (6:13–17). Once again divine intervention saves the life of the faithful person (6:19–22), and there is even a comic twist when the king, who had been tricked into sentencing Daniel to death, orders his unfaithful advisers to be cast into the lions' den (6:24; compare Esther 7:5–10).

Stories of Daniel as Diviner and Champion of Yahweh

In Dan. 2, 4, 5, Daniel exercises his ability as a diviner by interpreting a series of dreams and signs. Each story demonstrates the insight given to this *hakam* ("wise man"), which far exceeds that of the king or any of his advisers (compare Gen. 41:1–45). In that sense, Daniel's special God-given ability (Dan. 2:19) might be compared to the empowering of Isaiah (6:5–7), Jeremiah (1:6–9), and Ezekiel (2:1–7) to speak God's message to the people. In the first story, Nebuchadnezzar has had a troubling dream of a mighty statue, divided into four separate sections of different metals (Dan. 2:31–35), which is destroyed by a stone thrown from heaven. When "the magicians, the enchanters, the sorcerers, and the Chaldeans" fail to provide an answer, Daniel steps forward with confidence and provides the interpretation, identifying the four metals in the statue as representations of the successive kingdoms that have conquered and ruled Israel and/or Judah. The statue's destruction marks Yahweh's intervention into history and heralds the establishment of an eternal kingdom (2:36–45). Nebuchadnezzar is greatly impressed, promotes Daniel, and praises the power of his God, a clear example of the universalism theme (2:47–49).

Nebuchadnezzar's second troubling dream begins and ends much like the first. He sees a bounteous tree that, like the statue, is ordered to be destroyed by the "decree of the Most High" (4:10–17). Daniel, whom the king acknowledges "is endowed with a spirit of the holy gods" (4:8–9), identifies the tree as Nebuchadnezzar himself. He tells the king that he has brought great blessings to his people, just as the tree has nurtured the creatures that inhabited its branches. However, because Nebuchadnezzar failed to recognize Yahweh's power, he is doomed to be humbled by a period of insanity, after which he will freely acknowledge the power of Yahweh above all else (4:24–37).

The story of Belshazzar's feast in Dan. 5 is the last example of Daniel's interpretative abilities. Belshazzar, coregent in Babylon with his father, Nabonidus, stages a magnificent feast and attempts to impress his guests by serving them from the sacred vessels taken from the Jerusalem temple (2 Kings 24:13; Jer. 28:3). In response to this sacrilege, a spectral hand materializes and writes a series of Aramaic words on the wall of the banquet hall: "Mene, Mene, Tekel, and Parsin" (5:2–9, 25). Although the guests can read the words of the message, they cannot determine its importance. At his queen's urging, Belshazzar summons Daniel to interpret the meaning of these mysterious words. Daniel predicts the destruction of a kingdom whose days have been numbered (*mene*), whose sins have been weighed on the scales (*tekel*), and who will be "divided [*parsin*] and given to the Medes and Persians" (5:25–28). This story differs from the other two because it does not result either in Belshazzar's praising Yahweh or in Daniel's personal advancement. It may be that the writers have chosen to use only the great king Nebuchadnezzar as the model for the monarchs who will "prostrate themselves" before the power of Yahweh (Isa. 49:7). In any case, Daniel's stature as a true seer is proved once again when the predicted events occur and Babylon falls to the Persian conquerors (Dan. 5:30; compare Gen. 41:46–57).

Apocalyptic Visions

The apocalyptic visions in Daniel can be treated as a whole, more so than the earlier instructive tales can. They share the common **eschatological** theme that the present age is evil. All good things have been subverted, and corruption seems to be spreading everywhere. The righteous are being oppressed, and they need encouragement to continue in their faith. One ancient Egyptian text, the "Visions of Neferti," describes a similar disintegration of Egyptian society prior to the breakup of the Old Kingdom (1991–1786). It contains the same gloomy appraisal of a world gone mad. This Egyptian sage sees Egypt "in chaos," a land where "no order remains" and in which "no one sheds a tear for Egypt" (*OTPar* 336).

In the face of such a disaster, the climactic intervention of God is the last hope of the righteous. Since this age cannot be expected to survive much longer, the whole world becomes the stage for divine actions. Just as in the

---

Characteristics of Apocalyptic Literature

Primary Characteristics

- dualism (a universe constantly divided between the forces of good/light and evil/darkness)
- eschatology (emphasis on "final days")

Secondary Characteristics

- visions interpreted by angelic being
- animal symbolism (often a bizarre mixture of images)
- numerology (significant numbers assigned to forecast events or enumerate past events)
- angelic and demonic armies in perpetual struggle

case of Zechariah's frightening apocalyptic vision (Zech. 14:1–5), great persecution, turbulence, and global warfare must precede the end. The more intense the conflict, the more evident it is to the righteous that the end of the age is approaching.

This understanding of the end of the world, as well as the use of angels as the leaders of Yahweh's forces, may have been influenced, or at least been reinforced, by **Zoroastrianism**, the dualistic Persian religion that viewed the history of the world as a continuous struggle between the forces of light (good) and darkness (evil). The apocalyptic visions in Daniel contain many similarities to Zoroastrianism, and it can be said that Judaism underwent some marked changes during the Persian and Hellenistic periods. These include the addition, among at least a segment of the population (i.e., the Pharisees), of the concept of resurrection and final judgment. This concept is clearly reflected in Dan. 12:2: "Many of those who sleep in the dust of the earth shall awake, some to everlasting life, and some to shame and everlasting contempt." And according to the Jewish historian Josephus, many Pharisees adopted this belief (*Jewish Antiquities* 18.14–15).

Summary of the Visions

The visions in Dan. 7–12 are filled with reports of conflict on earth and cosmic struggles fought by the angel armies of Yahweh and Persia. They end with the eventual downfall of the kingdoms that have oppressed Israel over the centuries and the final emergence of Yahweh as the supreme God over all the earth (compare Mal. 4; Zech. 14:16). In typical apocalyptic fashion, Dan. 7 contains a vision of deliverance from an oppression symbolized by four fantastic beasts: a lion with eagle's wings, a bear with three tusks, a leopard with four wings and four heads, and a beast too terrible to describe, with iron teeth and ten horns (7:3–8). Like the multilayered statue in Dan. 2, each beast represents a kingdom that has successively oppressed Judah and Israel, and the various wings, heads, and horns represent the individual kings of these empires. The general consensus among scholars today is that the beasts represent, in this order, Babylon (Chaldea), Media, Persia, and Seleucia. Finally, the Seleucid king Antiochus IV is the small horn who plucks out three others in the fourth beast (7:8, 23–25; 1 Macc. 1:8–10).

The reign of these kingdoms ends with the decree of the enthroned "Ancient One," who appoints a messiah-like figure to exercise everlasting dominion over all peoples and nations (Dan. 7:9–14; compare Zech. 12:1–9). One of the angelic attendants explains to Daniel that the fourth beast was the last to oppress Israel (Dan. 7:23–28). The reference to the attempt "to change the sacred seasons and the law" may well be a direct reference to Antiochus

Epiphanes's attempt to suppress Jewish worship and replace it with Hellenistic cultic practices and gods (1 Macc. 1:44–50).

The vision in Dan. 8 expresses a similar outcome for the reigning kingdoms. This vision depicts a warring ram, which represents the Medes/Persians, and a he-goat, which represents the successors of Alexander. The vision also introduces the angelic interpreter Gabriel, who softens the terrifying experience for the baffled Daniel (8:15–17). He is told that once again an agent of God, the "Prince of princes" (8:23–25), will extinguish the destructive efforts of the evil leaders. Daniel 9 reveals, however, that evil and oppression will last for "seventy weeks" (9:24); this odd expression seeks to apply Jeremiah's prophecy of a seventy-year exile (Jer. 25:11–12; 29:10) to the events of the mid-second century. Among these events is "the abomination that desolates" (Dan. 9:27; 11:31) committed by Antiochus IV, who orders the construction of an altar to the Greek god Zeus Olympios in the Jerusalem temple (1 Macc. 1:54; Matt. 24:15; Mark 13:14).

In the vision of Dan. 10–12, Daniel learns more about the last days from the angel Michael (10:13–14). The vision contains a series of episodes, each prefaced with the statement "in those times" or "at the time of the end" (11:6, 14, 20, 29, 40). The eschatological episodes describe the Seleucid period from the writer's own day and on into the immediate future. They are filled with descriptions of the disorder caused by uprising and the overthrow of Seleucid kings (11:2–45) and the self-exaltation by a king who "consider[ed] himself greater than any god" (11:36). In Dan. 12, Daniel is assured that, despite long periods of conflict, evil, and disorder, God will ultimately deliver those who remain faithful (compare Joel 2:30–32): "At that time Michael, the great prince, the protector of your people shall arise. There shall be a time of anguish, such as has never occurred since nations first came into existence. But at that time your people shall be delivered, everyone who is found written in the book" (Dan. 12:1).

In addition, the righteous can expect a divine promise of a reward beyond this life: "Happy are those who persevere and attain the thousand three hundred thirty-five days. But you, go your way, and rest; you shall rise for your reward at the end of the days" (Dan. 12:12–13).

These statements are intended to encourage the Jews to remain faithful to their ancestral religion despite the political oppression they are facing and the allure of Hellenistic culture (compare Sir. 2:15–17). They demonstrate the superiority of Yahweh, who is in control of everything, including the events of history and the gods of the other nations. Daniel's **theodicy** thus explains how the Jews can continue to face oppression without succumbing to cultural extinction. It also demonstrates the ways in which Judaism evolved out of the original Mesopotamian and Canaanite context that formed much of the early fabric of Israelite worship into a strictly monotheistic religion.

16

Final Thoughts

This survey has examined the phenomenon of prophetic activity as recorded in the annals, letters, and inscriptions of the ancient Near East and the Bible. For the most part, prophecy, like **divination** and other methods that seek to determine the will of the gods, is recognized among these ancient cultures as a valid and desirable communication. Of course, most of the prophetic figures made their audience uncomfortable, but they also tended to uphold the basic social values of the nation. Their message was intended to draw rulers and their subjects back into compliance with established norms. These efforts, then, raise the question why prophetic activity and prophetic figures officially cease to be a part of Jewish tradition after Ezra and Nehemiah (ca. 400) even though some of the prophetic literature was composed as late as the Hellenistic period. Although we do not have a reliable history of the events that led to the development of the Hebrew **canon** of Scriptures, it is quite apparent that at some point the decision was made to solidify the tradition that the age of the prophets had ended at that point. A caution is even recorded in Zech. 13:4 that the people should beware of those claiming to be prophets and who wear the "hairy mantle" (a reference to Elijah's garb in 2 Kings 1:8). The only prophetic figure or messenger predicted to carry on the role as God's representative is Elijah (Mal. 4:5), but he is of course an unusual character and one who is said to have never died (2 Kings 2:11–12). Even so, in this future age his task will not be prophetic, but rather instructive, turning "the heart of parents to their children and the hearts of children to their parents" in order to prevent a vengeful God from striking the "land with a curse."

Instead of a continuous stream of new prophetic figures, the postexilic prophets make the case that the message of the "former prophets" continues to be valid and needs no further elaboration. As a result no additional prophetic voices are needed. Instead, the people are admonished to "return to me" and "I will return to you" (Zech. 1:3). Thus Zechariah's visions (1:7–2:5; 3:1–6:8), each of which are interpreted for him by angelic messengers, restore a model of divine appearance missing since the time of the ancestors (e.g., Jacob's **theophany** at Bethel in Gen. 28:10–17). Prophecy officially comes to an end and is solidified within tradition as a fixed body of shared revelation along with the Law (Matt. 5:17; 7:12).

Of course, the idea that a prophet might yet appear remains a part of popular culture in subsequent periods. For instance, after the beheading of John the Baptist, Herod Antipas is given a variety of identifications of this figure, which include Elijah or "a prophet, like one of the prophets of old" (Mark 6:14–16). In a similar fashion, Peter's response to Jesus's question about his true identity includes the rumors that Jesus is "Elijah, . . . Jeremiah or one of the prophets" (Matt. 16:14). Furthermore, one of the signs of confusion in a later age listed in Matt. 24:11 is the rise of "false prophets," perhaps playing off of Zechariah's warning. All this suggests that despite the closing of the canon and the solidifying of tradition about the prophets, the desire to receive direct communication from God never ceases to spark human imagination. Thus to study the prophets and their messages can also be seen as a modern journey, seeking answers and hoping to come into closer contact with the God who called upon these ancient figures to speak to the people about their **covenant** obligations.

Glossary

The first occurrence in a chapter of the following glossary terms is in boldface type.

annunciation: a birth announcement that in the biblical account is made by a representative of God.

anthropomorphic: giving human characteristics and emotions to a god or other nonhuman creature or object.

apocalyptic: a type of literature dealing with end things and characterized by verbal or numerical symbols, monstrous visions, and predictions of final battles.

apology: a literary device used to defend an individual or to create a justification for rulership.

apostasy: any action that knowingly allows or condones false worship.

archaeology: the scientific process of examining the ancient remains of human settlements and the artifacts produced by these people.

ark of the covenant: the gold-covered box created during the wilderness period (Exod. 25:10–22) to house the Ten Commandments. It was carried by the Levites and kept in the holy of holies in the tabernacle during the wilderness period.

Asherah / Asherah pole: Asherah was the divine consort of the Canaanite god Baal. She was often represented by a sacred pole erected near an altar (Exod. 34:13) or by a sacred grove of trees (Deut. 16:21).

BCE: "before the Common Era"—used in place of BC, but the dates are the same; *note*: all dates in this book are BCE unless otherwise stated.

call narrative: the description of the circumstances in which a person is called by God to become a prophet. Some narratives are quite elaborate and include several steps (e.g., Isa. 6) while others provide few details (e.g., Amos 7:15).

canon: the books designated by the faith community as Holy Scripture and the standard for faith and practice.

casting his mantle: an action designed to designate someone as a person's successor (1 Kings 19:19).

CE: "Common Era"—used in place of AD, but the dates are the same.

Chronicler: the biblical editor or editors said to be responsible for the books of 1–2 Chronicles and possibly Ezra and Nehemiah. The work most likely dates to the late fifth century. It contains a revised history of Israel from David to the postexilic period.

city-state: a political unit comprising an urban center and its immediate environs and villages.

cognitive dissonance: a situation in which two completely credible and contradictive statements are made, one of which is necessarily false.

colophon: a statement or phrase placed at the end of a document (e.g., Hosea 14:9), to serve as a summary or simply an end marker.

corporate identity: a legal principle according to which an entire household is rewarded or punished for the righteousness or sins of the head of the household.

cosmopolitan: an attitude of cultural openness and sophistication generally found in large urban settings.

covenant: the contractual agreement between Yahweh and the people, in which Yahweh promises land and children in exchange for the people's exclusive worship and obedience.

covenant renewal ceremony: a ritual used several times by Israelite leaders to reinforce the importance of the covenant with Yahweh. It involves an assembly of the people, reading of the law, reaffirmation, and sacrifice (Exod. 24:3–8).

Deuteronomistic Historian: the name given to the author/authors associated with the book of Deuteronomy (the D-source in the Documentary Hypothesis) and a layer of editing in Joshua–2 Kings. Dated to ca. 600, this source reflects a strict moralism and a view of Israelite history in which the people continually fail to obey the covenant and therefore deserve Yahweh's punishment.

Diasporic Judaism: the conservative strand of Judaism that evolved during the exile and is characteristic of the Jews who remained in the lands of the exile.

divination: a set of practices that attempt to determine the future and the will of the gods. These practices include casting lots, examining animal entrails, and seeking patterns in natural phenomena.

divine assembly: the divine company that serves Yahweh in the form of messengers and is portrayed surrounding Yahweh enthroned (1 Kings 22:19).

Divine Warrior: the role of Yahweh in warfare as the champion of the people of the covenant.

ecstatic: a physical and mental condition sometimes experienced by the prophets that caused them to lose full control of their bodies as they spoke a divine message.

egalitarian: denoting a social system in which all persons have equal status.

enacted prophecy: a prophecy that uses an action or a form of street theater by the prophet to draw attention and reinforce the message.

endogamy: a policy of marrying only within a certain identifiable group.

Ephraim: son of Joseph and the generic political name synonymous with the northern kingdom of Israel.

eponymous: a term used for a heroic character considered to be the founding father of a tribe or nation.

eschatology: the study of last things or events just prior to the end of time.

execration ritual: a set of actions designed to curse a person or place (e.g., Jer. 19).

framework: a narrative that shows an outline structure that can be applied whenever a similar set of events occurs or can be used as the basis for a drama.

genre: a category of literature (e.g., short story, poetry).

hegemony: a political situation in which a powerful nation or empire exercises extensive influence over the policies and actions of neighboring states.

herem: holy war in which all captured property and persons are destroyed as a dedicatory sacrifice to God (e.g., the conquest of Jericho in Josh. 6).

hesed: a covenantal term meaning "everlasting love" and the basis for Yahweh's willingness to make a covenant with the people.

high place: Hebrew *bamah*, a nearby hill or local shrine that served both the needs of the village culture as well as cities such as Dan. Although Yahweh was worshiped at the high place, other gods were also worshiped here. They were banned by the kings of Judah, but continued in use in Israel through their history (part of the sins of Jeroboam in 1 Kings 12:25–33).

inclusio: a literary device, an envelope of sorts that encloses a portion of text within the same statement or material (e.g., Pss. 8:1 and 8:9). An inclusio may either set off the enclosed material or provide a thematic frame for a larger narrative.

juridical parable: a form of prophetic literature in which the prophet confronts either an authority figure or the nation with a legal situation that is designed to justify God's judgment on them (e.g., 2 Sam. 12:1–15).

King's Highway: the major international trade route traversing Transjordan that extends from Damascus in Syria in the north to Elath on the Gulf of Aqaba in the south.

lament: a genre, found principally in the Psalms and the book of Lamentations, that expresses the sorrow or suffering of an individual or a group.

liturgy: the outline and stages of a worship service.

Messiah: Hebrew *mashiyah* ("anointed"), a term used for individuals chosen by Yahweh for leadership positions.

motif: a repeated idea or theme within a narrative.

myth: a story that centers on the origin of events or things and usually involves the activities of gods.

omen text: texts based on previously observed signs in nature or through divining methods such as the examination of sheep livers. These were compiled in ancient Mesopotamia and consulted as references by divining priests for interpretation of the will or intent of the gods.

oracles against the nations: a type of prophetic speech designed to pronounce judgment on Israel's neighbors. For example, Ezek. 25–32 contains a series of proclamations against various countries, including Ammon, Tyre (Phoenicia), and Egypt.

prophetic immunity: a traditional form of protection given to prophets when they speak in a god's name and that in principle is designed to prevent the people from killing the messenger because of a negative message.

proselytes: converts to a faith community.

remnant: the portion of the community who will, according to the prophets, survive God's wrath and rebuild the nation.

ritual purity: the steps (including diet and bathing) taken to transform persons or objects into a clean or pure religious state.

sabbath: the celebration of Yahweh as the creator God and the commemoration of the creation event by ceasing work one day each week.

sackcloth: a roughly woven garment worn as a sign of mourning or repentance.

Septuagint: the Greek translation of the Hebrew Bible made by the Alexandrian (Egypt) Jews between the fourth and second centuries; abbreviated LXX, it contains the Apocrypha, or Deuterocanonical books of the Bible.

seventy elders: the group of men originally selected to help Moses administer the Israelites and who later represent them at major events.

Shephelah: a ten-mile-wide region lying between the coastal plain and the hill country of Judah that consists of rising plateaus and is one of the most fertile areas of ancient Canaan.

sin(s) of Jeroboam: the action(s) taken by King Jeroboam I to establish a separate identity for the northern kingdom, which become the hallmark of an "evil king" in the estimation of the Deuteronomistic Historian.

sons of the prophet: a support group who serve Elijah and Elisha as messengers and represent the faithful during the reigns of Ahab and his sons.

superscription: an instruction containing information on orchestration, instrumentation, and melody, placed before the first verse of a psalm.

syncretism: the practice of borrowing or adopting cultural ideas and traits from neighboring peoples.

theodicy: an explanation why God allowed the nation to be punished or took certain actions to demonstrate to the people the power of the deity.

theophany: the appearance of God to a human being (e.g., the burning bush in Exod. 3:2–4).

transcendent: of a deity—separate from the creation and not affected by the forces of nature.

universalism: in the biblical narrative, a theme that attempts to demonstrate that Yahweh is a universal god by having a non-Israelite make a statement of faith or remark about Yahweh's power.

Via Maris: the name of an international highway that extended at least from Upper Galilee to the Mediterranean coast of Palestine by way of the Jezreel valley; it may have also extended south along the coast to Egypt and north to Damascus.

wisdom (literature): a type of literature that concentrates on the basic values and common sense of a culture; its genres include proverbs, jokes, and philosophical treatises.

woe oracle: a prophetic exclamation of divine judgment or rebuke of either an individual or a group/nation (e.g., Isa. 3:9, 11; Jer. 13:27; Ezek. 24:6, 9).

Yahweh: one of the names for the Israelite God in the Bible. Sometimes anglicized into Jehovah, it is associated with the J-source in the Pentateuch, according to the Documentary Hypothesis. In the English translation of the Bible, Yahweh is often translated "Lord."

Yehud: during the Persian period (539–332) the province of Judah was named Yehud (a term found on the coin inscriptions of this era). It extended from Bethel south to Engedi, and from Emmaus in the west to the Jordan River, with Jerusalem as its capital.

Zoroastrianism: a dualistic religion associated with the Persians that viewed all of creation in a continuous struggle between the forces of light and darkness. Its beliefs in cosmic conflict, resurrection of the dead, and a last judgment influenced the development of some branches of Judaism (see Dan. 12:1–2) including the Pharisees.

Bibliography

I have relied on the work of many other scholars in writing this survey of the Hebrew prophets. However, I have chosen to provide only a select bibliography. General works and the major commentaries written on individual prophetic books dominate this list so that students may come to recognize the principal works in the field. The literature on ancient Near Eastern and biblical prophecy is quite rich, and any bibliography will be out of date as soon as it is published. As a result, I have created several online bibliographies to assist students. Since they are continually updated, they provide a more vibrant source for further reading on the prophets:

Hebrew prophecy in general
    http://courses.missouristate.edu/VictorMatthews/bib/PROPHET.html

Isaiah
    http://courses.missouristate.edu/VictorMatthews/bib/ISAIAH-02.html

Jeremiah
    http://courses.missouristate.edu/VictorMatthews/bib/JERBIB-02.html

General References

Anchor Bible Dictionary. Edited by D. N. Freedman et al. 6 vols. New York: Doubleday, 1992.
Ancient Near Eastern Texts. Edited by James Pritchard. Princeton: Princeton University Press, 1969.
Cambridge Ancient History. Edited by J. Boardman et al. Cambridge: Cambridge University Press, 1970–.

Civilizations of the Ancient Near East. Edited by Jack Sasson. 4 vols. New York: Scribner, 1995. Repr. in 2 vols. Peabody, MA: Hendrickson, 2001.

Context of Scripture. Edited by W. W. Hallo and K. L. Younger. 3 vols. Leiden: Brill, 1997.

Dictionary of Biblical Imagery. Edited by L. Ryken et al. Downers Grove, IL: Inter-Varsity, 1998.

Dictionary of Deities and Demons in the Bible. Edited by K. van der Toorn et al. Leiden: Brill, 1995.

New Encyclopedia of Archaeological Excavations in the Holy Land. Edited by E. Stern. New York: Simon & Schuster, 1993.

New Interpreter's Dictionary of the Bible. Edited by K. Sakenfeld et al. 5 vols. Nashville: Abingdon, 2006–9.

Oxford Encyclopedia of Archaeology in the Near East. Edited by E. Meyers et al. 5 vols. New York: Oxford University Press, 1997.

Particular Aspects of Bible Background

Berquist, J. *Judaism in Persia's Shadow.* Minneapolis: Fortress, 1995.

Blenkinsopp, J. *Sage, Priest, Prophet: Religious and Intellectual Leadership in Ancient Israel.* Louisville: Westminster John Knox, 1995.

Borowski, O. *Agriculture in Iron Age Israel.* Winona Lake, IN: Eisenbrauns, 1987.

———. *Every Living Thing.* Walnut Creek, CA: Alta Mira, 1998.

Bottéro, J. *Mesopotamia.* Chicago: University of Chicago Press, 1992.

Cook, S. L. *Prophecy and Apocalypticism: The Postexilic Social Setting.* Minneapolis: Fortress, 1995.

———. *The Social Roots of Biblical Yahwism.* Atlanta: Society of Biblical Literature, 2004.

Cross, F. M. *Canaanite Myth and Hebrew Epic.* Cambridge, MA: Harvard University Press, 1971.

Cryer, F. H. *Divination in Ancient Israel and Its Near Eastern Environment.* Sheffield, UK: JSOT Press, 1994.

Davies, W. D., et al. *The Persian Period.* Cambridge History of Judaism 1. Cambridge: Cambridge University Press, 1984.

Dearman, A. *Religion and Culture in Ancient Israel.* Peabody, MA: Hendrickson, 1992.

Dempsey, C. J. *The Prophets: A Liberation-Critical Reading.* Minneapolis: Fortress, 2000.

Eshkenazi, T., and K. Richards, eds. *Second Temple Studies.* Journal for the Study of the Old Testament Supplement 175. Sheffield: Sheffield Academic Press, 1994.

Gershevitch, I., ed. *The Median and Achaemenid Periods.* Cambridge History of Iran 2. Cambridge: Cambridge University Press, 1985.

Gowan, D. E. *Theology of the Prophetic Books: The Death and Resurrection of Israel.* Louisville: Westminster John Knox, 1998.

Grabbe, L. *Judaism from Cyrus to Hadrian*. Minneapolis: Fortress, 1992.

———. *Priests, Prophets, Diviners, Sages: A Socio-historical Study of Religious Specialists in Ancient Israel*. Valley Forge, PA: Trinity, 1995.

Hoerth, A., G. Mattingly, and E. Yamauchi. *Peoples of the Old Testament World*. Grand Rapids: Baker, 1994.

Horowitz, W. *Mesopotamian Cosmic Geography*. Winona Lake, IN: Eisenbrauns, 1998.

Jacobsen, T. *The Harps That Once*. New Haven: Yale University Press, 1987.

———. *Treasures of Darkness*. New Haven: Yale University Press, 1976.

Keel, O. *The Symbolism of the Biblical World*. New York: Seabury, 1978.

Keel, O., and C. Uehlinger. *Gods, Goddesses, and Images of God in Ancient Israel*. Minneapolis: Fortress, 1998.

King, P. *Amos, Hosea, Micah: An Archaeological Commentary*. Philadelphia: Westminster John Knox, 1988.

King, P., and L. Stager. *Life in Biblical Israel*. Louisville: Westminster John Knox, 2001.

Kuhrt, A. *The Ancient Near East, 3000–330 BC*. London: Routledge, 1997.

Lambert, W. G. *Babylonian Wisdom Literature*. Oxford: Clarendon, 1960.

Lichtheim, Miriam. *Ancient Egyptian Literature*. 3 vols. Berkeley: University of California Press, 1980.

Matthews, V. H. *A Brief History of Ancient Israel*. Louisville: Westminster John Knox, 2002.

———. *Manners and Customs in the Bible*. 3rd ed. Peabody, MA: Hendrickson, 2006.

———. *Old Testament Turning Points: The Narratives That Shaped a Nation*. Grand Rapids: Baker Academic, 2005.

———. *Studying the Ancient Israelites: A Guide to Sources and Methods*. Grand Rapids: Baker Academic, 2007.

Matthews, V. H., and D. C. Benjamin. *The Social World of Ancient Israel*. Peabody, MA: Hendrickson, 1993.

Mazar, Amihai. *Archaeology of the Land of the Bible*. New York: Doubleday, 1990.

Miller, J. M., and J. Hayes. *A History of Ancient Israel and Judah*. 2nd ed. Louisville: Westminster John Knox, 2006.

Nemet-Nejat, Karen Rhea. *Daily Life in Ancient Mesopotamia*. Westport, CT: Greenwood, 1998.

Overholt, T. W. *Channels of Prophecy: The Social Dynamics of Prophetic Activity*. Minneapolis: Fortress, 1989.

Peckham, B. *History and Prophecy: The Development of Late Judean Literary Traditions*. New York: Doubleday, 1993.

Pleins, J. D. *The Social Visions of the Hebrew Bible*. Louisville: Westminster John Knox, 2001.

Rainey, A. F., and R. S. Notley. *The Sacred Bridge: Carta's Atlas of the Biblical World*. Jerusalem: Carta, 2006.

Redford, D. B. *Egypt, Canaan, and Israel in Ancient Times*. Princeton: Princeton University Press, 1992.

Reiner, E. *Astral Magic in Babylonia*. Philadelphia: American Philosophical Society, 1995.

Roaf, M. *Cultural Atlas of Mesopotamia and the Ancient Near East*. New York: Facts-on-File, 1990.

Snell, D. *Life in the Ancient Near East*. New Haven: Yale University Press, 1997.

Sweeney, M. A. *The Prophetic Literature*. Nashville: Abingdon, 2005.

Toorn, K. van der. *Sin and Sanction in Israel and Mesopotamia*. Assen, Netherlands: Van Gorcum, 1985.

Van de Mieroop, M. *A History of the Ancient Near East, ca. 3000–323 BC*. London: Blackwell, 2004.

Weinfeld, M. *Social Justice in Ancient Israel*. Minneapolis: Fortress, 1995.

Wiseman, D. J. *Nebuchadrezzar and Babylon*. New York: Oxford University Press, 1985.

Wright, C. J. H. *God's People in God's Land*. Grand Rapids: Eerdmans, 1990.

Yamauchi, E. *Persia and the Bible*. Grand Rapids: Baker, 1990.

Commentaries

Isaiah

Blenkinsopp, J. *Isaiah*. 3 vols. Anchor Bible 19. New York: Doubleday, 2000–2003.

Childs, B. *Isaiah*. Old Testament Library. Louisville: Westminster John Knox, 2001.

Oswalt, J. *The Book of Isaiah*. 2 vols. New International Application Commentary on the Old Testament. Grand Rapids: Eerdmans, 1986–97.

Watts, J. D. W. *Isaiah*. 2 vols. Word Biblical Commentary 24. New York: Nelson, 2005.

Wildberger, H. *Isaiah 1–27*. 2 vols. Continental Commentaries. Minneapolis: Fortress, 1991–98.

Jeremiah

Allen, L. C. *Jeremiah*. Old Testament Library. Louisville: Westminster John Knox, 2008.

Carroll, R. P. *Jeremiah: A Commentary*. Old Testament Library. Louisville: Westminster, 1986.

Holladay, W. *Jeremiah*. 2 vols. Hermeneia. Minneapolis: Fortress, 1986–89.

Keown, G. L., P. J. Scalise, and T. G. Smothers. *Jeremiah 26–52*. Word Biblical Commentary 27. Waco: Word, 1995.

Lundbom, J. R. *Jeremiah 1–52*. 3 vols. Anchor Bible 21. New York: Doubleday, 1999–2004.

Stulman, L. *Jeremiah*. Abingdon New Testament Commentaries. Nashville: Abingdon, 2005.

Thompson, J. A. *The Book of Jeremiah*. New International Commentary on the Old Testament. Grand Rapids: Eerdmans, 1980.

Ezekiel

Allen, L. *Ezekiel*. 2 vols. Word Biblical Commentary. Waco: Word, 1990–94.

Block, D. I. *The Book of Ezekiel*. 2 vols. New International Commentary on the Old Testament. Grand Rapids: Eerdmans, 1997–98.

Bodi, D. *The Book of Ezekiel and the Poem of Ezra*. Orbis Biblicus et Orientalis 104. Göttingen, Germany: Vandenhoeck & Ruprecht, 1991.

Greenberg, M. *Ezekiel 1–37*. 2 vols. Anchor Bible 22. New York: Doubleday, 1983–97.

Zimmerli, W. *Ezekiel*. 2 vols. Hermeneia. Minneapolis: Fortress, 1979–83.

Daniel

Baldwin, J. G. *Daniel*. Tyndale Old Testament Commentaries. Downers Grove, IL: InterVarsity, 1978.

Collins, J. J. *Daniel: A Commentary on the Book of Daniel*. Hermeneia. Minneapolis: Fortress, 1993.

Goldingay, J. E. *Daniel*. Word Biblical Commentary 30. Waco: Word, 1989.

Hosea

Andersen, F. I., and D. N. Freedman. *Hosea*. Anchor Bible 24. New York: Doubleday, 1980.

MacIntosh, A. A. *A Critical and Exegetical Commentary on Hosea*. International Critical Commentary. Edinburgh: T&T Clark, 1997.

Stuart, D. *Hosea–Jonah*. Word Biblical Commentary 31. Waco: Word, 1987.

Wolff, H. W. *A Commentary on the Book of the Prophet Hosea*. Hermeneia. Minneapolis: Fortress, 1974.

Joel

Allen, L. C. *The Books of Joel, Obadiah, Jonah, and Micah*. New International Commentary on the Old Testament. Grand Rapids: Eerdmans, 1976.

Barton, J. *Joel and Obadiah: A Commentary*. Old Testament Library. Louisville: Westminster John Knox, 2001.

Crenshaw, J. *Joel*. Anchor Bible 24. New York: Doubleday, 1995.

Hubbard, D. *Joel and Amos: An Introduction and Commentary*. Tyndale Old Testament Commentaries. Downers Grove, IL: InterVarsity, 1989.

Stuart, D. *Hosea–Jonah*. Word Biblical Commentary 31. Waco: Word, 1987.

Wolff, H. W. *Joel and Amos*. Hermeneia. Minneapolis: Fortress, 1977.

Amos

Andersen, F. I., and D. N. Freedman. *Amos*. Anchor Bible 24. New York: Doubleday, 1989.

Jeremias, J. *The Book of Amos: A Commentary*. Old Testament Library. Louisville: Westminster John Knox, 1998.

Paul, S. M. *Amos: A Commentary on the Book of Amos*. Hermeneia. Minneapolis: Fortress, 1991.

Wolff, H. W. *Joel and Amos*. Hermeneia. Minneapolis: Fortress, 1977.

Obadiah

Allen, L. C. *The Books of Joel, Obadiah, Jonah, and Micah*. New International Commentary on the Old Testament. Grand Rapids: Eerdmans, 1976.

Barton, J. *Joel and Obadiah: A Commentary*. Old Testament Library. Louisville: Westminster John Knox, 2001.

Raabe, P. R. *Obadiah*. Anchor Bible 24. New York: Doubleday, 1996.

Wolff, H. W. *Obadiah and Jonah*. Hermeneia. Minneapolis: Fortress, 1986.

Jonah

Limburg, J. *Jonah: A Commentary*. Old Testament Library. Louisville: Westminster John Knox, 1993.

Sasson, J. *Jonah: A New Translation*. Anchor Bible 24. New York: Doubleday, 1990.

Walton, J. *Jonah*. Bible Study Commentary. Grand Rapids: Zondervan, 1982.

Wolff, H. W. *Obadiah and Jonah*. Hermeneia. Minneapolis: Fortress, 1986.

Micah

Andersen, F. I., and D. N. Freedman. *Micah*. Anchor Bible 24. New York, Doubleday, 2000.

Ben Zvi, E. *Micah*. Forms of the Old Testament Literature. Grand Rapids: Eerdmans, 2000.

Hillers, D. *Micah*. Hermeneia. Philadelphia: Fortress, 1983.

Mays, J. L. *Micah: A Commentary*. Old Testament Library. Philadelphia: Westminster, 1976.

Nahum

Baker, D. W. *Nahum, Habakkuk, and Zephaniah*. Tyndale Old Testament Commentaries. Downers Grove, IL: InterVarsity, 1988.

Roberts, J. J. M. *Nahum, Habakkuk, and Zephaniah: A Commentary*. Old Testament Library. Louisville: Westminster John Knox, 1991.

Habakkuk

Andersen, F. I. *Habakkuk*. Anchor Bible 25. New York: Doubleday, 2001.

Roberts, J. J. M. *Nahum, Habakkuk, and Zephaniah: A Commentary*. Old Testament Library. Louisville: Westminster John Knox, 1991.

Smith, R. L. *Micah–Malachi*. Word Biblical Commentary 32. Waco: Word, 1984.

Zephaniah

Berlin, A. *Zephaniah*. Anchor Bible 25. New York: Doubleday, 1994.

Roberts, J. J. M. *Nahum, Habakkuk, and Zephaniah: A Commentary*. Old Testament Library. Louisville: Westminster John Knox, 1991.

Smith, R. L. *Micah–Malachi*. Word Biblical Commentary 32. Waco: Word, 1984.

Haggai

Meyers, E. M., and C. L. Meyers. *Haggai and Zechariah 1–8*. Anchor Bible 25. New York: Doubleday, 1987.

Petersen, D. *Haggai and Zechariah 1–8: A Commentary*. Old Testament Library. Louisville: Westminster John Knox, 1984.

Verhoef, P. A. *The Books of Haggai and Malachi*. New International Commentary on the Old Testament. Grand Rapids: Eerdmans, 1986.

Wolff, H. W. *Haggai*. Hermeneia. Minneapolis: Fortress, 1988.

Zechariah

Meyers, E. M., and C. L. Meyers. *Haggai and Zechariah 1–8*. Anchor Bible 25. New York: Doubleday, 1987.

Meyers, E. M., and C. L. Meyers. *Zechariah 9–14*. Anchor Bible 25. New York: Doubleday, 1993.

Petersen, D. *Haggai and Zechariah 1–8: A Commentary*. Old Testament Library. Louisville: Westminster John Knox, 1984.

———. *Zechariah 9–14 and Malachi*. Old Testament Library. Louisville: Westminster John Knox, 1995.

Malachi

Glazier-McDonald, B. *Malachi: The Divine Messenger*. Atlanta: Scholars Press, 1987.

Hill, A. E. *Malachi*. Anchor Bible 25. New York: Doubleday, 1998.

Petersen, D. L. *Zechariah 9–14 and Malachi*. Old Testament Library. Louisville: Westminster John Knox, 1995.

Index of Names and Subjects

229

Index of Scripture and Ancient Sources